FORGING

THE

WARRIOR'S
CHARACTER

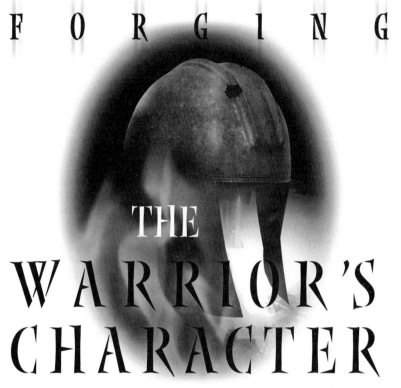

FORGING

THE
WARRIOR'S
CHARACTER

MORAL PRECEPTS FROM THE CADET PRAYER

Don M. Snider
Project Director

Lloyd J. Matthews
Editor

Foreword by General Eric K. Shinseki, US Army, Retired

 **Learning Solutions**

Boston   Burr Ridge, IL   Dubuque, IA   New York   San Francisco   St. Louis
Bangkok   Bogotá   Caracas   Lisbon   London   Madrid
Mexico City   Milan   New Delhi   Seoul   Singapore   Sydney   Taipei   Toronto

The **McGraw·Hill** Companies

FORGING THE WARRIOR'S CHARACTER
MORAL PRECEPTS FROM THE CADET PRAYER

4 5 6 7 8 9 10 11 DOC 1 5 4 3 2 1 0

ISBN-13: 978-0-07-812154-8
ISBN-10: 0-07-812154-X

Learning Solutions Manager: JD Ice
Learning Solutions Specialist: Michael Hemmer
Production Editor: Nina Meyer
Cover Photo: Flames in a furnace © DEX IMAGE
Cover Design: Fairfax Hutter
Printer/Binder: RR Donnelley

Contents

List of Illustrations. vii

Acknowledgments ix

Foreword. xiii
Eric K. Shinseki

Introduction. xvii
F. L. Hagenbeck

Part I. The Role of Character Development in the West Point Experience. 1

1. Developing Leaders of Character at West Point. 3
   Don M. Snider

2. The Domain of the Human Spirit 23
   Patrick J. Sweeney, Sean T. Hannah, and Don M. Snider

3. Reflections on Moral Development at West Point. 51
   Erica Borggren and Donna M. Brazil

Part II. The Role of Character in Military Leadership 63

4. Frameworks of Moral Development and the West Point Experience:
   Building Leaders of Character for the Army and the Nation. 65
   Sean T. Hannah and Patrick J. Sweeney

5. High-Impact Military Leadership: The Positive Effects
   of Authentic Moral Leadership on Followers 91
   Patrick J. Sweeney and Sean T. Hannah

6. Moral Principles and Moral Reasoning in the Ethics
   of the Military Profession. 117
   Anthony E. Hartle

**Part III. Moral Guidance for Military Leaders from the
Cadet Prayer: Interfaith Perspectives.** **143**

7. The Cadet Prayer: A Catholic Perspective. 145
   Edson J. Wood

8. Prayer and Leadership in the Tradition of Moses
   Our Teacher, Peace Be Upon Him 159
   Carlos C. Huerta

9. Islam and The Cadet Prayer: An Islamic Reflection on
   Prayer and Moral Leadership 173
   Sherifa Zuhur

10. Four Sermons on the Cadet Prayer: The Protestant Perspective 191
    John J. Cook III and James R. Carter

About the Contributors **221**

List of Illustrations

Figure 1-1. Definition of Officership 9

Figure 1-2. Definition of a Leader of Character...................... 15

Figure 2-1. Conceptualization of the
Domain of the Human Spirit........................... 28

Figure 4-1. Model for the Development of
Authentic Moral Leaders............................... 70

Figure 5-1. An Interdependence Model for the
Development of Trust 93

Figure 5-2. Attributes of a Leader Who Can Be Trusted in Combat....... 96

Figure 6-1. Factors Shaping the Military Ethic 125

Figure 8-1. Jewish Leadership Model 165

Acknowledgments

This book is the product of several stout hands, the absence of any of which would have prevented its creation. They are the USMA Class of 1946, which initiated a project to bring renewed emphasis to the Cadet Prayer at West Point; the USMA staff and faculty, which responded with alacrity to the opportunity to strengthen character development of cadets and officers; the Academy's leaders, who provided an environment richly receptive to intellectual inquiry; and, lastly, those who sacrificed personally so that this volume could come to fruition.

In the fall of 2002, three members of the USMA Class of 1946 and their wives banded together to seek renewal of the traditional prominence of the Cadet Prayer in West Point life. Though the three represented different religious faiths—Roland Catarinella, Protestant; John Donahue, Roman Catholic; and Jesse Cohen, Jewish—their life experiences all converged on a common conclusion. Each believed that their lives, their very essence, had been shaped profoundly by what they had internalized from the moral precepts so eloquently set forth in the Cadet Prayer. They sought the same outcome for future generations of graduates. In the words of Catarinella:

> I was disappointed to learn in 2001 at the 55th reunion of my Class that the Cadet Prayer was unknown to some cadets. They had never read it and knew nothing about it. When I discussed this matter with my classmates John Donahue and Jesse Cohen, they agreed that if the Academy continued without the Cadet Prayer, West Point would have lost a powerful force with which to develop leaders of character committed to the values of Duty, Honor, Country.

With Catarinella in the lead, they approached the USMA Chaplain with the general idea of underwriting the production of a book about the prayer. Sensitive to the current status of church-state relations in America, particularly as affecting the service academies, they offered on behalf of the Class of 1946 to provide enough copies for a substantial initial presentation to cadets without charge. Remarkably, nearly a score of classmates and wives have since joined them in this endeavor: MG (Ret.) and Mrs. Richard A. Bresnahan, BG (Ret.) J. C. Burney, Mr. Corbin J. Davis, BG Clyde R. Denniston, Mr. and Mrs.

Robert J. Eichenberg, Col. (Ret.) and Mrs. George E. Hall, Col. (Ret.) C. F. Horton, Jr., Mr. Donald R. Lynch, Jr., Mrs. Mildred Posvar, Mr. John E. Sterling, Mr. John R. Treadmill, Mr. Harlan W. Tucker, Mr. and Mrs. Robert B. Tully, Mr. Joe H. Warren, Jr., and Col. (Ret.) William J. Whitener.

When I returned from medical leave in the late spring of 2005, the USMA Chaplain, Colonel John Cook, asked me if I would take on the project of creating a book about the Cadet Prayer. That request coincided with my own abiding interest in the Cadet Leader Development System (CLDS) which, in the cadet developmental reforms of 2000–2002, had specified a new domain— the spiritual—as one of the three areas in which the Academy facilitates the formation of character in future Army officers. In the ensuing years, however, as little had been done to advance cadet development in that new domain, I became ever more convinced that the Academy's faculty, effectively the professoriate of the Army profession, would itself need to create the expert knowledge necessary to support development of the spiritual domain.

I therefore agreed to undertake the task provided that I could assemble an interdisciplinary team of thinkers from the USMA staff and faculty who shared my interest in character development. We were all enthusiastic over the opportunity to combine in common cause the Class of 1946's Cadet Prayer initiative and the Academy's own initiative to buttress cadet moral and character development. In aiming to address this developmental void at West Point and within the Army, we sought new ideas, models, and language that would enhance the ability of future officers and their mentors to analyze and critique their own moral and characterological development, particularly those entering the Army from Generation Y.

Gratifyingly, my stipulation was quickly met, as attested by the many members of the USMA faculty, both past and present, who eagerly stepped forward to do the arduous work involved. Such enterprise was an outgrowth of our professional calling—it certainly wasn't dictated by anyone's job description. As the Army's "university at large," West Point is privileged to have had some very remarkable scholars and professionals among its staff and faculty, some still at West Point, some retired. Of singular mention as one such remarkable scholar and former Army professional is the editor of this book, Lloyd Matthews. This is our third book together since 2002, and one of the delights of my days has been to hear from Lloyd and see what he and his gracious wife Phyllis have been able to do with the often hurried prose we provided them.

Contributors cooperated so wholeheartedly because of the uniquely hospitable intellectual environment that prevails here at West Point. It is one that encourages honest inquiry into topics critical to the Army profession, even if they are as potentially controversial as the subject of the warrior's spirituality. The flourishing of such an environment is testimony to the wisdom of the leader teams assembled here in recent decades by the Academy's Superintendents—Lieutenant Generals Howard Graves, Daniel Christman, William Lennox, and, most recently, Lieutenant General F. L. Hagenbeck.

As with all such endeavors, someone has to pay the bill in terms of the fugitive moments wrested from crowded days in completing such an undertaking. Each author has his or her own story to tell of relationships and endeavors that were encroached upon to make room for this book. So far as I personally am concerned, Caroline, my Army wife of 42 years, has once again unstintingly shared my load. That said, however, we have both been richly remunerated by the satisfaction that comes from serving the cause of West Point and the Army in this manner, which we are both so privileged to do.

Don M. Snider
West Point, New York
April 2008

Foreword

My generation arrived on the world scene late in the first half of the 20th century. We grew up in the shadows of giants, those who fought and won World War II and saved our Nation and the world from tyranny. Born in Hawai'i about a year after the attack on Pearl Harbor, I was raised on the fringe of what was called the Pacific Theater of Operations. My personal heroes, whose shadows touch me even today, came from the 100th Infantry Battalion, the 442nd Regimental Combat Team, and the Military Intelligence Service, those highly decorated Nisei units whose Soldiers also fought to prove the loyalty of Americans of Japanese ancestry. On the heels of World War II came Korea. Once again, I sensed what preserving freedom and liberty meant, this time on the Korean Peninsula, and internalized the great sacrifice, courage, and heroism displayed by the Americans who fought there.

Following my graduation from the United States Military Academy and commissioning with the distinguished Class of 1965, I deployed to Vietnam for my own tours in a war zone. A first tour, without benefit of the Officer Basic Course, and a second tour, during which I dealt with a combat refusal, provided early grounding in the leadership challenges of the profession of arms. Service in Europe followed, the first time at the height of the Cold War and the second during its final days, when the Berlin Wall was breached and the Iron Curtain fell on November 9, 1989. Then-LTG Fred Franks, Commander of VII Corps, taught all of us about courage and toughness and seeing one's duty clearly, no matter what the General Defense Plan mandated. During this period of uncertainty, when the outbreak of freedom was preceded by indicators of an impending military invasion, he and his chain of command, with characteristically cool heads, held us in our garrison locations rather than take the provocative step of marshaling our units and deploying them to defensive positions along the inter-zonal German border. For leaders, the harder right usually involves risk, sometimes significant risk.

When I retired from the Army in August 2003, young Americans were fighting once again, this time in Afghanistan and Iraq. I had come full circle in a life that began at the height of World War II and an Army career that concluded during America's first war of the 21st century.

Throughout my 38 years as a Soldier, the responsibilities of leadership were underscored time and again by the words of the Cadet Prayer—words

I was inspired by when I first heard them 46 years ago. They remind that ethics is about the unwavering demand of duty—our responsibility for knowing what needs to be done, for understanding the difference between right and wrong, and then for doing what is right without fail. They still reflect some of the finest insights into ethical leadership I have ever encountered:

> Strengthen and increase our admiration for honest dealing and clean thinking, and suffer not our hatred of hypocrisy and pretence ever to diminish. Encourage us in our endeavor to live above the common level of life. Make us to choose the harder right instead of the easier wrong, and never to be content with a half truth when the whole can be won. Endow us with courage that is born of loyalty to all that is noble and worthy, that scorns to compromise with vice and injustice, and knows no fear when truth and right are in jeopardy. Guard us against flippancy and irreverence in the sacred things of life.

For those who listen, these imperatives drum an insistent cadence. All these many years later, the words from the Cadet Prayer still resonate with me because they foster ideas and actions that not only reinforce the fundamental values of the profession of arms, but also remind us of our sacred duty to uphold them.

In February 1997, the Army's senior 4-star generals gathered at a Winter Senior Commanders Conference in the Pentagon. The conference was organized around a select number of 30-minute decision briefings tightly managed by the Vice Chief of Staff. One briefer mentioned in passing the Army's new institutional values. Time seemed to stand still as the senior generals confronted one another about those attributes—for over three hours. "Why isn't Competence on the list?" asked one General. "What do you mean by Honor?" asked another. "How do we measure integrity?" asked a third. And on it went until they had addressed their concerns. I sensed that they understood they were defining their Army for generations to come, and they wanted to get this right. They seemed to think that, if they were able to do that, all else would follow. They were right. Today, those seven Army Values—Loyalty, Duty, Respect, Selfless Service, Honor, Integrity, Personal Courage—define our Army and its service to the Nation, both in peace and in war. Sitting in on that conference as a note-taker, I wondered then, as I've wondered on other occasions since, whether similar discussions occurred in other institutions and other militaries around the world. I felt incredibly good about my profession, and I have always believed that those general officers treated me to a privileged moment.

Dick Cavanagh, the highly respected President and CEO of the Conference Board, once described a dinner party that took place in 2001 at the Four Seasons Restaurant in Manhattan. Peter Drucker, the distinguished "Father of Modern Management," and Jack Welch, the former CEO of General Electric, led a discussion about who best develops leaders. In Cavanagh's words, "To my surprise, the usual suspects so often cited for finding and training leaders didn't figure—not the Harvard Business School, or Goldman Sachs, or McKinsey & Company, or General Electric, or IBM, or Procter & Gamble. The enthusiastic choice of both of these management legends was the United States military."[1] He went on to remind that the high regard in which the military is held represented a recent reversal in standings between military leaders and their business counterparts.[2] Discussions like this one led to a partnering endeavor between the Army, the Conference Board, and the Leader to Leader Institute, led by its inspirational Chairman, Frances Hesselbein, to find common ground in developing inspired and inspiring leaders across the various sectors of America.

This growth in respect was important to the U.S. Army, which had left Vietnam some 28 years earlier, after having fought successfully at the tactical level without achieving the strategic outcomes desired by a Nation that had lost its way and its will in that brutal conflict. We were led out of the dark days of Vietnam by tough, smart, and determined military leaders, who saw their duties clearly. Their mission was to rebuild the Army quickly into a force capable of dealing with the massive threat presented by Warsaw Pact forces in Europe. Many gifted Soldiers had a hand in rebuilding the Army and its non-commissioned officer corps, but the men who led this turnaround were the Army's successive Chiefs of Staff. It was the continuity of their investments in leader development that produced the conclusions that were arrived at in the Four Seasons Restaurant during that evening in 2001. At the heart of the Chiefs' determination were the skills, knowledge, attributes, and values underscored by the words of the Cadet Prayer.

In this collection of essays intended for the development of future Army officers, Don Snider and Lloyd Matthews provide, yet again, another important contribution to the Army's study of the ethical leadership that will sustain the Army and our Nation in peace and war for years to come.

Eric K. Shinseki
General, U.S. Army Ret.
West Point, N.Y.
September 2006

Notes

1. Richard Cavanagh, foreword to *Be-Know-Do: Leadership the Army Way,* by the Leader to Leader Institute, with introduction by Frances Hesselbein and General Eric K. Shinseki, USA Ret. (San Francisco, CA: Jossey-Bass, 2004), xi.
2. Ibid.

Introduction

The Army profession, like all others, creates its own expert knowledge. That knowledge is then mastered and embedded in professional Soldiers in the form of expertise to be practiced whenever and wherever the American people direct the Army to serve, in peace or in war. This book is a part of that evolving expert knowledge of the U.S. Army.

The specific knowledge addressed herein is the modus operandi for developing moral character in the Army's officer leaders, particularly those who are commissioned here at the U.S. Military Academy each spring after completing the 47-month West Point experience. Our mission here at the Academy is "to educate, train, and inspire the Corps of Cadets so that each graduate is a commissioned leader of character committed to the values of Duty, Honor, Country and prepared for a career of professional excellence and service to the Nation as an officer in the United States Army."

We understand the development of our graduates, including their moral character, to be the result of carefully integrated activities fulfilling all three of the verbs in the mission statement—educate, train, inspire. And it is the third of these, to inspire leaders, that serves as the focus of this book—the inspiration to do their duty as Soldiers and leaders regardless of circumstances or obstacles to mission accomplishment. Such inspired motivation comes from the leader's human spirit.

Having commanded the 10th Mountain Division in Afghanistan and subsequently served as the manager of the Army's human resources as the Deputy Chief of Staff for Personnel-G1, I am very well aware of the unique demands this Long War against radical Islamic terrorists is placing on our Army's leaders, particularly its junior leaders. These terrorists are an adaptable, cunning, and utterly immoral enemy whose tactics and techniques in battle flout all the international laws of war. In the desperate straits of battle, then, the urgent temptation for our forces to respond in kind is thwarted only by Soldiers and leaders of such high moral character that they can be relied upon to "choose the harder right instead of the easier wrong."

That quotation is one of the seven nonsectarian moral precepts within the Cadet Prayer, written in 1924, to illuminate for all cadets, regardless of faith, denomination, or spiritual disposition, the type of moral character they needed to acquire in order to become maximally effective leaders. This humble fragment of military lore has become a transcendent didactic and cultural force here at the Academy. As you will witness within this volume, its moral precepts have inspired and guided generations of West Point graduates in peace and war, and continue to do so to this day, including, with all humility, myself.

But even if the inspiring words of the Cadet Prayer point to the necessary behavioral outcomes, how are these particular outcomes, as manifested in strengthened moral character, developed? And how should our faculty, staff, and cadets think about the relevant developmental processes, and with what ideas and words should they discuss their own development within the domain of the human spirit? Our inability to achieve such development with sufficient conceptual clarity sparked the interest of our faculty in explicating for the Army profession how moral character can be further strengthened in the newest generations who come to West Point from diverse cultural backgrounds and spiritual assumptions.

Thus, an interdisciplinary group of USMA staff and faculty under the leadership of Dr. Don Snider has produced still another landmark text for use not only within the Army profession itself, but within any institution of higher education and leader development where the character of the leaders produced is the paramount concern. Given that West Point understands the significance of the human spirit in preparation for war, it should not be surprising that the disciplines of cognitive psychology, social psychology, leadership theory, philosophy and ethics, theology, political science, and Islamic studies are represented in the eclectic group of contributors.

Obviously, we have no pretense that what our contributors have produced is the last word on the theory of moral development, which remains a dynamic and rapidly evolving field of research. But in elaborating the methods currently employed at the U.S. Military Academy to produce leaders of character—methods validated daily by reports reaching West Point from the battlefields of Afghanistan and Iraq on the performance of its graduates—we have every confidence that the Academy continues on the right path.

F. L. Hagenbeck
Lieutenant General, U.S. Army
Superintendent.

I

The Role of Character Development in the West Point Experience

1

Developing Leaders of Character at West Point

Don M. Snider

Introduction

In his book titled *Honor Unvarnished: A West Point Graduate's Memoir of World War II* (2003), General Donald V. Bennett, USA Ret., who earlier served as the Academy's 47th Superintendent, spoke these eloquent words: "It is to the Point that I shall finally return and where I shall rest, with Bets at my side. Nearby will be the Chapel, where long ago I heard the words that shaped my life." Then, General Bennett quoted in full the Cadet Prayer:

> O God, our Father, thou Searcher of human hearts, help us to draw near to Thee in sincerity and in truth. May our religion be filled with gladness and may our worship of Thee be natural.
>
> *Strengthen and increase our admiration for honest dealing and clean thinking, and suffer not our hatred of hypocrisy and pretence ever to diminish. Encourage us in our endeavor to live above the common level of life. Make us to choose the harder right instead of the easier wrong, and never to be content with a half truth when the whole can be won.* Endow us with courage that is born of loyalty to all that is noble and worthy, that scorns to compromise with vice and injustice and knows no fear when truth and right are in jeopardy. Guard us against flippancy and irreverence in the sacred things of life. Grant us new ties of friendship and new opportunities of service. Kindle our hearts in fellowship with those of a cheerful countenance, and soften our hearts with sympathy for those who sorrow and suffer. *Help us to keep the honor of the Corps untarnished and unsullied and to show forth in our lives the ideals of West Point in doing our duty* to Thee and to our Country. All of which we ask in the name of the Great Friend and Master of all. Amen. (Italics added to original by author of this chapter)

Following the Prayer, General Bennett continued: "As long as those words are spoken, acted upon, *and believed in*, I know that all of the sacrifices of those who sleep the eternal sleep on the Plain of West Point will not have been in vain."[1]

As the moral precepts italicized in the Prayer make clear, there is a unique character required of the members of the Long Gray Line of West Point. Not all attain it, but the vast majority of them do, and it bonds them together in a manner unlike that of the graduates of other elite colleges and universities in America. In those institutions the bond is more tenuous, focused on the individual graduates and their storied achievements across the many vocations that make up the various sectors of American life, public and private. West Point graduates, however, are not being prepared for those activities, though they may pursue them later in life. Their preparation, as we shall see, is to enable them to serve as commissioned officers in the U.S. Army, leading America's sons and daughters into the crucible of mortal combat, to fight the nation's "wars" wherever and however the society they serve chooses to define a war. Thus, the bond among the members of the Long Gray Line is focused on their common understanding of their duty and whether they, individually, have the attributes of moral character necessary to fulfill that duty. To betray their commission, the Army, and America's soldiers, and thus the Nation, by poor individual leadership is also to betray the other members of the Long Gray Line. The quality of moral character counts in an officer, and thus it counts in all Academy graduates.

General Bennett knew of what he spoke when he noted that the moral precepts within the Cadet Prayer must be "acted upon and believed in" if the necessary personal character in West Point's graduates is to be built. After graduation and commissioning with the Class of 1940, he deployed to North Africa in 1942, then to Casablanca, Tunisia, and Sicily, then on to England and across the Channel, landing on Omaha Beach on June 6, 1944. He led his soldiers through the killing zones of the beach, through the breakout, across the lowlands, and, with his battalion, held the northern shoulder of the Bulge during the terrible winter months of 1944. They then crossed the Rhine and by May of 1945 had fought on to the Elbe River in Czechoslovakia.

Then, after three years of war, he observed the start of another war—the Cold War—as, under the terms of Yalta, Russian troops moved up to the demarcation line along the Elbe and rounded up the columns of wretched humanity fleeing the occupation. He watched as they were marched eastward toward the gulags. He watched as what Churchill would famously call the Iron Curtain descended between eastern and western Europe.

General Bennett's story demonstrates, as do the many thousands of other silent narratives of wartime officers, that military leaders in war need a very special quality of personal character. In a deeply self-directed way they must discern their duties rightly and fully and then manifest the courage and resilience to persevere in fulfilling them, often under the most adverse of conditions for months and even years at a time.

Great military leaders have commented frequently on this inner quality of personal character that is a necessity for combat leaders and their soldiers alike. General of the Army George C. Marshall noted:

> The soldier's heart, the soldier's spirit, and the soldier's soul are everything. Unless the soldier's soul sustains him, he cannot be relied on and will fail himself, his commander, and his country in the end. It is not enough to fight.

It is the spirit that wins the victory. Morale is a state of mind. It is steadfast-ness, courage, and hope. It is confidence, zeal, and loyalty. It is élan, esprit de corps, and determination. It is staying power, the spirit which endures in the end, and the will to win. With it all things are possible, without it everything else—planning, preparation, and production—count for naught.[2]

More recently, another well respected leader, General Colin Powell, used the metaphor of the heart in describing the quality of character requisite for effective military leaders. Speaking to the Corps of Cadets in 1998, he noted:

Our Army is truly a people's Army. This simple code [Duty, Honor, Country] is not something West Point gives to you. It is something that West Point helps you give to yourselves. For all its beauty and history, West Point is a pile of stone until you bring it to life every day. You can inscribe Duty, Honor, Country, on every granite block and it would mean nothing unless those words are engraved in your heart. You bring the code alive every day by the dozens of decisions you make. . . . Always live by the code inscribed in your heart.[3]

While developing the moral character of its graduates is accepted as a necessity at West Point, that is not the case for many elite colleges and univer-sities in America today. They simply do not see this as a task for themselves. For example, in 1997 during the well-known "Aims of Education" oration presented annually to incoming freshmen at the University of Chicago, Professor John Mearsheimer observed:

Not only is there a powerful imperative at Chicago to stay away from teach-ing the truth, but the University also makes little effort to provide you with moral guidance. Indeed, it is a remarkably amoral institution. I would say the same thing, by the way, about all other major colleges and universities in this country. . . . Today, elite universities operate on the belief that there is a clear separation between intellectual and moral purpose, and they pur-sue the former while largely ignoring the latter. There is no question that the University of Chicago makes hardly any effort to provide you with moral guidance. . . . I am not saying that moral questions are unimportant and that you should pay them little attention in the years ahead. On the con-trary, individuals and societies they live in constantly run up against trou-bling ethical questions, and they have no choice but to wrestle with them and attempt to find the right answers. However, for better or worse, we do not provide much guidance in sorting out those issues. That burden falls squarely on your shoulders.[4]

Subsequently, Mearsheimer's faculty colleague, Professor Andrew Abbott, confirmed Mearsheimer's point in 2002 in a similar oration to freshmen, but with a very interesting twist:

My friend, John Mearsheimer, had the guts to stand where I am standing four years ago and argue forcefully that college education is not moral education. Theoretically Mearsheimer may have been right—he argued from a strong libertarian and positivist viewpoint—but empirically he was dead wrong. Willy-nilly moral learning will be central in your college experience. You will do a lot of moral learning, even in the classroom, much of it learning to dissemble your real views in discussions that are more apparent than real. . . . Now my point is that for you as individuals, your responsibility for finding education is not limited to the cognitive matters to which the University—following Mearsheimer's argument—largely restricts itself. You need to become educated in morals and emotion as well. And in those areas, I am sad to say, we do not really provide you with anything like the systematic set of exercises in self-development that we provide on the cognitive side. So you are on your own.[5]

What Abbott recognized, and Mearsheimer did not acknowledge, is that postadolescent students are conducting their own search for moral meaning and their own understanding of truth, irrespective of whether the university recognizes that to be the case or not. Fortunately, at West Point, that fact is well understood and, even more importantly, is being acted upon.

The purpose of this chapter is to explain how West Point goes about developing what it calls "Commissioned Leaders of Character," and the role that such precepts as those highlighted in the Cadet Prayer play in character development. I will present this story in four parts. First, I will review the process the Academy went through at the end of the Cold War to reset its development programs in cognizance of the new demands and missions its graduates would face in the 21st century. The process resulted in the renewed concept of "officership," a shared professional identity toward which all developmental activities at the Academy are now directed. Second, we will look more specifically at some of those developmental techniques as comprehended within the Cadet Leader Development System (CLDS), specifically noting the establishment of two new domains of development, the spiritual and the social. Third, we will focus on the spiritual domain, and how it is designed to facilitate the personal moral development of future Army Leaders. In the fourth and last part, I will relate the content of this chapter to the remainder of the book, adumbrating for the reader the scope and intent of the larger project.

In the Wake of the Cold War: West Point Renovates Its Approach to Leader Development[6]

As the Cold War came to a close and the full implications of this historic tectonic shift in relations among nations began to dawn on attentive thinkers, it became apparent that both the type of wars in which the Army would fight and the demands placed on future Academy graduates had fundamentally changed. The first Gulf War in 1990–1991 had shown that American Army divisions were the most professional and devastating land force ever to fight, particularly in armored battles in open terrain. But it was also clear that the Cold War era of great power conflict was at least in a state of strategic pause, and that America no longer faced any real land-power threats. This development had produced much debate, both within the Army and outside it, over the employment of Army forces in Haiti, Rawanda, Bosnia, and Kosovo in the mid-1990s in what were called humanitarian interventions. At its core, this debate went to the root of the self-concept of the Army officer. Was he or she in the late 1990s a war-fighter or a peacekeeper; and were the demands on the leader the same in both cases, or were they so specialized and different that an Army officer could be competent only in one or the other, but not both? For officers who believe, rightly, that professional competence is in fact a moral imperative, this was a matter of deep concern, and so it was for those who led and served at the Academy during that period of change.

It was at this point that Lieutenant General Daniel Christman entered the scene as Superintendent of the Academy, serving in that capacity during the critical years 1996–2001. For roughly two years a faculty committee established by Christman studied with the Academy's leadership team the Nation's external security environment on one hand, and the internal processes by which cadets were developed into officers on the other. In brief, how should the new security environment affect the Academy's development goals for cadets? The committee's conclusions were straightforward, accompanied by four major recommendations for the Superintendent. First, it recommended that the Academy adopt a broader self-concept as the developmental goal for its graduates, moving well beyond that which had been used at the Academy during the Cold War decades—one in which graduates had seen themselves as confined to the roles of "war-fighter" and "leader of character." The larger debate within the Army had already convinced many senior Army leaders, including those at the Academy, that "war-fighter" was too restrictive to describe the martial role of future graduates, with "warrior" becoming the preferred alternative. But even with this refinement, "warrior" and "leader of character" formed too narrow a goal according to the analysis presented to General Christman.

To create this broader officer identity, the committee recommended the addition of two additional roles—those of "member of a profession" and "servant of the Nation." With regard to membership in a profession, concurrent research, some of which was done in the field among active-duty Army majors, had shown clearly that during the force drawdown of the 1990s, after the first Gulf War, the Army had lost many of the attributes of a profession and was coming to behave in many ways more like a governmental bureaucracy.[7] It had been a difficult time for the Army, called upon to do more with less as its end-strength and its budget were reduced by over one-third during the decade. This change in the institution's culture and behavior produced an exodus of captains[8] and contributed to a loss of professional self-concept among the remaining officers of the middle grades.[9] Thus, it was recommended to General Christman that the Academy address this malady directly by instilling more deeply in future Academy graduates an explicitly professional identity, one based on the understanding that the Army is to be a vocational profession and each officer within it an aspiring or practicing professional.

As to the second added role, servant of the Nation, the committee was responding to several factors. First and foremost, the concept of a graduate's duty to the country had long been a part of the Academy's ethos, most recognizably in the Academy's traditional motto, "Duty, Honor, Country." Thus the committee wanted to codify formally in the new development system that long-term aspect of the Academy's, as well as the Army's, ethos. But in the nearer term, the Academy was resetting its developmental system in the midst of the economic bubble of the late 1990s. Hyper-materialism was rampant at that time in America as members of the boomer generation were "getting theirs" before the bubble burst. Throughout the Army, attractive offers, many by former Academy graduates themselves, were being made to graduates at the rank of captain as they approached the end of their five-year mandatory service obligation. Such recruiters argued that graduates had "paid their contractual obligation" to the Academy and the Nation for their "free education," and it was only fair for them to earn something for themselves in the booming private sector. The effect on retention rates of Academy graduates was distinctly negative. Thus the recommendation to the Superintendent was to counter this environment of materialistic self-centeredness by reinforcing explicitly within the new developmental goal the servant concept with its inherent suggestion of self-sacrifice in a noble calling—that of spending a lifetime in service to one's countrymen. This addition also brought the newly broadened developmental goals directly in line with the Academy's mission:

> To educate, train, and inspire the Corps of Cadets so that each graduate is a commissioned leader of character committed to the values of Duty, Honor, Country; professional growth throughout a career as an officer in the United States Army; and a lifetime of selfless service to the nation.[10]

Note that within the mission statement, the objective—the target of the Academy's efforts—is to be a "commissioned leader of character." While quite accurate, this is a rather wordy way of saying, "Officer," but it does indicate clearly that the mission focus at West Point is to be on the officer's commission and character rather than on the Academy's diploma and the graduate's intellect. To accomplish such a mission, the Academy must produce graduates of such competence and character as to be able to fulfill the obligations of a commission in line with the Nation's expectations of what it means to be an Army officer. Thus, the third recommendation to General Christman was to renew at the Academy use of the term "officership" as the inclusive self-concept subsuming the four individual roles, and making it—officership—the new developmental goal for the Academy entering the 21st century.

Originally coined by Professor Samuel Huntington in the 1950s, the term "officership" had served quite well the early generations of officers in the Cold War.[11] But, with the push toward egalitarianism in America and her civic institutions in the revolutionary post-Vietnam era, the term had fallen out of favor in the Army as being too elitist.[12] The committee recommended reversing that trend by making clear the unique role that commissioned officers play in the Army and in the Nation's civil-military relations by instilling a deeper understanding of officership in the Academy's future graduates. The Superintendent agreed and subsequently promulgated as strategic guidance for all developmental programs for the decade, 2000–2010, the definition of officership set forth in Figure 1-1.

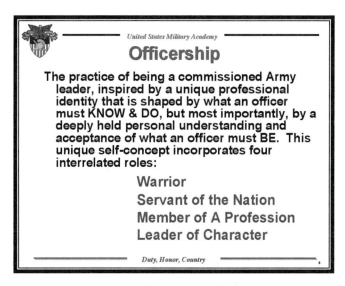

Figure 1-1. *Definition of Officership.*

Thus, *USMA Strategic Vision—2010* envisions future Academy graduates as officers "prepared for the uncertainty and ambiguity of military service . . . because they will have reflected upon and developed *a personal understanding of the unique characteristics of their chosen profession and the principles that govern the fulfillment of their office.*"[13] The italicized phrase captures the essence of officership—a self-concept, a professional identity, and a personal understanding of the unique characteristics of what it means to be an Army officer within a unique profession. Moreover, the phrase also acknowledges a set of principles that "govern the fulfillment of their office." The Oath of Commission charges an officer to "well and faithfully discharge the duties of the office I am about to enter." But since cadets have not yet served in a commissioned status, the definition of officership was augmented with a set of eight principles intended to guide the cadets' personal development and conduct day by day, both at the Academy and later on active duty. As the vision document states, "To meet these responsibilities, commissioned officers are guided throughout their lifetime of service, from lieutenant to general to civilian-servant, by the following eight principles: Duty, Honor, Loyalty, Service to Country, Competence, Teamwork, Subordination, and Leadership" (see Appendix 1–A to this chapter for definitions of these principles).[14]

Returning to the Academy's mission statement, we must also note that it emphasizes three verbs—"educate, train, and inspire." Taken together, these three verbs define human development—the holistic means by which the Academy accomplishes its mission, the processes by which cadets are introduced to, experience, reflect on, and internalize the defining fundamentals of officership.[15] Thus, the fourth recommendation of the committee was to embed the redefined goal of officership within the Academy's educational and training programs in a manner that was consciously, effectively, and systematically developmental.

This may sound like mere common sense, but in fact the issue was much more urgent at the Academy during General Christman's tenure than it might now appear. Other faculty studies and internal assessments of cadet life had indicated clearly that cadets had become over-committed and over-scheduled. Many cadets were going from activity to activity over their four years, from academics and sports or club activities to summer training and back to academics, in such a hurried and frenetic manner as to preclude the essential processing necessary for human learning and maturation. They had little time, opportunity, or encouragement to reflect on their everyday experiences, often to the point that many activities that should, and otherwise would, have been developmental for them simply were not.

Thus in 2001, the Academy initiated the implementation of a new Cadet Leader Development System (CLDS), one that was specifically tailored to implement the "officership" goal. Far more than in the past, the approach taken was to unify the efforts of staff and faculty across the breadth of the Academy and the vast number of very different activities they led and mentored—from football team, to chapel choir, to physics class, to debate team. The single, common, unifying goal for all was to develop graduates who, as noted above, had thought carefully about what it meant to be an officer and had internalized as their own the four-fold self-concept of officership.

The term "officership" provided the vision, a common developmental goal. But the greatest challenge to the implementation of the new CLDS was to get the institution's staff and faculty to understand that the new goal concerned far more than education and training per se. More important, it dealt with inculcation, inspiration, and transformation. The new goal of officership would be attained only to the extent that all activities worked to change how cadets saw themselves and their place in the world and to bring them to accept for themselves the new meanings that these changes entailed for their lives.

The staff and faculty thus needed to have more than a goal; they also needed a common understanding of human learning and maturation. Moreover, they needed a conceptual framework or model for officer development. Not surprisingly, no such common understandings existed at the Academy at the time (nor were there models describing the process of human development in any published Army doctrine). To be sure, those responsible for individual components of the Academy's programs had their own conceptions of how cadets developed—intellectually, physically, and militarily. But there was no integrating concept, nor was there any documented understanding of how cadets developed morally in terms of their individual character.

Therefore, the final version of the CLDS manual provided for the staff and faculty such a model, one built around what it calls the "five keys to human development": (1) the individual readiness of each cadet to be developed, understanding that they do not all develop at the same rate either by age or class; (2) a series of experiences that are meaningful, varied, and marked by difficulty and conflict such that individuals are moved out of their comfort zones to challenge their own worldviews, understandings, and capabilities; (3) consistent support and feedback from staff and faculty acting credibly as role models and mentors to enable individual cadets to make sense of their world in new ways as they transit the demanding and potentially developmental experiences; (4) facilitated reflection on these experiences to allow the cadets to become more self-aware, both of themselves and where they are in the development process as an apprentice officer; and (5) availability of time, recognizing that while education and training are normally rather short-term interventions, human development is a continuous and open-ended process that will extend well beyond the tenure of cadets at West Point.[16] In fact, for the aspiring officer, such development and commitment to life-long learning is a true mark of a professional.

The CLDS redesign, and particularly the conceptual model outlined above, were deliberately made to accord with the Army leadership doctrine that has long been cast in the BE-KNOW-DO framework. As we shall see in subsequent chapters, the Army defines leadership as influencing people by providing purpose, direction, and motivation while operating to accomplish the mission and to improve the organization.[17] The BE-KNOW-DO framework sets forth the characteristics necessary for an effective Army leader in terms of character, skills, and actions. Attributes and values describe personal character (BE); professional knowledge provides the foundation for, and is manifested in, the officer's skills and expertise (KNOW); and the resultant of BE and KNOW is ultimately seen in the officer's actions (DO). To be authentic to their followers, the actions of Army leaders (DO) must be an accurate reflection of who they are (BE) and what they have learned professionally (KNOW). In other words, an officer's "walk" must match his or her "talk."

Given this framework, it was clear that, far more than in the Academy's past, the redesigned CLDS focused intentionally on the BE component. The reason for this was straightforward to the committee and quite explicit in their discussions with General Christman. Their studies had shown that in an information-age Army, the rate of technological advance would cause rapid and continuing changes in the American way of war and thus in what a leader must KNOW and DO. Constant reeducation and retraining were to be the norm now that knowledge and skills once learned were increasingly perishable in information-age warfare. But what would remain constant within this welter of change was the necessity, particularly in combat, for a deeply moral character in the commissioned leader, the BE component of Army leadership. Thus, given the Academy's unique opportunity to develop cadets over a 47-month period (no other full-time educational or training experience for an Army officer exceeds 12 months save for civilian graduate schooling), it was logical to place greatly increased emphasis on the BE component of developing leaders. The officership concept with its four interrelated identity roles provided, by design, specifically for such emphasis.

To move now from the abstract to the concrete, let me offer two examples of how this intentional focus on the BE component was implemented in the Academy's developmental programs. The first example is known as the cadet's "cemetery walk," which was intentionally focused on the third verb in the Academy's mission, "to inspire." To help cadets personalize what it means to join the Long Gray Line, sophomore cadets were given the name and obituary of a graduate who had made the ultimate sacrifice for his or, as we are seeing today with increasing frequency, *her* country. They were assigned to go to the Post Cemetery, locate the graduate's headstone, and meditate on the life and sacrifice of their assigned graduate, answering such questions as what he or she accomplished by military service and whether or not the graduate's death was in vain. They subsequently wrote a reflective essay, to be discussed with a mentor, as to what meaning they could attach to such a life and how it might help them understand their own evolving commitment to officership. Mentors were often astounded at the insights that young cadets displayed, especially given there were no "right" answers. Meaning is what the individual cadet made it to be, but in the process of meaning-making, terms like sacrifice and service lost their hazy abstraction and took on flesh-and-blood significance. At the same time, the cadet's moral character took another stride forward along the path of realization and maturation.[18]

For a second example of how the CLDS program was implemented, we turn to the academic program. The Dean of Academics, Brigadier General Daniel Kaufman, requested that in preparing core courses, course designers be especially mindful of the evolving needs of the Army officer. In other words, without at all vitiating the liberal arts experience of broadening the mind and liberating the intellectual spirit, officership was to touch the academic encounters of cadets through the recognition that they are not entirely like college students on other campuses, say at Penn State. Rather, they had chosen to be different, to become officers, and their core education should reflect that choice and their evolving identity *within the flexibility offered by existing accreditation standards.* In the Department of Social Sciences, the core American Politics course was modified by amplifying the treatment of American civil-military relations, a sub-discipline of political science and a subject about which Army officers should be quite familiar. As a result, the opportunities for classroom discussions between role-model instructors and cadets over the place of the Officer Corps within the American political system were materially increased, exactly the intention of the redesigned CLDS. Education was still education—superb education—but now it was also contextualizing for future officers within the discipline of political science the role their profession and its leaders properly play in the American political system.

Inside CLDS—Developmental Domains for Competence and Character

There are two fundamental ways to describe the total developmental process at West Point, the sum of all those scheduled and unscheduled activities that offer the potential for human learning and change over 47 months. One is to describe it as experienced by the cadets; the second is to describe it as it is organized, planned, and implemented by officials at the Academy. I will use here the first approach, covering the six developmental domains within which cadets experience targeted growth opportunities: the intellectual, military, physical, spiritual, ethical, and social domains. While each domain has been designed to facilitate a particular aspect of growth, to the individual cadet the experiences tend to blend together holistically. However, to the Academy, it is recognized that growth must occur within each discrete domain if the institutional mission of producing commissioned leaders of character is to be accomplished.

Within the Army, leadership, and specifically officership, has always been understood to be a combination of individual competencies and character. Thus three of the domains—the intellectual, military and physical—are associated with the development of professional competence, while the remaining three—the spiritual, ethical, and social—relate to the development of personal character.[19]

Compared to past conceptions of leader development at West Point, there are now two new domains—the spiritual and the social. The Academy has long promoted leader development in the other four domains, which produce attributes essential to all military leaders—the intellect, military skills, physical capabilities, and an internalized ethic. But now, consistent with the committee's recommendation to refine graduates' understanding of what it means to BE an officer, the Academy has two new domains.

This step was not taken without considerable debate, usually focused on why a spiritual domain was needed when the Academy already had an ethical domain. How the Academy resolved that issue in the redesigned CLDS is our final task in this chapter.

The Spiritual Ingredient in Character Development at West Point

Human spirituality is a subject of increasing interest to American society today, not only with regard to individuals but also regarding its role in institutional life as well. Of particular interest to the Academy is the research proceeding in three areas—higher education, leader development, and the American workplace. Each of these areas intersects with the mission of the Academy and the roles its graduates will fill.

Definitions of human spirituality abound. Here is an example proposed by a group in higher education:

> Spirituality points to our interiors, our subjective life, as contrasted to the objective domain of material events and objects. Our spirituality is reflected in the values and ideals that we hold most dear, our sense of who we are and where we come from, or beliefs about why we are here—the meaning and purpose we see in our lives—and our connectedness to each other and to the world around us. Spirituality also captures those aspects of our experience that are not easy to define, the mysterious, the sacred, and the mystical. Within the very broad perspective, we believe spirituality is a universal impulse and reality.[20]

Then we have an example suggested by a prominent theorist on leadership in the workplace:

> Our individual sense of who we are—our true, spiritual self—defines us. It creates our mindset, defines our values, determines our actions, and predicts our behavior. As such, spirit is a part of leadership and always has been, whether the individual leader knows it or consciously uses this fact in developing his or her leadership approach. As our work world expands in importance and becomes, for many, the central activity of our lives, relating personal spiritual values with work values becomes the central task of leadership. Leaders must get in touch with their own spiritual nature. They must sense the spiritual essence of their followers and must deal directly with the task of creating an organization—defined as a group of people in voluntary relationship—where the essential spiritual needs of each member is considered and made a part of the group experience.[21]

For its part, the Academy has newly included the spiritual domain in CLDS, consistent with the increased focus on the BE component of leadership, that is to support development toward the fourth identity of the officer—the Leader of Character. As portrayed in the CLDS manual, that identity is defined in Figure 1-2.

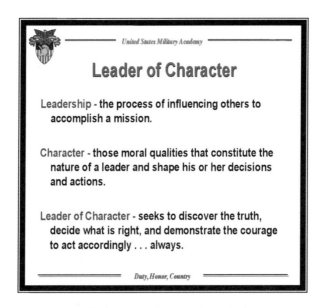

Figure 1-2. *Definition of A Leader of Character.*

This definition was carefully crafted to unite both dimensions of this role—capacity to lead and character—in a vital and indivisible whole.[22] Cadets must come to understand that their actions as officers will flow naturally from their moral character and that only leaders of high moral character can be expected consistently to take actions that the profession and the client it serves will consider ethical. That is the essence of their personal integrity, taking actions that are consistent with and motivated by their own beliefs and fully consistent with the ethics, now internalized, of the profession they have chosen to embrace.

The definition also carefully arrays (bottom entry in Figure 1-2) the full range of moral development required for an officer's actions to be integral with his or her own and the profession's values and beliefs. If leaders are not looking for the truth, if situations resonant with moral implications are not recognized as such, then leaders may base decisions on purely expedient grounds with potentially unethical results. But moral sensitivity alone is not enough. Once leaders know that they are facing a decision with a moral component, they have to invoke moral reasoning and judgment to decide what is right and just. Even then, moral sensitivity, reasoning, and judgment do not always produce ethical behavior. Without the courage to follow through and *take* the right action—the DO component of leadership—such discerning and reasoned assessments may go for naught. The final element in developing the leader's character, then, is molding the fortitude to do the right thing over and over in the course of a duty day.[23]

One brief but effective method of illustrating this necessary range of moral development to cadet discussion groups is set forth in the following linked sequence:

Personal Truth => Professional Ethic => Leader Actions

Starting from the right, it is easy to engage cadets in a discussion about how an officer's "walk" (the leader's visible actions) must match his or her "talk" (the leader's spoken or written affirmation of the profession's ethic). One reason it is so easy is that history offers all too many examples of officers whose walk has not matched their talk and who are therefore rightly disregarded by the cadets as role models. Toss such an example to a group of cadets for discussion and the heuristic effect is remarkable. They literally teach themselves.

The walk-talk connection also lends itself to edifying discussion because of persistent questions as to what the Army's professional ethic really is. Over the years, the Army has not seen fit to codify the ethic into a single document for officers; rather, parts are to be found in the Declaration of Independence; the Constitution; the officer's Oath of Commission and other legislated statutes which govern the services, particularly the Uniformed Code of Military Justice; the Army's own Seven Values; and the Army's deeply engrained customs and traditions, particularly the now broadly assimilated West Point motto, "Duty, Honor, Country."[24] Thus, the uncodified nature of the Army's ethic is initially challenging to young officers and apprentices as they seek to find out exactly what "the rules" are. Though it is far too general to be a complete ethical prescription, a useful base for them to touch is the "Requirements of Exemplary Conduct" in the United States Code, Title 10— Armed Forces (3583) which establishes *as a matter of law* the commander's responsibility for the moral and ethical stewardship of his unit:

All commanding officers and others in authority in the Army are required:

1. to show in themselves a good example of virtue, honor, patriotism, and subordination;
2. to be vigilant in inspecting the conduct of all persons who are placed under their command;
3. to guard against and suppress all dissolute and immoral practices, and to correct, according to the laws and regulations of the Army, all persons who are guilty of them, and;

4. to take all proper and necessary measures, under laws, regulations, and customs of the Army, to promote and safeguard the morale, the physical well-being, and the general welfare of the officers and enlisted persons under their command or charge.[25]

But how do young cadets develop in a few short years to the point of being able to fulfill this very demanding set of legal duties and obligations, which are far more stringent than the relativistic, postmodern value structure that in many cases characterized their education and acculturation prior to arriving at West Point? The Academy believes that in order to do so, they must continue, while at West Point, the individual search for meaning, values, and personal understanding of truth that is a natural part of postadolescent maturation.[26]

Glancing now at the left side of the Truth=>Ethic=>Action diagram broached above, we note the results of that search, i.e., the individual cadet's conception of his or her personal truth and beliefs. The challenge, then, is for individuals to continue that search over the 47 months while also reconciling any differences between their own beliefs and the values inherent in the Army's professional ethic, *before* they accept their commission. Once commissioned, as noted above in the excerpt from Title 10, officers are expected to enforce the norms of the professional ethic, even in the most desperate straits of mortal combat. Long experience, validated by scientific research, has taught the Army that young officers cannot do this well if they have assimilated the profession's moral virtues in a shallow manner due to dissonance with their own beliefs.[27]

Returning to the two additional developmental domains identified by the faculty for inclusion in CLDS—the spiritual and the social—we note that they were added specifically to amplify, for cadets and staff and faculty alike, the full range of character development needed in Academy graduates—particularly to fulfill the role of the leader of character. The previous approach simply lumped together the widely dispersed elements of requisite moral-ethical development as a single entity, often thought of as a mere penumbra of the traditional domains of competence. However, such an approach failed to provide the needed degree of definition and saliency to moral inquiry within the totality of cadet development.

In sum, Army officers must be aware of their human spirit and essence, knowing who they are, what they believe, and what they personally understand "truth" to be. They need a personal worldview that is solidly informed and purposefully evolving, thus the addition of the spiritual domain. They also must be grounded in what the profession considers to be "right" conduct in peace and in war, thus the traditional ethical domain of development. And they must lead through the interpersonal relations they develop with the soldiers under their command and with others, thus the social domain. Such development requires cadets to seamlessly join their personal search for meaning—which for each cadet is inherently a *spiritual* and moral endeavor—with their profession's *ethical* norms and expectations, and then take actions within a *social* context. Throughout, cadets transitioning to officership must be mindful that all moral and ethical impulses, indeed all professional activities themselves, occur within a social context.[28] Thus, the rationale is complete for the three domains that support West Point's goal of character development.

The Chapters to Follow

Returning now to the spiritual domain, which broadly speaking this book is mainly about, it is the case that for many cadets the search for moral truth will be faith-based.[29] But that is not the case for all. Moreover, as a U.S. Government institution the Academy has no official interest as to whether that is the case or not; the Academy is not in the business of telling cadets that they must be religious or, conversely, that they may not be so. However, as with all Army posts and major commands, there are chaplains present to facilitate the free exercise of religion for those cadets so interested. There are also many other avenues within the undergraduate curriculum for cadets to pursue their inner search through the study of philosophy, history, literature, the arts, the physical and social sciences, and even military traditions. Additionally, there are competitive sports galore to test and strengthen moral fiber (cadets referee their own intramural sports) and many forums of a dialectical nature, e.g., the intercollegiate Debate Council and Forum, where cadets can defend their own conceptions of justice and truth in competition with those of their collegiate peers. The Academy's developmental interest in all such activity extends only so far as assuring that cadets be aware of the search they are pursuing, a search that will continue long after they are commissioned and that warrants Academy support through a broad range of alternatives. The specific "making of meaning" rests at all times with the individual cadet.

Given this developmental interest, the purpose of this book, as stated in the introduction, is two-fold: (1) to explain how leaders of character are developed at West Point, and (2) to explain, from the perspectives of the traditional faiths, how the moral precepts found in the Cadet Prayer may influence the development of individual cadets pursuing a faith-based search for personal meaning.

We should pause to emphasize also that generations of cadets who have freely chosen not to pursue a faith-based approach to their moral development have, according to their own testimony, found profound meaning, guidance, and inspiration from the moral ideals so eloquently stated in the Cadet Prayer.

This book is divided into three parts. Chapter 2, Part I, will amplify the preparatory discussion of Chapter 1 with a more focused look at the human spirit. Chapter 3 will move from the abstract to the real world of concrete particulars in the form of two narratives by Academy graduates treating their own moral search while cadets. The graduation years of the two cadets were some two decades apart, lending greater longitudinal validity to their combined perspectives. Chapter 3 is intended to provide the reader a more complete understanding of just what goes on in the minds of cadets as they develop, as recollected in the tranquility of later years.

Part II continues with three chapters in an analytical vein by current or former Academy faculty. Chapters 4 and 5 are by psychologists and leadership theorists, while Chapter 6 was prepared by a philosopher trained in military ethics. Considering the three together, the reader will come to understand in more detail how and why the Cadet Leader Development System is shaped the way it is. They should not be surprised to learn that most of the system is focused on developing the commissioned leader of character.

Part III of the book devotes a chapter to the perspective of each of the four dominant faiths represented at West Point—Chapter 7, Roman Catholic; Chapter 8, Jewish; Chapter 9, Muslim; and Chapter 10, Protestant— explaining how the moral precepts within the Cadet Prayer influence the inner development of inquiring cadets. These four chapters are thus largely the work of current or past members of the USMA Chaplain's staff at the Academy.

I believe readers will agree after digesting the contents of this book that the moral precepts written into the Cadet Prayer in 1924, its year of composition, are as relevant and apt today as they were then, judged in light of the unique developmental needs of those young Americans called to the professional vocation of officership. The Prayer serves equally for all, whether developing the moral character of warriors like Donald Bennett and his classmates graduating in 1940 bound for the bloody fields of World War II, or those deploying to Afghanistan and Iraq during the period 2003–2007. We can be absolutely certain it will be just as useful for America's future warriors in the inevitable wars to come.

Notes

1. General Donald V. Bennett, U.S.Army Ret., and William R. Forstchen, *Honor Untarnished: A West Point Graduate's Memoir of World War II* (New York, N.Y: Forge, 2003), 303-304.
2. General George C. Marshall, quoted in Department of the Army Pamphlet 600-63-12, *Spiritual Fitness: Fit to Win* (Washington, DC: U.S. Government Printing Office, September 1987), 1.
3. Colin L. Powell, Comments on the Receipt of the USMA Association of Graduates Thayer Award, West Point, NY, September 15, 1998, accessed August 6, 2006, at http://www.aogusma.org/aog/awards/TA/98Speech.html.
4. John J. Mearsheimer, "The Aims of Education Address, 1997," accessed on January 1, 2006, at http://www.uchicago.edu/docs/education/record/10-23-97/aimsofeducation.html.
5. Andrew Abbott, "Welcome to the University of Chicago," The Aims of Education Address, 2002, accessed on January 11, 2006, at http://www.ditext.com/abbott/abbott_aims.html.

6. This section of the present chapter is an abbreviated version of chap. 1 in Don M. Snider, project director, and Lloyd Matthews, editor, *The Future of the Army Profession*, 2d ed. (Boston: MA, McGraw-Hill, 2005). That chapter deals with how West Point revamped its approach to leader development in the late 1990s.

7. See Don M. Snider, John A. Nagl, and Tony Pfaff, *Army Professionalism, the Military Ethic, and Officership in the 21st Century* (Carlisle Barracks, PA: U.S. Army War College, Strategic Studies Institute, 1999); and Don M. Snider and Gayle Watkins, project directors, and Lloyd Matthews, editor, *The Future of the Army Profession* (Boston, MA: McGraw-Hill, 2002), 537-546.

8. See Mark Lewis, "Transformation and Junior Officer Exodus," *Armed Forces and Society* (Fall 2004): 63-93.

9. See Gayle L. Watkins and Randi C. Cohen, "In Their Own Words: Army Officers Discuss Their Profession," in *The Future of the Army Profession*, 2d ed., chap. 5.

10. Office of Policy, Planning, and Analysis, U.S. Military Academy, *Strategic Vision – 2010* (West Point, NY, 2000), 7. This mission statement has been modified by a few words in subsequent versions.

11. Professor Huntington began his classic treatise as follows: "The modern officer corps is a professional body and the modern military officer a professional man. This is, perhaps, the most fundamental thesis of this book." See Samuel P. Huntington, *The Soldier and the State: The Theory and Politics of Civil-Military Relations* (Cambridge, MA: Belknap Press of Harvard University, 1957), 7.

12. "Fallen out of favor" is, perhaps, an understatement. For example, the 2001 version of FM 22-100, *Army Leadership,* addressed the role of the commissioned officer only in an appendix, and did not even use the noun "profession."

13. *USMA Strategic Vision-2010,* xx.

14. Ibid., 8. I should note that the development of the eight principles was no easy task. They were originally formulated as 12 principles in Snider, Nagl, and Pfaff, 36-42, but subsequent vetting within the committee, with Academy leaders, and ultimately with a host of senior retired Army officers including former Chiefs of Staff, eventually reduced the list to eight.

15. The committee was well aware that the Academy had always educated and trained its graduates quite well. But, as discussed earlier, educating and training them for "what" was now less clear. Thus we accepted that the Academy must do much better at "inspiring" them to service in whatever future might eventuate. See CLDS Manual, 17, 24.

16. CLDS Manual, 21-24.

17. Field Manual 1, *The Army* (Washington, DC: Department of the Army, 2005), 1-18, 1-19.

18. Scott Snook, "Be, Know, Do: Forming Character the West Point Way," *COMPASS: A Journal of Leadership* (March 2004): 16-20.

19. CLDS Manual, 27-28.

20. Higher Education Research Institute, *The Spiritual Life of College Students: A National Study of College Students' Search for Meaning and Purpose* (Los Angeles: University of California, 2005), accessed June 2005 at http://www.spirituality.ucla.edu.

21. Gilbert W. Fairholm, *Capturing the Heart of Leadership: Spirituality and Community in the New American Workplace* (Westport, CT: Praeger Publishers, 2000), 1.

22. CLDS Manual, 16.
23. One very useful definition of the professional practice of Army Officers is "the repetitive exercise of discretionary judgment," which is continuous for those in combat operations. See Don M. Snider, "The Multiple Identities of the Professional Army Officer," in *The Future of the Army Profession*, 2d ed. (New York, NY: McGraw-Hill, 2005), 139-146.
24. See chap. 6 of the present book for a more complete discussion of the uncodified nature of the ethic. For a listing of the most salient elements of the Army ethic as winnowed from the authoritative sources, see Lloyd J. Matthews, entry titled "Ideals, Military" in *The Oxford Companion to American Military History*, ed. John Whitehead Chambers II (Oxford, England: Oxford University Press, 1999), 324. See also Keith E. Bonn, *Army Officer's Guide*, 49th edition (Mechanicsburg, PA: Stackpole Books, 2002), 67-81. Though unofficial, the various editions of this book have provided useful and accessible information to Army officers on their professional/ethical responsibilities since 1930.
25. See *Perspectives on Officership: The Commissioned Army Leader*, 3d ed., published by the William E. Simon Center for the Professional Military Ethic, United States Military Academy (New York: McGraw-Hill Publishing, 2005), *xxxi*.
26. See chap. 4 of the present volume for a discussion of the cognitive processes inherent within this moral search.
27. See chap. 5 of the present volume for an example of such research.
28. CLDS Manual, 28.
29. Longitudinal data collected voluntarily from incoming freshmen (Plebes) indicate consistently that over 90 percent of Academy cadets do identify a religious preference among the 75 faiths and denominations listed. Data received by author from Office of the USCC Chaplain, West Point, NY, August 18, 2006.

Appendix 1–A, Chapter 1
The Principles of Officership

(1) Duty. Professional officers always do their duty, subordinating personal interests to the requirements of the professional function. They are prepared, if necessary, to lay down their own lives and the lives of their soldiers in the Nation's interest. When an officer is assigned a mission or task, its successful execution is first priority, above all else, with officers accepting full responsibility for their actions and orders in accomplishing it—and accomplishing it in the right way. The officer's duty is not confined, however, to explicit orders or tasks; it extends to any circumstance involving allegiance to the commissioning oath.

(2) Honor. An officer's honor is of paramount importance, derived historically from demonstrated courage in combat. It includes the virtues of integrity and honesty. Integrity is the personal honor of the individual officer, manifested in all roles. In peace, an officer's honor is reflected in consistent acts of moral courage. An officer's word is an officer's bond.

(3) Loyalty. Military officers serve in a public vocation; their loyalty extends upward through the chain of command to the President as Commander in Chief and downward to all subordinates. Officers take care of their soldiers and families. This loyalty is central to the trust that binds together the military profession for its public servant role.

(4) Service to Country. An officer's motivations are noble and intrinsic: a love for the technical and human aspects of providing the Nation's security and an awareness of the moral obligation to use that expertise self-sacrificially for the benefit of society. The officer has no legacy except for the quality of his or her years of service.

(5) Competence. The serious obligations of officership—and the enormous consequences of professional failure—establish professional competence as a moral imperative. More than proficiency in the skills and abilities of the military art, professional competence in this sense includes attributes of worldliness, creativity, and confidence. Called to their profession and motivated by their pursuit of its expertise, officers commit themselves to a career of continuous study and learning.

(6) Teamwork. Officers model civility and respect for others. They understand that soldiers of a democracy value the worth and abilities of the individual, both at home and abroad. But because of the moral obligation accepted and the mortal means employed to carry out an officer's duty, the officer also emphasizes the importance of the group as against the individual. Success in war requires the subordination of the will of the individual to the task of the group. The military ethic is cooperative and cohesive in spirit, meritocratic, and fundamentally anti-individualistic and anti-careerist.

(7) Subordination. Officers strictly observe the principle that the military is subject to civilian authority and do not involve themselves or their subordinates in domestic politics or policy beyond the exercise of the basic rights of citizenship. Military officers render candid and forthright professional judgments and advice and eschew the public advocate's role.

(8) Leadership. Officers lead by example always, maintaining the personal attributes of spiritual, physical, and intellectual fitness that are requisite to the demands of their profession and which serve as examples to be emulated.

2

The Domain of the Human Spirit

Patrick J. Sweeney, Sean T. Hannah, and Don M. Snider

Introduction

Anyone with experience in close combat knows that in the face of the paralyzing fear that it brings, not all soldiers, sailors, and airman acquit themselves with the same degree of inner strength. This is not just a phenomenon of wars past. By one recent account from Iraq, American land forces have conducted in Anbar Province alone over 200 firefights within the confined rooms of concrete houses. In contrast, in Vietnam during the Tet Offensive of 1969, at the height of the urban battle for Hue U.S. forces conducted only two confined firefights of such intensity.[1]

They had no right to win. Yet they did, and in doing so they changed the course of a war . . . even against the greatest of odds, there is something in the human spirit—a magic blend of skill, faith, and valor—that can lift men from certain defeat to incredible victory.

—WALTER LORD, INSCRIPTION, BATTLE OF MIDWAY PANEL, WORLD WAR II MEMORIAL

Today the outcome of such close combat is still determined as it was in ages past, by the will, courage, and perseverance of the stronger combatants and the society they represent. To prevail, Army leaders need to be individually strong of spirit, called to their professional service, and fortified by the support of the American people. Notwithstanding the advantages offered by modern high technology, we see no chance that the nexus between soldierly spirit and success in close combat will weaken in the future. And neither did those who recently redesigned the developmental processes for the cadets at West Point.

Americans also accept the primacy of spirit, taking care to enshrine it in their most prominent war memorials. The epigraph at the beginning of this chapter recounts for all visitors to the National World War II Memorial in Washington, DC, that the Battle of Midway would have been lost save for the indomitable spirit of those who fought there. The inscription by Walter Lord makes clear that our servicemen not only won the battle, but also changed the course of history in the Pacific theater of that war. On the other side of the Memorial's ellipse, where the war in Europe and the Atlantic is portrayed, is an inscription for the Ardennes. During the Battle of the Bulge fought in that area, soldiers of the 101st Airborne Division—men of equally indomitable spirit—held out, as we read in Chapter 1, against overwhelming odds even as divisions on both their flanks crumbled under the harshness of freezing blizzards and the German Army's winter offensive.

Today, the Army expects all of its soldiers, and particularly its officer leaders under commission, to manifest the Warrior Spirit and to adhere to the demands of the Warrior's Ethos:

- I will always place the mission first.
- I will never accept defeat.
- I will never quit.
- I will never leave a fallen comrade.[2]

As emphasized in the Memorial inscription alluded to above, this ethos reflects accurately the expectations of the society the Army profession serves. In turn, the Academy is vitally concerned with how best to instill such an indomitable, winning spirit in its graduates, a goal pursued, as we saw in Chapter 1, by the various developmental activities cadets experience during their 47-month preparation to receive their commission to lead.

From the time in 2002 when two additional domains of development—spiritual and social—were added to the Cadet Leader Development System (CLDS), a major challenge has been to create among cadets and their faculty mentors a common understanding and language for development within these new domains. Simply stated, human spirituality is a topic with which many Army officers are not viscerally familiar, particularly as it relates to leader development. Regardless of its central role in the warrior ethos as enacted in the combat zone, it is fair to say that the topic is seldom seriously addressed, even in Army schools. All too often this is because of concerns that it might be misinterpreted as institutional support for religious spirituality, with any number of church-state issues attached thereto. Thus, neither the Army nor the Academy currently has such language or other tools of pedagogy for development of the human spirit broadly construed.

But it is not just within the Army profession that understanding of the human spirit is needed. An interview was recently conducted with the parents of the first Naval Academy female graduate to be killed in Iraq, Marine Maj. Megan McClure. The journalist conducting the interview was at a loss for words to explain what he learned from her parents. When he offered condolences, Megan's mother replied that "she had died doing what she believed in and that's a great gift." The journalist continued:

> There's an incredible eloquence and depth in these words. . . . There are certain irreducible elements in a person's essence that cannot be separated out and conveniently lent to arguments over politics and war. One of the irreducible elements of Major McClure's life was her belief in the cause, her

dedication to the mission. That's military talk that a lot of people don't understand, but it's a point of view that should be draped in honor. I'm not talking about medals or other trappings, but the honor of being true to one's self.[3]

In this chapter, then, we seek to explain that ineffable something the journalist could only describe as "military talk." We do this by presenting very briefly a proposed framework to further understanding of human spirituality and what it means to "be true to one's self." We hope that such a framework will assist cadets and their faculty and staff mentors in discussing their own development in these newly defined domains.

Narrowing the Topic

Obviously, the subject of the human spirit is immensely broad. The etymology of the word spirit indicates a source in the Latin, *spiritus,* meaning breath, later moving to the English language via the Old French *esprit,* from which we derive esprit de corps to mean the élan or spiritedness of a military organization.[4] The spirit has traditionally been understood to be the animating force, or the energy, within living beings. It has therefore been strongly linked with the occurrence of life itself, distinguishing a living from a nonliving person.

More recently, the subject of the human spirit and its role in mortal combat has been usefully adapted within the Army's own professional literature. As two respected soldier-scholars deeply versed in psychological studies of soldiers following the terrorist attacks of September 11, 2001, and Operation Iraqi Freedom have written: "All soldiers have human needs and most have spiritual needs broadly defined, and converting these needs into strengths of will and character is an important part of combat leadership."[5]

Thus the Army profession has historically considered it important to understand how soldiers could persevere, as at Midway and the Battle of the Bulge, under the most daunting and demoralizing circumstances to produce victory in battle when all rational calculation seemed to indicate that defeat was inevitable. And what the profession has learned is that soldiers who have strong, indomitable spirits can face the unimaginable dangers, horrors, and hardships of combat and still persevere to complete the mission.[6] Indeed, it is the spirit that drives soldiers to self-sacrifice and to prevail. The result that flows from the presence or absence of such spirit can be contrasted across armies, as for example the case of the Iraqi soldiers during the first Gulf War, whose readiness to surrender caused their lines to rapidly fold, leading to a swift defeat.[7]

A leader's spirit imbues in his soldiers the purpose, direction, will, and courage to do the right thing in the very complex and chaotic environment of combat, where life, death, and strategic interests of the country hinge on the leader's decisions.[8] Leaders who nurture their own and their followers' spirits are preparing their soldiers to meet the harsh rigors and stresses of combat, thereby enhancing the combat power of their unit, promoting the growth of their followers as humans, and helping protect soldiers from post-traumatic stress disorder (PTSD) and other battle-induced pathologies.[9] In its published doctrine, the Army has recognized the critical importance of developing the human spirit, incorporating it, among other places, in its master plan for promoting soldier well-being in its totality.[10]

In the balance of this chapter, we will offer a conception of how the human spirit is developed, including a model that explicates the domain of the human spirit, discuss how innate human needs drive the development of the human spirit, and explain how one's spiritual development is experienced and manifested.

In doing so, we have reduced the complexity of spirituality so as to establish a common framework, one that can be implemented and utilized in various belief systems. We recognize some limitation to this model as it may relate to any specific belief system, but do hold that it captures many of the innate core processes that produce a leader's spirit. We acknowledge that some individuals, such as those whose moral quest in based on a specific religious faith, may find this model insufficiently complete to encompass their full definition of spirituality. We believe, however, that it is a model which they can individually add to, thus accommodating it to their own value systems.

The reader will find that, once rightly understood, development of the human spirit is thoroughly manifested in who we are now, in who we seek to become, and in most of our thoughts and actions in between. In other words, our spirit represents our evolving human essence from which we cannot divorce ourselves; it will always be an integral part of our being, our actions, and our social interactions.

A Definition of the Domain of the Human Spirit

Returning to the definition offered earlier, we can define spirit as "the vital animating force within living beings; the part of a human being associated with mind, will, and feelings; and the essential nature of a person."[11] According to this definition, the human spirit influences how one thinks, acts, and feels about life. Thus, the development of the human spirit should form the cornerstone of any leader development program.

To advance our understanding of how the human spirit develops, we revisited the literatures of humanist psychology and human spirituality. The humanist psychologists view such development in terms of realizing one's full potential, or self-actualization. To do so, people must determine their purpose in life, discover who they truly are, and develop the strength to pursue activities that will develop the true or authentic self regardless of any contrary expectations from others.[12] Similarly, scholars of spirituality, particularly as regards college students, view individual spiritual development as the inward quest to discover one's identity, purpose, meaning, truth about the world and life after death, and how to live a life that matters.[13] Integrating the concepts from both the humanist psychology and spiritual literatures, we offer the following definition of the development of the human spirit:

It is an individual's search to find:

- *one's true self in terms of core values and beliefs (character);*
- *meaning and purpose in life, making a difference and thus making life worth living;*
- *truth about the world, enlightenment;*
- *relationships that bring fulfillment, and*
- *the autonomy to pursue realization of one's full potential.*[14]

Psychological Components of the Domain of the Human Spirit

To discuss the development of the human spirit, we focus on identifying the psychological structures and states that comprise an individual's spirit. Common themes found in both literatures were the following:

- To develop the spirit, one must engage in self-reflection and introspection; self-awareness is critical.
- Increased self-awareness allows one to solidify his/her values and belief system (character), which forms the foundation of one's personal philosophy or worldview.
- One's evolving worldview is used to determine truth and make meaning out of experiences.
- Spiritual development is the individual's responsibility; institutions can only provide conducive conditions.
- In order to establish positive relationships and further refine one's worldview, one must develop social awareness (empathy and respect), which is necessary to understand others' emotions and viewpoints.
- An individual must have a strong conviction (faith) that living according to one's values and beliefs and striving to realize one's potential will lead to a fulfilling and satisfying life.

Since development of the human spirit is universal and occurs in all cultures,[15] we accept Abraham Maslow's proposition that innate human needs drive the process.[16] We will return to this proposition after we present a model of the domain of the human spirit.

We propose that the domain of the human spirit consists of the psychological components as depicted in Figure 2-1: *a worldview, self-awareness, a sense of agency, social awareness,* and *faith.* These components are interrelated, and taken together they foster the growth of the human spirit. We believe that an understanding of these components and the relationships between them can facilitate cadets' individual journeys toward spiritual development while also providing leaders and mentors insights as to how best to contribute to or otherwise facilitate these explorations.

Before we proceed, we need to clarify the semantic distinction between *human spirit* and the complementary noun *spirituality*. While we view the former as a product—i.e., the vital animating force or essence defining us as uniquely human—that one may choose to develop over time, the latter can be viewed as the degree of receptivity one feels toward undertaking such development. Specifically, the human spirit is a leader's current state as it relates to possession of the components of the framework in Figure 2-1. At any point in his career apprenticeship, a leader has a certain level of agency, faith, self-awareness, and social awareness, and his aim should be to gradually increase the level and integration of these qualities. *Spirituality,* by way of comparison, can be seen as a leader's inclination and orientation to pursue such development and enlightenment within the domain of the human spirit.

In certain contexts, it is useful to use the noun *spirituality* (along with its adjectival cognate *spiritual*) in a second sense, that is, as applying to the *process* whereby the components of worldview, sense of agency, self-awareness, social awareness, and faith interact to promote growth of the human spirit, as depicted by the bi-directional influence arrows in Figure 2-1. Thus, the ameliorative transformation we seek in the human spirit of leaders can well be described as a *spiritual* quest or an adventure in *spirituality.*

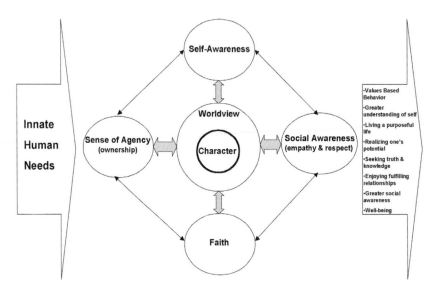

Figure 2-1. *Conceptualization of the Domain of the Human Spirit.*

We turn now to a description of each component of the domain of the human spirit:

Worldview. A person's worldview can be understood as the lens through which he/she views the grand stage of human existence. It is an individual's personal life philosophy used to make meaning out of experiences and to provide direction and purpose in life.[17] This complex cognitive framework determines what one attends to, how one interprets information and events, the knowledge and experiences one seeks out, and how one behaves.[18] Not static, but dynamic, a person's worldview actually influences every aspect of his/her current life and future goals. Thus, a person's worldview is the foundation upon which the development of the human spirit rests.

This cognitive framework contains at any point in time an individual's collection of knowledge and assumptions about how the world operates; truths about the world based on learning and experiences; a system for determining truth and meaning; values and beliefs that one should live by; a vision of a life rendered worth living by making a meaningful contribution; reflections on one's mortality; and beliefs about what comes after death.[19] Individuals continuously refine and develop their worldviews through the acquisition of new knowledge, reflection on their own and others' experiences, introspection concerning their values, beliefs, and meaning-making systems, and discussing with others topics about their human essence.

Worldviews are largely shaped through the socialization processes of the mediating institutions of family, school, and church, among others. Parents' childrearing techniques, the community's cultural expectations, educational and life experiences, and religious or philosophical practices all play a role in the development of the early worldview of children. The cornerstone of a person's worldview, as depicted in Figure 2-1, is one's values and beliefs system or character. This system defines who the person is and what the person stands for, serves as a guide for determining behavior—especially in ambiguous and chaotic situations—and also provides the courage and will to act in accordance with one's beliefs and values.[20] For most people, adolescence is the time they begin their struggle to discover their own identity and character and to establish themselves as independent and unique individuals.[21] Thus, the college or post-high school experiences are critical periods in which to establish coherent and soundly evolving worldviews.

From the military perspective, the soldier's character provides the physical courage to fight in close combat and the moral courage to act in accord with, and to enforce, the profession's ethics. A major insight offered by Lord Moran in his classic book, *The Anatomy of Courage,* is that "a man of character in peace is a man of courage in war."[22] A strong character provides a person with a sense of continuity and stability in one's day-to-day life.[23] It is here that the moral precepts of the Cadet Prayer resonate so strongly, serving as a moral compass for guiding future behavior. The compass points are the attributes that all officers require—e.g., "Make us to choose the harder right instead of the easier wrong and never to be content with a half-truth when the whole can be won." In Chapter 4, we shall propose and discuss in some detail a model for how to develop one's values and belief system, worldview, and sense of moral agency.

Finally, in the interpersonal realm, an officer's worldview is central to his/her leadership as it provides the cognitive lens through which the officer experiences and makes meaning of personal experiences as well as those of followers. It is this ability to make meaning and communicate that meaning to their followers that enables officers to provide purpose, motivation, and direction amid the stress of combat.

Self-Awareness. Reflection and introspection are the processes individuals use to enhance development of their human spirits.[24] Through reflection and self-examination people gain insights into life's most pregnant questions, such as: Who am I, what is my purpose in life, what is a life worth living, who do I want to become, what can I believe in, how do I live a life that will make a difference, and how can I be happy?[25] Answers to these pressing introspective questions help form and shape one's worldview and identity.

Indeed leaders cannot separate their own self-concept from their concept of the external world. The self-concept is in fact an idiosyncratic "construct" leaders develop over their lifespan as they interpret and encode their personal experiences into memory.[26] In essence, leaders learn who they are as they interact with and receive feedback from their social environment. It is through dedicated reflection about these experiences that the self with its human essence becomes "known" to the individual. We argue that to the extent leaders' developmental experiences contain elements of the spiritual, the more they reflect on these elements the greater will be the growth of their own human spirit. This drive for reflection and self-awareness—to know oneself—is part of one's spiritual orientation, a part of one's *spirituality.*

Reflection and introspection allow leaders to make sense out of their own and others' experiences and in the process create new meaning or knowledge. Reflection and introspection also help organize and integrate the content of their worldviews. Therefore, everyone, especially young adults, should set aside time for reflection, particularly in solitude, to gain a penetrating view of their inner lives. Leaders can use various activities as opportunities to facilitate reflection and introspection: journaling, sitting in a quiet location, writing a paper on a topic that requires introspection, listening to music, walking, hiking, trail running, meditating, biking, praying, participating in a retreat, watching the sun rise or set, and lifting weights.[27] The venue or type of activity is not important; the keys are solitude and quiet time to reflect and assess one's inner life.

These periods of reflection and introspection provide leaders with the opportunity to question and evaluate aspects of their worldviews, which were mostly shaped for them through early socialization and learning processes. It is through continuous reflection and introspection that leaders gain the ability to step outside those handed-down worldviews shaped largely by parents and culture, and then to self-author their own unique worldviews.[28] These processes of enhancing self-awareness provide leaders with a greater understanding of who they truly are, who they want to become, how to determine truth and meaning, and how they should lead their lives. All of this promotes the development of their worldview schemas. It is thus through self-awareness that leaders gain the ability to chart and focus their quest to develop their human essence.

Such spiritual self-awareness is critical to leadership. Before they can provide value-based leadership and facilitate idealization and inspiration in others, leaders must have a firm grasp of who they are, what their core values and beliefs are, and their self-concept as it relates to their role as a leader. During combat, a leader's self-concept will be challenged as his/her values, beliefs, needs, and other elements of the self are strained to make meaning of and reconcile their chosen profession with the horrors of warfare. It is only the self-aware and resolute leader who can operate effectively under such challenges and provide the moral compass for their followers' actions.

Sense of Agency. The development of the human spirit is an active, dynamic, and very personal journey that the individual owns exclusively. Agency involves assuming ownership of and responsibility for one's spiritual development and having a sense of confidence that one can successfully guide this developmental quest. Individuals who assume responsibility for such development and actively engage in activities that foster the growth of their spirits tend to live satisfying and contented lives.[29] Those who fail to take responsibility for the development of their human spirit are forced to live with the worldviews that society imposes on them, which can cause extreme psychological distress.

A sense of agency empowers people to reflect, evaluate, and self-author their own worldview. It provides the independence of thought to chart their own path for the development of their spirit and to step away from the expectations of others.[30] In a sense, such agency provides them with essential control over their own destiny. Individuals with a sense of agency will actively seek out activities that impart new knowledge, create new experiences that reinforce or challenge their existing worldview, and promote self-reflection and introspection in order to develop and strengthen the human spirit.[31] These empowered individuals will demand the freedom to develop their spirit in the way they see fit. Freedom of thought and action are necessary conditions for one's sense of agency to grow.[32]

Educational institutions, the Academy included, can better facilitate their students' sense of agency by providing access to various resources: a broad curriculum that exposes students to topics on the human spirit, e.g., comparative philosophy and courses about religions, libraries that are well resourced with diverse materials, interfaith and philosophical forums for exchanging ideas, opportunities for community service, quiet places for reflection, and physical fitness facilities that offer a wide variety of athletic pursuits.[33] Perhaps most importantly, they should also provide faculty who are able to aid students in their journeys regardless of the path.[34] Educators can also assign writing requirements such as essays or journals that require students to reflect on and evaluate the content of experiences as they relate to their worldview. Such faculty should encourage and respect the free exchange of questions and ideas relating to the human spirit in the classroom as students learn of the world beyond their own experience.[35]

However, educational institutions and faculty must keep in mind that spiritual development is an individual journey; therefore, they must be very careful not to promote one path of spiritual development over another. They should recognize that a majority of college students will use religious practices as a primary, but perhaps not sole, vehicle for spiritual development. A national study conducted in 2003 by the University of California found that over two-thirds (74,073) of the 112,232 college freshmen surveyed resorted to some sort of religious practice for their development within the domain of the human spirit.[36] Other students may anchor the development of their spirit in the pursuit of various philosophies. Students will more than likely use a combination of activities to promote the development of their spirit. The important point is that the willingness of institutional leaders to provide freedom, resources, and activities to facilitate the journeys of all students does enhance the students' sense of agency. Conversely, without such institutional support, the growth of such agency can be frustrated.

Social Awareness. Social awareness is important to the development of the human spirit because without respect and empathy a person will have trouble forming connections with other people and ideas. This will in turn hinder the ability to form new relationships and to gain new knowledge about diverse cultures and ideas. Without such experiences there can be little broadening or refinement of one's worldview.

Thus, the quest to develop the human spirit requires people to develop the social skills necessary to establish positive relationships with others. Respect for others is the first social skill one must develop. Respect is simply recognizing and acknowledging that others have the right to hold different values, beliefs, and customs and that one must, without giving up one's own beliefs and values, show them due consideration and be open to learn from alternative views. This form of toleration is bedrock to democratic pluralism, the Constitutionally founded form of government that the Army profession is sworn to defend. Respect also entails the ability to appreciate others and their beliefs without immediately judging them as being inferior because they differ from one's own. Showing respect for others' views communicates that they are acknowledged, valued, and accepted as humans, which sets the conditions for positive interactions and learning from each other.[37]

Moreover, to truly understand others an individual must have the empathic ability to place himself/herself in the shoes of others and view the world through their lens. Social-awareness enhances empathy by increasing the person's capability to recognize emotions in others.[38] Empathy allows one to see the situation as others see it, to feel the emotions that others feel, and to experience the motivational forces that compel behavior by others as they experience these forces.[39] This is a daunting challenge for all of us! But a person can use insights into others' perspectives to expand and refine his/her own worldview and to develop positive relationships that communicate understanding, acceptance, and care for others.[40]

Such social awareness is central to effective military leadership. We discussed at the beginning of this chapter the importance of the leader's human spirit in facing the perils of combat while behaving within the bounds of the warrior ethos. To be able to do so, leaders must be aware of, accepting of, and able to leverage and draw upon their followers' inspired motivations, their human spirits. Indeed, we suggest that such leadership should be seen and valued as a unit combat power multiplier.

Faith. Faith is defined in *Webster's Universal Encyclopedic Dictionary* as "something that is believed especially with strong conviction; allegiance to duty or to a person; a firm belief in something for which there is no proof; complete trust; or fidelity to one's promises." Such faith is critical because it provides the *direction* and *will* to persist in the continuous, often arduous, journey of life and the *trust* and *hope* that the journey will produce a life worth living.

Simply stated, faith is what keeps us striving toward life's goals, the striving that fuels our hope for a successful, meaningful life. For many soldiers and cadets, such faith will be grounded primarily in one of the world's religions, but if not that is a personal choice to be respected by all. As mentioned earlier, many college-age individuals place their faith in several belief systems at once during the intense interactions between higher education and spiritual awareness and growth.

For the purposes of this discussion, then, the kind of faith we are interested in is intrapersonal; it is a person's confident belief in and commitment to a life-long quest to develop and to live in accordance with one's values and principles—to be true to self as was Maj. Megan McClure. Otherwise, what motivation leads us to live and strive, or even more, to serve others? As the epigraph to this chapter reminds us, such faith was an element evident in the indomitable spirit of those who won the Battle of Midway and other battles critical to national survival.

At the intrapersonal level, then, such faith provides a strong sense of conviction or expectancy that there is a path which, if followed, will lead to enjoying the experiences of truth, happiness, fulfillment, and, if one so believes, nonworldly rewards such as eternal life. That path consists of living by one's own values and principles; continuously refining knowledge of the inner self through reflection and introspection; striving to develop one's full potential by seeking out new knowledge and experiences; working for noble pursuits that have a positive impact on others; developing positive relationships with family, friends, and associates; and appreciating and respecting others. Thus, the kind of faith we are addressing here keeps the person moving forward to develop his/her essence, to seek truth, and to live above the common level of life out of the firm belief that it is the right thing to do.

For the Army officer in particular, such faith works in the same way except that it does so within the context of the profession's service to the American people. Such faith provides officers the courage to behave according to their values and principles and according to the profession's ethic in the face of bureaucratic pressures to do otherwise; to seek growth experiences that stretch capabilities instead of "playing it safe" with the next assignment; to explore and understand new cultures despite initial discomforts; to engage in self-reflection and introspection even when it is painful; to join a noble and prosocial profession such as the Army instead of pursuing financial wealth; to focus on the good in the world when the news media focus on the negative; and to continue to strive to have a positive influence when others do not seem to value or appreciate it.

In sum, we suggest that these five components, as diagramed in Figure 2-1, provide the needed model for understanding the domain of the human spirit. With this model explained, we now turn to a discussion of the innate human needs that drive the processes within the model.

Innate Human Needs and Development of the Human Spirit

As we mentioned earlier, people from every culture are engaged in the quest to develop their essence, so it is logical to accept the hypothesis that innate human needs drive the development of the human spirit (see left side, Figure 2-1). In his theory of human motivation, Abraham Maslow proposed that the following hierarchy of human needs, ranging from the most basic to the most advanced, drive the development of the human spirit:

- physiological (survival needs),
- safety or security (control and predictability),
- belongingness and love (affiliation),
- esteem (efficacy and respect),
- knowing and understanding (curiosity and insights),
- experiencing the aesthetic (order, symmetry, and closure), and
- self-actualization (reaching one's full potential).[41]

It is in striving to satisfy these innate needs that the development of the human spirit is advanced. According to Maslow's theory, as each level of need is met, the need at the next level of advancement becomes more dominant as a source of motivation. Thus, once a given need is mostly satisfied (e.g., safety), that need diminishes as a source of motivation, while advanced-order needs (e.g., belongingness) take over as more dominant sources of motivation. If an individual is working to satisfy advanced needs and satisfaction of a more basic need is threatened, the person may redirect efforts to meet the basic need.[42] Ultimately, assisting developing leaders in their spiritual growth toward the most advanced level, self-actualization, will be facilitated when leadership development experiences provide broad opportunities to advance through the complete hierarchy of human needs in a progressive manner. We turn now to a discussion of how an individual's striving to meet the various needs contributes to development of the psychological structures and states that, as earlier posited, comprise the domain of the human spirit.

Need for Safety. Beyond the most basic need of all—survival—a person's need for safety compels him/her to develop a worldview or personal life philosophy in order to understand and accommodate to the immediate environment. There are two aspects of the safety need: physical and psychological. The physical aspect is met when people feel secure and protected against threats from criminals, nature, and anything that could do them harm. We cannot imagine a physical context wherein this need is more salient than that of combat. Regarding the psychological aspect, people feel safe when they have a means to organize circumstances in an orderly and predictable manner so that unexpected, unmanageable, and dangerous events are less likely to happen. Thus, they innately seek a sense of control over the events of life.[43]

A leader gains a sense of control over such events through the establishment of a worldview, enabling prediction and sound expectation as to what is coming. As stated earlier, this schema contains knowledge and assumptions about how the world operates, a values and beliefs system, ideas about one's role or purpose in the world, and a vision of who the person is striving to become. Thus, a worldview provides the ability to reasonably extrapolate to a provisional view of future situations and how others will act and react, thus providing a sense of control and predictability in life.

Need to Belong and Be Loved. The innate affiliation need manifests itself in a desire to connect to something, or someone, outside and more powerful than the self. The key to meeting this innate need is the ability of individuals to transcend the self and subordinate their own interests. This transcendence involves the humbling realization that one is but a small actor in this vast universe and that a connection with a more powerful force can empower, enrich, and inspire one's life. The source of this connection could be an individual, a group, a supreme deity, an idea, a philosophy, or a calling to vocation such as the officer's calling to the Army profession.

This innate desire to connect with someone or something more powerful than the individual serves an adaptive function because it contributes to one's sense of safety through physical and psychological support and also enhances one's worldview by serving as a source of new knowledge and inspiration for one's purpose in life. Being loved, valued, and accepted by others reaffirms one's perceptions of self-worth and also contributes to feelings of wholeness. Thus, individuals'need to seek connections with people, groups, ideas, or deities outside of themselves to help shape and develop their human spirits.[44]

The military profession has long recognized the empowering benefits of a greater sense of confidence, safety, and purpose gained from meeting soldiers' innate need for affiliation. This is why the U.S. military places such great emphasis on unit heritage, unit integrity, promoting selfless service and teamwork, and demanding loyalty in terms of taking care of one's buddy and the unit. For example, a soldier who has established positive relationships (connections) with other members in the squad has eight other people looking out for his safety and sharing the burdens of combat, which boosts his sense of confidence and safety and also greatly increases the soldier's probability of survival.[45] In addition, the connection with others provides a social support network that helps the soldier deal with the fears and stresses of combat.

Through this social network, a soldier can learn new knowledge about how to deal with stress; express fears and other emotions; receive understanding, acceptance, and validation for emotions experienced; learn combat survival techniques; and, most important, learn new ways to come to terms with traumatic events.[46] The collective meaning-making that takes place in social networks tends to enhance soldiers' worldviews. Thus, by forming these connections with other soldiers and the group, each soldier gains a greater sense of confidence in his/her own ability as well as the unit's to successfully complete the mission and survive in doing it. Soldiers who fail to make connections with others tend not to last long in the combat zone. They either succumb to stress or are injured or killed early in their tours because they are not fully connected to the social support system in the unit.[47] Most importantly, these connections between soldiers serve as the primary source of motivation for them to fight.[48] This is why cohesion continues to play such a critical role in individual and unit performance in combat.

Need for Esteem. The innate need for esteem plays a significant role in the development of a person's sense of agency (responsibility for and ownership of one's destiny) and also impacts the development of one's worldview. Maslow proposed that the innate need for esteem entailed two interrelated components: self-esteem and gaining the esteem of others.[49] Self-esteem consists of a person's feeling that he/she has the ability to act independently to achieve life goals and to handle life's challenges. Thus self-esteem is very important in the development of a sense of agency. Individuals who feel confident that they can chart and master their own life journeys are more likely to assume the responsibility for developing their human spirit. They will actively seek out and engage in activities that promote the development of their worldviews. On the other hand, people with low self-esteem are more likely to have a lesser sense of agency regarding the development of their human spirit because they do not feel they have the ability to control their destiny. Individuals with low self-esteem are more apt to let society and others influence or even dictate the development their human spirit.

Receiving the esteem of others in terms of praise, recognition, status, and appreciation provides external verification of one's abilities and worth to others. This validation of one's value to others enhances self-esteem and a sense of agency, and facilitates positive emotions and human flourishing. In addition, being valued by others provides individuals with the sense that they are important and that their presence in the world makes a difference, all of which bolsters faith in their developmental journey and their evolving worldviews.[50] Soldiers must be imbued not only with such personal esteem, but also with pride and esteem in their unit, which promotes cohesion and a collective sense of purpose.

Need to Know and Understand. The innate human need to know and understand significantly contributes to the development of a person's worldview and feelings of safety. Individuals' curiosity and desire to seek out and learn new knowledge helps them gain a greater understanding of how the world works and how people live in it, which adds to the richness and complexity of their own worldview (see Chapter 4 for a fuller explication of moral complexity). In turn, a more refined worldview helps them to perceive more orderliness, meaning, and predictability in both themselves and the world, thus contributing to a greater sense of safety.

The innate need for knowledge and understanding also contributes to individuals' motivation to engage in self-reflection and introspection with the hope of discovering insights about themselves. This increased self-awareness helps people answer life's pressing questions concerning identity, purpose, a worthy contribution, and how to achieve happiness. Lastly, the need for knowledge and understanding plays a role in promoting a sense of agency in people to develop their own essence and inner strength. Such people will likely attribute their knowledge-seeking behaviors to internal states, thus providing the perception of agency or self-directed development.[51] Particularly during stressful times such as combat, leaders and their soldiers must find a level of coherence and acceptance, hence satisfying the innate need for understanding.

Need for Self-Actualization. Self-actualization is the most advanced level of Maslow's hierarchy. The need for self-actualization contributes to the growth of the human spirit by motivating people to develop themselves to become "who they must be" in order to have a life that is meaningful and makes a difference.[52] Carl Rogers, a noted humanist psychologist, proposes that the need for self-actualization is the "mainspring of life" that propels people to seek out activities that cause them to grow, mature, and become autonomous in their quest to reach their full human potential.[53] According to Rogers, to achieve self-actualization a person must: (1) determine his/her purpose in life; (2) live a responsible, moral, and self-restrained life (positive values and beliefs system); (3) be confidently proactive in initiating change to promote growth and independence (agency); (4) engage in reflection to develop one's self-awareness (introspection); (5) form connections to sources outside of the self (affiliation); and (6) learn to enjoy the simple pleasures of life (achieving happiness).[54] Thus, according to the views of both Rogers and Maslow, the innate drive towards self-actualization will develop a person's full human potential and, as well, one's human spirit.

Self-actualization is central to the identity of an officer and his/her development as a leader. Leaders tend to envision their *current self* and also a more distant *possible self* which they would like to become—their ideal self.[55] It is through envisioning, most likely by use of a role model, and by lucidly visualizing the "gaps" between the current and possible self, that leaders will be motivated to develop and actualize that possible self. It is through such processes that an officer's roles and identity as favored by both the Army and Academy will be internalized.

To the extent that leaders and their followers envision a possible self with higher capabilities for faith, agency, self-awareness, and social awareness—as integrated in Figure 2-1—they will have greater drive toward development in the domain of the human spirit. More specifically, we suggest that this drive and its developmental manifestations will be experienced as a heightened sense of *spirituality*.

Experiencing the Development of the Components of the Human Spirit

In the last portion of this chapter, and in Appendices 2–A, 2–B, and 2–C that follow, we present various emotional, cognitive, and behavioral indicators of how the development of the human spirit is manifested and experienced. The purpose is to assist cadets and their mentors to recognize and assess the development of the human spirit as they proceed through the 47-month experience at the Academy. Indeed, we believe these indicators should serve both as a rudimentary road map to chart the development of the human spirit, and as milestones to chart progress toward the possible self. Research has shown that development will occur through vicarious learning such as observing role models and imagining instructive experiences, e.g., having followers imagine themselves successfully engaging in positive spiritual behaviors and achieving their own envisioned possible selves.[56] More than likely, multiple indicators from each one of the three areas—emotional, cognitive, and behavioral—will apply. The more indicators that do apply, the greater will be the progress.[57]

Emotional Indicators (See Appendix 2–A). Development of the *worldview* manifests itself in feelings of safety, orderliness, and peace. The growth of a more complex worldview provides individuals with a greater ability to predict and make meaning out of their experiences. Thus, events do not surprise and/or shock them as much as they did earlier, and individuals no longer feel naïve regarding how the world operates. The cornerstone to one's sensation of safety and peace is the feeling that one has the correct values and beliefs (character) to function effectively in the world and to live a life that makes a difference. As individuals experience progress in becoming who they want to be and realizing their potential, they assume a sense of well-being and contentment with life. Furthermore, individuals know that their *sense of agency* is developing when they feel a sense of empowerment to self-author their own values and beliefs and to control their journey to realize their potential. Individuals feel they own and have control over their destiny because they have the capability to create the lives they seek. Growth in *social awareness* manifests itself with feelings that one has the ability to read and understand other people, see the world from others' point of view, and establish positive relationships with them. Individuals feel a greater sense of respect and appreciation for human life and also a greater sense of compassion towards others. They feel that their own lives are enriched by other people, who aid them in their journey of self-actualization.

Growth in *self-awareness* manifests itself in feelings that one is getting to know and understand oneself better. Such individuals are not afraid to reflect on and evaluate their inner lives because they feel increasingly comfortable with who they are and what they want to become. Finally, they know their *faith* is developing when they feel a strong conviction that living a life based on one's values and beliefs is right and will lead to fulfillment in spite of social pressures to live otherwise.

Cognitive Indicators (See Appendix 2–B). Individuals know that their *worldview* is developing when they generally understand how the world operates, accepting the existence of both good and evil. They become more open to, and not threatened by, new ideas, experiences, cultures, and beliefs. They develop a thirst for knowledge. Such individuals increasingly consider their own values and beliefs when making decisions because their need to maintain integrity to self outweighs the desire to meet the expectations of others. When this occurs, individuals have the autonomy to control their journey to develop their human essence.

Moreover, such individuals know they are developing their *self-awareness* when they regularly reflect on their strengths and weaknesses, their life goals, and the progress they are making toward developing their potential. They question and evaluate their values and beliefs because they want to know truth. They reflect on experiences to make meaning out of them and evaluate the implications for their worldview. The cognitive indicators of *social awareness* entail a greater understanding of people and a willingness to view others as individuals rather than applying prejudicial group stereotypes. One also develops a greater understanding of the frailty of human nature, resulting in a greater sense of compassion and desire to help others (altruism). Individuals understand and accept that others have a right to have different viewpoints, values, and beliefs, and that just because these views are different, they are not necessarily wrong, bad, or inferior.

Cognitive indicators of the development of one's *sense of agency* are thinking routinely of activities to develop the spirit, monitoring the progress of the journey, and making adjustments as needed. Individuals know and accept that they are fully responsible for and in control of their own spiritual development. As discussed earlier in connection with the emotional indicators, they feel a sense of autonomy enabling them to step away from the expectations of others and pilot their own journey with an increasingly strong belief, or faith, that the quest to develop the spirit will lead to a meaningful, noble, and fulfilling life. Such a person more and more lives a principle-centered life, even in the face of social pressures to do otherwise, because such is the right thing to do to be true to one's self.

Behavioral Indicators (See Appendix 2–C). Individuals know that their *worldview* is developing when they find themselves behaving in a more authentic manner based on their own values and beliefs. They engage naturally in activities that promote learning about new subjects, people, and cultures, such as reading about or experiencing different philosophical and religious beliefs in a search to find truth. They realize their *sense of agency* is growing the more they engage regularly in activities that help realize their full potential. Likewise, their *self-awareness* is growing when they take time routinely to engage in reflection and introspection, particularly regarding their experiences, values, beliefs, and goals in life. This can take the form of journaling, documenting life visions and goals, carrying on internal, positive dialogues with themselves, praying, or meditating on life's eternal questions.

Behavioral indicators of a developing *social awareness* are treating all people with respect, engaging in volunteerism to help others, cooperating with difficult people, and being more understanding, tolerant, and forgiving of others and their weaknesses, including being less judgmental. Greater social awareness is also manifested in the formation of positive and cooperative relationships. The main indicators of the strengthening of an individual's *faith* is a more consistent, daily striving to live a value-based life, and taking action to follow one's developmental journey despite the arduousness of the task—more often doing "the harder right instead of the easier wrong," as enjoined by the Cadet Prayer.

Conclusion

By applying a model for the domain of the human spirit, we believe cadets and the Academy's faculty and staff can achieve a needed level of commonality in understanding and articulating the development of the inner self. Individuals can understand what psychological components and states are involved and how they interact as they develop (see again Figure 2-1). These tools will provide the ability to tailor individual developmental efforts, targeting specific components of the human spirit and using applicable indicators to track progress.

With diligent application of such tools, we believe that at least five outcomes are feasible, all clearly supporting the development of commissioned leaders of character for the Army:

- An increased self-awareness by each leader, most often enhancing the ability to understand and to self-author the values and beliefs that define his/her character;
- An evolving worldview or personal life philosophy that seeks truth and justice, appreciates diversity, and continuously seeks out new experiences and knowledge to promote growth;
- A growing social awareness that fosters respect for others' viewpoints and the ability to see and understand the world through the eyes of others, an attribute critical to understanding subordinates, allies, and enemies;
- An empowered sense of control and responsibility for one's own being, existence, and development, thus fostering inner strength and fortitude; and
- A sense of conviction or faith that one is part of a noble profession, providing intrinsic motivation to service and a fulfilling life as an officer.

We have outlined spirituality as a central facet of an officer's existence and a key driving force in the behavior and meaning-making systems of both leaders and followers—especially under conditions that most try the human spirit, such as close combat. Development of the human spirit must therefore be recognized as inextricable from any development program for leaders or leadership. We propose that such development should be purposive and that it can be made so by application of this model.

As stated earlier, the military requires its members to have a strong inner strength to withstand the stresses and rigors of combat and also to achieve psychological well-being; therefore, it is absolutely imperative for military leaders to understand how to develop their own human spirit, thus facilitating the moral journeys of both themselves and their soldiers toward full possession of the Warrior Spirit.

Notes

1. F. J. Bing, "American Military Performance in Iraq," *Military Review* (September/October 2006): 2-7.
2. Department of the Army, Field Manual 1, *The Army* (June 2005), iv.
3. Dana Parsons, "Orange County Marine's Death Transcends Tragedy," *Los Angles Times,* December 14, 2006, accessed December 15, 2006 at http://ebird.afis.mil/ebfiles/e2061214473768.html.
4. *The American Heritage College Dictionary,* 3rd ed. (Boston: Houghton Mifflin, 1997).

5. John M. Brinsfield and Peter A. Baktis, "The Human, Spiritual, and Ethical Dimensions of Leadership in Preparation for Combat," in Don M. Snider, project director, and Lloyd Matthews, editor, *The Future of the Army Profession,* 2d ed. (Boston: McGraw-Hill, 2005), 464.

6. Samuel A. Stouffer et al., *The American Soldier: Combat and Its Aftermath, Vol. 2* (New York: John Wiley & Sons, 1965), 105-191.

7. Leonard Wong, "Combat Motivation in the Iraq War," in Don M. Snider, project director, and Lloyd Matthews, editor, *The Future of the Army Profession,* 2d ed. (Boston: McGraw-Hill, 2005), 491-514.

8. Department of the Army, Field Manual 22-100, *Army Leadership* (Washington, DC: US Government Printing Office, 1999), 2-2.

9. Patricia A. Resick, *Stress and Trauma* (Philadelphia: Taylor & Francis Inc., 2001), 117.

10. US Army War College, *A Well-Being Framework for the US Army* (Carlisle, PA: US Government Printing Office, 2000), 26-27.

11. *The American Heritage College Dictionary,* 3rd ed. (Boston: Houghton Mifflin, 1997), 1313.

12. Carl R. Rogers, *On Becoming a Person* (Boston: Houghton Mifflin, 1961), 164-181; and Abraham H. Maslow, *Motivation and Personality* (New York: Harper & Brothers, 1954), 80-96.

13. Jon C. Dalton et al., "Inward Journeys: Forms and Patterns of College Student Spirituality," *Journal of College and Character* 7 (October 2006): 1-22, retrieved November 13, 2006 from http://collegevalues.org/pdfs/dalton.pdf.

14. Ibid.; Rogers, 164-181; and Maslow, 80-96.

15. Christopher Peterson and Martin E. P. Seligman, *Character, Strengths, and Virtues: A Handbook and Classification* (New York: Oxford University Press, 2004), 599-622.

16. Maslow, 80-97.

17. Ibid., 94.

18. Susan Fiske and Shelley Taylor, *Social Cognition* (Reading, MA: Addison-Wesley, 1984); and, Robert Lord and Roseanne Foti, "Schema Theories, Information Processing, and Organizational Behavior," in Henry M. Sims and Dennis A. Gioia, eds., *The Thinking Organization: Dynamics of Organizational Social Cognition* (San Francisco: Jossey-Bass, 1986), 20-48.

19. Ibid., 94; and William McCoy, *Under Orders: A Spiritual Handbook for Military Personnel* (Ozark, AL: ACW Press, 2005), 173-174.

20. Leader to Leader Institute, *Be-Know-Do: Leadership the Army Way* (San Francisco: Josey-Bass, 2004), 26; and H. Dale Burke, *How to Lead and Still Have a Life* (Eugene, OR: Harvest House, 2004), 63–64.

21. Eric Erikson, *Identity: Youth and Crisis* (New York: Norton, 1968); and Rogers, 164-181.

22. Lord Moran, *The Anatomy of Courage* (Garden City, NJ: Avery Publishing Group, 1987), xii.

23. Dalton et al., 1-21.

24. Rogers, 164-165; and Dalton et al., 1-21.

25. Ibid.

26. John F. Kihlstrom, Jennifer S. Beer, and Stanley B. Klein, "Self and Identity as Memory," in Mark J. Leary and June P Tangney, eds., *Handbook of Self and Identity* (New York: Guilford Press, 2003), 68-90.

27. Arthur Schwartz, "Growing Spirituality During the College Years," *Liberal Education* 87 (2001): 30-35.

28. Robert Kegan, *The Evolving Self* (Cambridge, MA: Harvard University Press, 1982), 184-220.

29. Rogers, 170.

30. Ibid., 170-172.

31. Ibid., 33.

32. Maslow, 92.

33. Dalton et al., 1-21.

34. Carney Strange, "Spirituality at State: Private Journeys and Public Visions," *Journal of College and Character* 2 (2006): 1-7, retrieved November 9, 2006 from http://collegevalues.org/articles.cfm?a=1& id=134.

35. Dennis Holtschneider, "All the Questions: Spirituality in the University," *Journal of College and Character* 8 (2006): 1-3, retrieved on November 20, 2006 from http://collegevalues.org/pdfs/Holtschneider.pdf.

36. Higher Education Research Institute, "The Spiritual Life of College Students: A National Study of Students' Search for Meaning and Purpose" (2004), retrieved November 13, 2006, from http://www.spirituality.ucla.edu/spirituality/reports/.

37. Rogers, 37-38.

38. Daniel Goleman, *Emotional Intelligence* (New York: Bantam Books, 1995), 96.

39. Rogers, 34.

40. Ibid., 34; and Goleman, 100.

41. Maslow, 80-98.

42. Ibid., 80-84.

43. Ibid., 87.

44. Sharon D. Parks, *Big Questions, Worthy Dreams: Mentoring Young Adults in Their Search for Meaning, Purpose, and Faith* (San Francisco: Jossey-Bass, 2000), 90.

45. Stouffer et al., 142-149.

46. Roger W. Little, "Buddy Relations and Combat Performance," in Morris Janowitz, ed., *The New Military: Changing Patterns of Organizations* (New York: Russell Sage Foundation, 1964), 195-223.

47. Franklin D. Jones, "Traditional Warfare Combat Stress Casualties," in The Surgeon General, *Textbook of Military Medicine: War Psychiatry* (Washington, DC: Walter Reed Army Institute of Research, 1995), 38.

48. Stouffer et al., 179.

49. Maslow, 90.

50. Ibid., 91.

51. Daryl J. Bem, "Self-perception: An Alternative Interpretation of Cognitive Dissonance Phenomena," *Psychological Review* 74 (1967): 183-200.

52. Maslow, 91-92.

53. Rogers, 35.

54. Rogers, 164-166.

55. Robert G. Lord and Douglas J. Brown, *Leadership Processes and Follower Self-identity* (Hillsdale, NJ: Erlbaum, 2004).
56. Albert Bandura, *Self-Efficacy: The Exercise of Control* (New York: Freeman, 1997); and Allen E. Kazdin, "Covert Modeling-Therapeutic Application of Imagined Rehearsal," in Jerome. L. Singer and Kenneth S. Pope, eds., *The Power of Human Imagination: New Methods in Psychotherapy—Emotions, Personality, and Psychotherapy* (New York: Plenum, 1978), 255-278.
57. The work of Abraham Maslow was the primary source used to develop the categories of indicators outlined below and in the appendices to the chapter.

Appendix 2–A: Emotional Indicators of Development of the Human Spirit

Indicator	Human Spirit Component	Innate Need
You feel a sense of safety, peace, orderliness, and understanding in life.	Worldview	Safety
You feel that you are on the right path in life.	Worldview/ Self-actualize	Self- awareness
You feel that you have a greater ability to make meaning out of your experiences.	Worldview	Know and understand
You feel that your vocation contributes to your sense of purpose in life.	Worldview	Self-actualize
You feel that you have created a good and true set of values and beliefs to guide your life.	Worldview/ Self-awareness	Know and understand
You feel a sense of confidence to interact with people from different cultures.	Worldview/ Self-awareness	Safety
You feel driven to seek out new knowledge and experiences.	Worldview	Know and understand
You feel that you have the power to achieve your goals and dreams in life.	Sense of Agency	Esteem

Indicator	Human Spirit Component	Innate Need
You feel that you control your journey to develop your spirit.	Sense of Agency	Esteem
You feel that you are making progress towards becoming the person you would like to be.	Sense of Agency	Esteem
You feel a sense of curiosity for and excitement about learning.	Sense of Agency	Know and understand
You feel that you have the power to author your own values and beliefs and not have society or others dictate them for you.	Sense of Agency	Esteem
You feel that others accept you for who you are.	Social Awareness	Affiliation
You feel connected to and understood by others.	Social Awareness	Affiliation
You feel that others respect, value, and trust you.	Social Awareness	Esteem
You feel a greater sense of self-control.	Self-awareness/ Sense of Agency	Safety/ Esteem
You feel more integrated as a person.	Self-awareness	Know and understand
You feel that you have a greater understanding of who you are, your purpose, and direction in life.	Self-awareness	Know and understand/ Self-actualize
You feel that your values and beliefs are right and will lead you to a fulfilling life.	Faith	Self-actualize
You feel commitment to living a principle-centered life and developing your potential.	Faith	Self-actualize

Appendix 2–B: Cognitive Indicators of Development of the Human Spirit

Indicator	Human Spirit Component	Innate Need
You possess a greater understanding of how the world operates.	Worldview	Safety/Know and understand
You have more realistic expectations about what is coming your way.	Worldview	Safety/Know and understand
You are more open to new ideas, different cultures, and different belief systems.	Worldview	Know and understand/ Affiliation
You consider your own values and beliefs when making decisions regarding behavior.	Worldview/ Self-awareness	Safety
You have less need to impose control in relationships with others.	Worldview	Safety/ Affiliation
You have a sense of curiosity about the world.	Worldview	Know and understand
You think of activities to develop your spirit.	Worldview	Know and understand
You refine your developmental plan frequently to ensure that the direction of your life is on track.	Sense of Agency	Self-actualize
You have autonomy to develop your own values and beliefs.	Sense of Agency	Esteem/ Self-actualize
You believe that you have the ability to control your own journey to develop your spirit.	Sense of Agency	Esteem/ Self-actualize
You believe that you are capable and talented enough to accomplish your life goals.	Sense of Agency	Esteem
You believe that others have the right to hold differing views and that different does not mean incorrect or bad.	Social Awareness	Know and understand

Indicator	Human Spirit Component	Innate Need
You have a greater understanding of how others and groups operate in the world.	Social Awareness	Know and understand
You have the ability to read people's emotions.	Social Awareness	Know and understand
You understand that all humans have needs for being valued, accepted, and respected.	Social Awareness	Know and understand
You can understand others' perspectives when making decisions.	Social Awareness	Know and understand
You have fewer negative evaluations (prejudices) towards groups of people.	Social Awareness	Know and understand
Since all humans have value, you are more compassionate in your dealings with others.	Social Awareness	Know and understand
You accept others who differ from you and do not judge them because they are different.	Social Awareness	Affiliation
You are open to questioning and evaluating your own values and beliefs.	Self-awareness	Know and understand
You periodically reflect on and evaluate your values, beliefs, and life goals to ensure they they are true and lead to a life worth living.	Self-awareness	Self-actualize
You possess a greater understanding of who you are and who you want to be in the future.	Social-Awareness	Know and understand
You believe that your developmental journey will produce a meaningful, noble, and fulfilling life.	Faith	Self-actualize
You continue to consider your values and beliefs when deciding what is right even when others are encouraging you to do otherwise.	Faith/ Sense of Agency/ Self-awareness	Know and understand/ Self-actualize

Indicator	Human Spirit Component	Innate Need
You are optimistic about realizing your full human potential and creating a satisfying life.	Faith	Self-actualize
You look at obstacles and setbacks in life as means to grow and become stronger.	Faith	Esteem

Appendix 2–C: Behavioral Indicators of Development of the Human Spirit

Indicator	Human Spirit Component	Innate Need
You act in accordance with your beliefs and values to do the right thing.	Worldview/ Sense of Agency	Safety/ Self-actualize
You are authentic when dealing with others.	Worldview/ Sense of Agency	Safety/ Self-actualize
You seek activities to learn new knowledge.	Worldview	Know and understand
You associate with diverse people.	Worldview/ Social Awareness	Know and understand/ Affiliation
You engage others in discussions about the meaning and purpose of life.	Worldview/ Social Awareness	Know and understand/ Affiliation
You feed your passion for learning.	Worldview	Know and understand
You write out goals and objectives as part of a developmental plan to develop your human spirit.	Sense of Agency/ Self-awareness	Self-actualize
You actively seek out and engage in activities that develop your spirit (meditation, prayer, self-reflection, new experiences, etc.).	Sense of Agency	Esteem/Know and understand

Indicator	Human Spirit Component	Innate Need
When confronted with situations you cannot make meaning of, you seek out new knowledge or talk to friends, parents, or mentors to help.	Sense of Agency	Know and understand
You look for and take advantage of opportunities to gain exposure to differing viewpoints.	Sense of Agency	Know and understand
You take advantage of the opportunity to study abroad.	Sense of Agency	Know and understand
You make time for reflection and introspection.	Worldview	Know and understand
You regularly evaluate your values, beliefs, and life goals to ensure they are true.	Self-awareness	Know and understand/ Self-actualize
You periodically reflect on your progress in developing your full potential.	Self-awareness	Know and understand/ Self-actualize
You keep a journal of your inner thoughts.	Self-awareness	Know and understand
You reflect on new experiences to determine meaning and lessons learned, and to assess your strengths and weaknesses.	Self-awareness	Know and understand
You attend retreats to get in touch with your inner self.	Self-awareness	Know and understand
You join groups that have noble purposes.	Social Awareness	Affiliation
You associate with people for who do they are and not for what they can for you.	Social Awareness	Affiliation
You treat all people with respect and dignity.	Social Awareness	Affiliation
You act in the best interest of the group and its members.	Social Awareness	Affiliation
You volunteer your time or give money to help others.	Social Awareness	Affiliation

Indicator	Human Spirit Component	Innate Need
You work hard to establish positive relationships with others, especially family and friends.	Social Awareness	Affiliation
You actively listen to understand others and learn.	Social Awareness	Affiliation
You show more kindness towards others.	Social Awareness	Affiliation
Your behavior demonstrates more tolerance of others because of your greater appreciation for the frailty and vulnerabilities of being human.	Social Awareness	Affiliation
You are more forgiving of others.	Self-awareness	Affiliation
You strive to develop your full potential because that is the path to satisfaction, happiness, and well-being.	Faith/Sense of Agency	Self-actualize
You live your life in accordance with your values and beliefs.	Faith/Sense of Agency	Safety/ Self-actualize

3 | Reflections on Moral Development at West Point

Erica Borggren and Donna M. Brazil

As addressed in Chapter 1, the Cadet Leadership Development System at USMA recognizes that one of the developmental mandates of late adolescence and young adulthood is the search for a worldview. It is at this point in young people's lives that they begin to question many of the assumptions they have held since childhood. An individual cadet who might have grown up going to church with her parents each week now has the opportunity to question the value of church attendance and the very assumptions upon which this behavior is based. She might no longer blindly accept the tenets espoused by her parents and instead seek to determine for herself what "truth" is. While the search for a worldview often involves redefining one's own religiosity, a young person who has no religious affiliation will still find herself searching through these years to determine her connectedness to the world and her place in that world.[1]

Across the field of psychology theorists explain this stage of life in varying ways. One school of thought focuses on identity development, others on changes in cognitive development, and still others on stages of moral development. While approaching the phenomenon from different angles, all acknowledge that there is a developmental imperative—namely, to determine who "I really am" and what I personally value—that is met head-on in the late adolescent or early adult years associated with college life, including life at West Point.

Theories of Development

Perhaps the most well-known developmental psychologist, Jean Piaget, posited that the prime developmental mechanism throughout childhood is one of active construction. Through active construction, individuals learn and develop by interacting with their environment and by building mental models that explain the outcomes of those interactions. While the complexity of the mental models is constrained by age during the early years, Piaget believed that it is in meeting these challenges that an individual changes, redefines, and develops more complex mental models. This can be seen in the

10-year-old child who can order his world and think systematically, but only when confronted by concrete issues and challenges. However, if this child is never challenged by disorder or allowed the opportunity to organize thoughts, she will not develop in this domain at the same speed as a child who is so stretched. The child who is challenged has the opportunity to build more and more complexly differentiated structures by interacting with the environment. In this way, the child grows to understand her world and develops a view of how she fits into that world. Throughout the first three periods of development that Piaget posits, children are unable to comprehend abstract thoughts.[2]

With regard to the final period of development addressed by Piaget, he suggested that sometime after the age of 11, individuals begin to mature into what he referred to as "formal operations," a developmental stage that continues on into adulthood. This period of development is marked by the ability to engage in abstract and hypothetical thought. It is here that a young adult can begin to go past the simple black-and-white rules and question the environment she lives in. This new-found power to question the world sometimes leads adolescents and young adults to be focused on themselves and to have illusions of their own importance in the world. It should be noted that Piaget did not believe that all adults actually reach the level of formal operations, or that all those who do reach it function in this way all of the time.[3] The late adolescent search for a worldview that is seen in the college years seems to occur as individuals are struggling with advanced formal operations.

Lawrence Kohlberg continued the work of Piaget, reaching the conclusion that Piaget's stages, while accounting for a great deal of cognitive development, stopped short of describing the changes in moral reasoning and moral development that also occurred as this cognitive development increased. Kohlberg noted additional differentiated moral development stages that continue where Piaget's formal operations ended. In these continued stages, individuals are able to acknowledge the presence of a law or precept but then decide to obey or disobey it for a greater good—understanding that punishments might be imposed for disobedience but believing they can present their case for lesser sanctions if need be. The sixth and final stage of development described by Kohlberg is that of attaining an appreciation for universal justice. Reasoning and acting in this stage require that an individual be able to look at a situation from the point of view of all concerned and seek out a solution that meets the higher universal need. As they embark on their search for meaning and a worldview, college students struggle with their ability to see the world through different lenses and points of view in these last two stages.[4]

Robert Kegan describes the later stages of development as a struggle to be included in something bigger than oneself and yet at the same time to be independent. In Kegan's second stage individuals begin to form a self-concept, but in this early stage the self is still highly egocentric; in stage three an individual begins to acknowledge the needs of others and is able to work toward mutually beneficial outcomes. In stage four the individual begins to be able to reflect on personal roles, norms, and self-concept. Finally, in stage five individuals are able to see themselves as a fabric of many personal systems; they begin to understand that their roles are simply "what they do" and that these roles are constructs which can be distinct from "who" they actually are. Development in Kegan's framework is driven by meeting and resolving disequilibrium as individuals search back and forth between inclusion and independence.[5]

This human struggle described in the various ways above can be looked at as tasks of cognitive, moral, and identity development. Though approached from different perspectives and focusing on different challenges, all serve to describe continual challenge, sense-making, and reflection as essential for developing deeper moral reasoning, cognitive complexity, and sense of self. The college experience in general, and the West Point experience in particular, provide fertile ground for exploring these issues and facilitating the struggle necessary for individual growth in these areas.

In what follows, the authors, as former cadets—the first a recent graduate, the second a seasoned officer reflecting back 23 years—share our own developmental journeys, with both describing our postadolescent search for meaning and how we found it at West Point. We hope that our personal journeys, narrated in the first person, will illustrate many of the tenets for growth and maturation that we as authors discussed above on a theoretical basis, and will continue to discuss in our interpolated commentaries.

Erica's Journey

Late in the afternoon one day in my junior year of high school, I received a phone call that would prove to be life-changing. The tennis coach at West Point wanted to talk to me. Although I had only vaguely ever heard about USMA, I was immediately intrigued. Months later, during a recruiting trip to West Point, my interest became a lot more than intrigue. I would say I fell in love with the place, but more likely I fell in love with the idea of West Point. I loved the unity of purpose that radiated out of 1,000 cadets wearing identical uniforms, walking subconsciously in step. I loved the idea of service, and the nobility that seemed attached to this particular form of service. And I loved the fact that values at this place were normative and lived out, not just verbally batted around in a sea of equally viable values that would be "okay for you." For a girl with no military background in her family, this was all new and, for me, refreshing. Here, the values similar to those I grew up with were not thought of as quaint or blandly relative—they were instead something to be lived up to no matter the cost.

When I arrived at Beast Barracks in the summer of 2002, it was largely because I was won over by that for which West Point stood. I was in for the quick discovery, however, that West Point was about a whole lot more than ideas and values. Despite my preparation, Beast shocked my body, drained my emotions, and challenged my resolve with its physical and mental demands. I often found myself wondering, was all of this seemingly excessive challenge worth it? On top of all this, there was the fact that our cadre often led forthright and challenging discussions on the sacrifices required by military service. What got me was the frankness of the acknowledgment that one could die in this service! Was such sacrifice worth all this travail? I found that the crucible of the West Point experience pitched me headlong into the typical undergraduate search for "who I am."

The commencement of this search coincided with attendance at weekly chapel services (mostly, at first, because Sunday services were a refuge from the loud intensity of the rest of the week), encounters with an incredibly intelligent and loving chaplain, and an inexplicable feeling of peace at the thought of a higher power. This "coincidence" is something for which I will always be grateful. Thus began my earnest search into the question of who God was, if anyone. Because of the death of a friend during my senior year in high school, the question had already arisen. I had been to church a few times with a girlfriend, mostly out of desperate curiosity. My search intensified during Beast and my plebe year, however, fueled as it was by two important discoveries. First, I found that the Christian community of West Point had an unavoidable appeal; I really felt that the Christians I encountered had something I did not, something that made their faces shine with joy and their smiles radiate with sincerity and love. Second, and most important for a young woman with a very rationalist mindset, I found that at West Point conversation about God, no matter how dubious the tone or irreverent the questions, was encouraged and even welcomed.

Erica's search for meaning had begun before she entered USMA. Like many adolescents she was beginning to question her "fit" in high school. She was still concerned with belonging but beginning to question what that entailed. She had begun to define herself and her values and found, on arriving at West Point, that she was comfortable in the atmosphere provided there, namely, an environment where values are spoken about and freely questioned—not attacked. The West Point experience, from the classroom to chapel services, from the tennis court to the company area, was filled with open and lively debate about God, about right and wrong, and about the seriousness of commitment to serving your country. This openness of the community to challenge and discussion was critical to Erica's journey of faith and moral development.

After nearly a year of wrestling with the God that my heart felt despite the intellectual objections that my head catalogued, my search was rewarded. Long and intense conversations with the chaplain and others had helped me address enough of my rational objections to reduce the size of the leap of faith required. Finally, the bridge of heartfelt conviction that my heart offered was long enough to span the now smaller gulf of doubt that had separated me from genuine belief. Finally, God had brought me to true knowledge of Him.

As a brand new Christian, I probably did not yet relate the values demanded by West Point to the kind of life demanded by God. The ideals to me were still "shiny" and appealing in and of themselves. And while I believe drawing the association between being a good officer and being a faithful Christian was ultimately inevitable, the faith community and faith institutions in which I participated at West Point did much to urge along the process of linkage. The values of West Point—honest dealing, clean thinking, harder rights over easier wrongs, whole truth, loyalty, duty—were the very things that God wanted and had enabled me to live out.

In Wednesday evening chapel during Beast Barracks and in regular Sunday chapel services, these values and the challenges related to them were regularly underscored, not only in the Cadet Prayer but in the consistent messages of the sermons themselves. God had called us, they emphasized, to this more difficult life. Just as God willingly sacrificed in service to us, so also must we be willing to do so in service to the nation and to our soldiers. As the sermons acknowledged, it might seem impossible to be truthful when there are repercussions, to always fulfill the tiniest of duties when sometimes things seem trivial, and to always give our best when sometimes energy is difficult to find . . . but God calls us to and through Christ, giving us the strength and willingness to do these very things. Naturally, then, my prayer life at West Point was filled with these issues.

Thanks to these sermons and related conversations with chaplains, mentors, and friends, the tenets of the Cadet Prayer were the very subjects I began naturally to pray about as I worked out my new faith. At the time, I believed my impulse to live out these values stemmed not from my desire to be a better cadet or officer, but from my yearning to somehow be a bit more like Christ, to be close to God and as pleasing to Him as I could be. Regardless of what West Point asked, these were the kinds of things I wanted my mind transformed to be, my will conformed to do, my heart formed to love. Looking back, though, I recognize that it was never as simple as this bare dichotomy would suggest. God had called me to be a cadet and eventually an officer, and thus He and West Point were asking the same things of me. In a sense, then, my identification with the concept of officership (and its inherent moral tenets) was not just a by-product of following God but was rather an integral part of the calling toward which He had brought me.

Erica experienced the struggles of reconciling different roles and norms. As a Christian, she was called to be like Christ. She sought to emulate Christ in her actions and in her dealings with others. At the same time, she was being called to be an officer, to lead others and ask great sacrifices of them. She worked through each of these roles individually and came to the realization that the roles were completely compatible and complementary.

For me, one of the most important aspects of moral development through faith at West Point is that faith was never just a matter for Sundays and sermons. Instead, it was allowed to be part of my everyday interactions and conversations. At weekly gatherings of the Officers Christian Fellowship, in informal conversations with friends, and even in academic settings with professors and classmates, real life and God were freely allowed to relate. In short, God was allowed to be woven into every aspect of cadet life for all who desired Him to be. For me, it was particularly important that outside their classrooms professors were willing to discuss faith with me. There were those who encouraged faith and helped me reconcile intellectual dilemmas, and there were those who challenged it and forced me to challenge myself and God for answers and understanding. All of this exploration allowed God to be about not just the heart but also the mind (for is not one of God's primary gifts to us our rationality?). The more God can be about the mind, the more freedom one has to intellectually work out dilemmas and doubts with Him; this is particularly important in the age of postmodern doubt, cynicism, and relativism. Because West Point allowed me the space and provided me the resources to know God with my head as well as in my heart, I emerged with a faith more able to withstand the relativist pressures that exist even within the Army. I certainly found this to be important when, just months after graduating from West Point, I found myself in the midst of an environment at Oxford University where the only espoused values were those of learning and tolerance.

As I've mentioned, I entered West Point as a young adult with a definite value set but not one very clearly thought through. Looking back, I think that those values appealed to me for the same reason that God appealed to me. It always seemed to me that God imbued us with a certain nobility in serving something higher. A living God whose love I could feel seemed such a better thing to serve than a faceless ideal or value itself. An important link clicked in place as I connected in my mind the values I had always espoused to something that gave me a reason to espouse them—God.

Erica understood the many roles she was asked to enact—cadet, Christian, leader, friend—and she fulfilled these roles well. Through her developing relationship with God and her working through the challenges posed by fellow cadets and mentors, she began to discern who she was, apart from these roles. In her mind, she found that the values and virtues that she believed were required for the roles she had assumed, were the same as those she already had developed in her faith journey. While the journey to faith and the journey to moral development are not always parallel, for Erica they seemed to be mutually supporting.

Now, when I step back and analyze what guides my moral choices, I find that the continuing and difficult daily decisions involved in living out the tenets of the Cadet Prayer are something that takes place in the space between me and God. I have discovered that there are many more ethical dilemmas in the Army than I faced at West Point. Although they are never enjoyable, each is an opportunity to actually be the person that God and country have asked me to be.

Even while I was at West Point, though, there were plenty of such opportunities. In the summer of my firstie year, I stood face-to-face with an event that made quite clear to me just how important my faith was in living out the value of courage. The moment you are told to jump out the door of a flying plane is inevitably a moment of truth, no matter how much you trust your equipment and your training. That first step out the door, I found, required a definite knowledge of who I was and where I was (a child of God in His hands) and what would happen if the parachute did not open (I would go to be with Him). Had I not been able to accept that death was not the worst thing that could happen, somebody may have had to push me out of the plane. Every soldier must know how to find courage in the face of life's worst what-ifs; for me, I find that that courage comes from my identity in Christ. Whatever one's answer, it surely must be believed in the heart as well as the head.

The many Honor Classes we had during Commandant's hour at West Point were all geared toward enabling us to anticipate the types of situations in which we might be tempted by others or the system to deviate from truth. These classes encouraged us to precondition our reaction to that challenge. At the time, I thought these classes were a bit overdone, a bit too frequent, and at times forced in their overly serious tone. I have definitely found since, however, that these situations arise frequently in day-to-day Army life. When, as the Executive Officer for my company, I faced a decision of whether to raise the issue of false reporting occurring in my unit, I certainly felt for a moment like I was back in a West Point dayroom.

This, however, was the first time the possible consequences of a moral decision would be actual and mine to face. I could and did weigh the costs and benefits of reporting a commander to a senior commander. I could and did rationalize, dread, and worry through the decision. But when it came down to it, there really was no choice at hand, and I don't believe I ever really thought there was. Truthfulness and what is right could not be compromised. When I think about what causes me to cling to those guiding precepts so strongly, I conclude that it is because I have a God who Himself embodies the perfection of these ideals and who lovingly asks that I attempt to do the same. This highlights the importance, I believe, of being able to answer the question of why a value is important. I am not sure adherence would be such an absolute requirement, such a given, if there was not a why beneath the values themselves; for me, that value comes from my foundational beliefs in who I am, where I come from, and Whom I serve.

Accepting and meeting challenges are common requirements for development in each of these domains. Erica's experiences were indeed stretching for her, and challenged the earlier mental models she had developed. In meeting each of these she developed a deeper, more refined, and more complex sense of purpose and identity. It is interesting to note that development continues throughout our lives. Erica reflects on classes taught at West Point that seemed "overdone" when presented in the somewhat sterile classroom, but are now increasingly relevant as she meets new challenges.

Finally, there is the issue of servant leadership itself: never ask your soldiers to do something you would not do yourself, always keep in mind that you are there to serve and guide your subordinates, and always put the welfare of your soldiers before your own. These ideas were so constantly emphasized at West Point that they could seem harped on to the point of tedium. Even I, one of the least cynical people I knew at USMA, would roll my eyes at times. However, now that I am in the Army and have soldiers under me, I find to my satisfaction that these precepts are deeply ingrained. Sometimes the extent to which I take this concept makes other officers around me laugh; who else, they ask, would feel uncomfortable taking an extra 20 minutes at lunch just because others in her office did not have that option? Even I can recognize at times the apparent triviality of some of the issues I actually create. But when it comes down to it, nothing feels too trivial to consider. I joke now with my friends and mentors that there is more "West Point" in me than I thought, but in actuality I think it is the foundation of my admiration for and calling to servant leadership—Jesus Christ—that underpins it. Servant leadership is what Christ did and is thus what a good officer does.

Refusing to jump out of the plane, ignoring false reporting, getting out of a requirement my soldiers could not get out of—in the crucial moments, I found that these were all non-options, for the values underlying the decisions I made were simply a part of me. In the Cadet Prayer, we beseech God to give us the strength to "live above the common level of life." Living at that higher level, I believe, takes place in the small and numerous decisions of daily life just like these.

Erica's journey is a stirring tapestry of many of the cognitive, moral, and identity development theories described at the beginning of this chapter. She came to West Point with strong values and beliefs but could not fully explain the reasoning behind them. Throughout her Academy experience, mentors, chaplains, professors, and peers challenged her to achieve a deeper understanding of who she was and what she truly believed. That search brought her to understand Christ and in doing so to better understand the values that guide West Point.

Donna's Journey

My journey was a little different, though Erica and I traveled on the same roads and studied in the same buildings—Washington, Cullum, and Thayer Halls. Though we each entered college searching to find our identity and to understand our world, we entered with different backgrounds and different starting points. Our military experience has also been different. I prepared for the Cold War and an attack across the Fulda Gap; she has been called on to fight the Global War on Terror. However, despite our differences, there are many similarities in our personal development that occurred at West Point.

I am, in cadet terms, an Old Grad. For the cadets I teach, I find that I am old enough to be their mother and sometimes feel differences in the generations that define us. However, while I do not listen to the music they listen to nor watch the same movies, more often than not I find that real differences are not great and that the developmental journey they are traveling is quite similar to the one I traveled more than 20 years ago.

I was already a senior in high school in 1977 when I saw an advertisement for West Point. I remember commenting to my guidance counselor that "they don't let girls go there." She told me that they had changed the rules and that the first class of women had started the year before. Growing up in the Bronx, I had visited West Point as a child and been enamored of the grandeur, the strength. I viewed it as separate from the rest of the world, at least as I knew it. West Point was less than an hour from New York City, yet seemingly lifetimes away.

When looking for a college, I wanted to make something better of myself; to try something new, out of the ordinary. I was raised Catholic, attending Catholic schools through high school. I laugh now to think that I have been in uniform since I was 5 years old. I was the second oldest of six children, raised with four brothers and a sister by my parents and grandmother. By all accounts, I was a bit wild growing up, always pushing the limits but somehow always managing to stay just within the lines. In my mind the schools I attended gave me the much needed lines. I credit St. Barnabas and Mount St. Ursula with structuring my development in those early years when I needed it most. I was attracted to USMA at first because it offered both challenge and clearly defined lines. I had read about the honor code and the strict regulations at West Point and believed that once again having these regulations as lines would keep me balanced and on target. What I did not know was that as part of my development at West Point, the lines that I once thought so clear and defined would be blurred, and I would have to decide for myself where the hard and fast margins were—if they existed at all.

I was very comfortable with lines, with having a higher authority define for me what was right and wrong. I had experimented in high school, pushing against the lines to see how far they would give, but I think that I only did that because I felt confident that the lines were out there somewhere and that I would not stray through the hole I might have created. In hindsight, I realize that I was yearning and searching for the real limits, and beginning to question the origin of the rules. I would argue for hours in order to understand the rationale behind a decision or perhaps in the hopes of getting it changed. West Point continued to provide the environment for that search— once again with lines, but they were not as clear now. I was free and even encouraged to question my faith, to question my identity, to question my values and my reason for being. In developmental terms, in my first years at West Point I struggled both to belong to something bigger than myself and to be independent.

During plebe year cadets learn the rules, and the Academy acknowledges that often cadets obey the rules simply to avoid negative repercussions or to obtain small extrinsic rewards. However, over time and with a growing understanding of the premises supporting the rules, cadets come to identify with and eventually to internalize the values of West Point and the Army. As I reflect on my experiences and development, I can see how I followed such a course. First, I was very comfortable with the lines that kept me in check.

Then, as I developed at the Academy, I grew both in my faith and in my understanding of the underlying values that define the Academy and its graduates. I gradually grew from complying with the rules and sometimes resisting those rules, to adhering to them because the people I admired did so, to finally internalizing and acting out the rules and the values underlying them simply because they are right.

Many developmental theorists identify critical or crucible moments that have the possibility of accelerating one's development. Our reaction to these moments determines the trajectory of that development. As a sophomore, I was faced with the knowledge that a friend and fellow cadet had violated the Cadet Honor Code. I knew that I was likely the only person who had this knowledge. I struggled and prayed, knowing all along the "right" thing to do, yet not being confident enough in my own identity and my own internalization of the rules to actually do it. In the end, after a very difficult night, I confronted her and she acknowledged the violation and turned herself in.

Two years later, as a senior, I used a study guide for a course that I was struggling in. After taking a particular exam, I became concerned that the study guide, while commercially available, might not have been authorized, as many of the questions on the exam were similar to those in the guide. I spent another night thinking and praying. Had I violated the Honor Code? Had I inadvertently gained an unfair advantage over my classmates? Who would know? I had worked so hard and was scheduled to graduate in a few short months. In the end I knew in my heart that all of this did not matter. If I had violated the Honor Code, I had to report it. Though a difficult decision, it was no longer about getting caught or being punished. It was about violating what I believed, no, what I knew, to be the foundation of who I was. I reported it to the Honor Committee. A representative looked into the matter and discussed it with my instructor, who determined that there was not an unfair advantage since the guide was available to anyone. In the end, there was no board and no threat to the future I envisioned for myself as an officer in the Army, but there was real growth. Through the struggle I came out stronger in my faith and in my understanding of the values and beliefs that had been kindled in me as a child and reinforced at West Point.

The issues of whether I had violated the Honor Code and whether I should confront my friend over her honor violation were crucible moments for me, and I was fortunate to have friends and mentors who supported me and helped me to grow through these challenges to my worldview. Before those experiences, though I am quite sure that I could have spoken to someone about the values of West Point and explained the tenets of the Honor Code, I did not yet fully understand that acting out the tenets of honor truly defined who I was. While this second incident was also difficult, I grew because of it and emerged better prepared for the challenges of the future.

In addition to those two crucible moments during my cadet days at USMA, I had many opportunities to grow that were not as dramatic, yet were sufficient to gently nudge me along in my developmental journey. As a plebe I was invited to attend a retreat that focused on the mystery of the Passion— the sufferings of Christ between the Last Supper and His crucifixion. I signed up for the retreat, though I must admit now that my intentions were far from religious. As a plebe I was eager for any excuse to get a weekend away from West Point. What I found at this retreat was amazing. I found a group of cadets and local college students who shared a common faith, yet all had vastly different backgrounds. I found individuals who wrestled with the same issues that I did, who were also trying to find their place in the world, an identity similar to yet distinct from the one I was establishing. I found a values-based environment that encouraged this questioning and in fact made not questioning seem as if I didn't care about the issues.

This retreat and the many more I attended in the next few years gave me the opportunity to reflect on my struggles, my growth, and my development while I was at West Point. Once a semester, through the West Point Chaplain's Program, I was able to take a weekend retreat in order to help make sense of these changes and experiences. During these opportunities, I continued to struggle to find my place at West Point and in the Army and to question the changes I was experiencing. All the while I was surrounded by officers, cadets, and individuals from the local community who were willing to talk about the issues and help me reflect on their meaning in my life. As I advanced through the years at West Point, I took on leadership roles in this group. I became one of the mentors and leaders who assisted other cadets in their journey. My own development continued through this leadership experience. As is often the case, in attempting to help others find answers and meaning, I was forced to continually reevaluate my own identity and values.

Through these experiences and many more that are now so much a part of my being that I am unable to recall them as single events, I slowly grew from a teenager looking for answers to a young adult who had found meaning in who I was and in what I chose to do. Through these struggles I came out stronger in my faith and rock solid in my belief in the values and tenets of West Point. I learned that the values the Academy stood for are not simply rules, but instead are a way of life. As the USMA Chaplain says each year at new cadet reception day, "'Duty, Honor, Country' is not a way to see certain things, but a certain way to see all things." Though a simple motto, it is a rather complete worldview. The values of West Point are not rules or even lines—they just are. I understand that we are dedicated to doing the harder right. I understand that what is not corrected is condoned. I understand that when I say to myself, "Someone ought to take care of that"—I am that someone.

The other night I was driving in a storm and noticed that a traffic cone had blown away from the hole it was supposed to be warning motorists about. I asked my daughter to get out of the car and move it back in place. As she was getting out of the car, she muttered something like "Why do I have to have do-gooder parents?" The answer is simple—it's because both her dad and I "grew up" at West Point.

The Cadet Prayer, while not an overt part of my faith and life journey while I was a cadet, has become so in the years since I have returned to the faculty. Sadly, I have had the honor of attending far too many military funerals at West Point in the past few years, and at each of those services, no matter what denomination, the prayer was always part of the service. During these new moments of struggle and sense-making, I have had the opportunity to read and reflect on this prayer and the meaning of it in my life then and now.

Despite the generations that separate old grads from new grads, like Donna from Erica, we find that the precepts embodied in this prayerful petition are timeless and denominationally nonspecific. They reflect basic truths and values that our common experience at USMA allowed us the time and opportunities to inspect, dissect, and identify with, and eventually to own and internalize. Thanks to the unique developmental process that we were ready for upon arrival and for which USMA provided the groundwork, they now describe not only how we act but who we are. It is fitting to end this chapter by recalling some of the language that lends the prayer such transformative power:

- Strengthen and increase our admiration for honest dealing and clean thinking.
- Encourage us in our endeavor to live above the common level of life.
- Make us to choose the harder right instead of the easier wrong.
- Endow us with courage that is born of loyalty to all that is noble and worthy.
- Guard us against flippancy and irreverence in the sacred things of life.
- Help us to maintain the honor of the Corps untarnished and unsullied.

Notes

1. Louis W. Fry, "Toward a Theory of Spiritual Development," *Leadership Quarterly* 14 (December 2003): 693-727.
2. William Crain, *Theories of Development*, 4th ed. (New Jersey: Prentice Hall 2000), 113. A complete list of Piaget's periods of development is as follows: Sensory-Motor Intelligence (birth to 2 years); Preoperational Thought (ages 2 to 7); Concrete Operations (ages 7 to 11); and Formal Operations (ages 11 to adulthood).
3. Ibid.
4. Lawrence Kohlberg, *Essays on Moral Development,* Vol. II: *The Psychology of Moral Development* (San Francisco: Harper Row, 1981), 175-176. Kohlberg's stages of moral development are as follows: Stage 1-Heteronomous Morality; Stage 2-Individualism, Instrumental Purpose, and Exchange; Stage 3-Mutual Interpersonal Expectations, Relationships, and Interpersonal Conformity; Stage 4-Social System and Conscience; Stage 5-Social Contract or Utility and Individual Rights; and Stage 6-Universal Ethical Principles.
5. Robert Kegan, *The Evolving Self* (Cambridge, MA: Harvard University Press, 1982), 87. Kegan's stages of human development are as follows: Stage 0-Incorporative; Stage 1-Impulsive; Stage 2-Imperial, Stage 3-Interpersonal; Stage 4-Institutional; and Stage 5-Interindividual.

II

The Role of Character
in Military Leadership

4 Frameworks of Moral Development and the West Point Experience: Building Leaders of Character for the Army and the Nation

Sean T. Hannah and Patrick J. Sweeney

Introduction

The West Point experience is a transformational one in which cadets are changed in positive and lasting ways. To provide a better understanding of this transformation, this chapter integrates the sciences of leadership, moral decision-making, social, cognitive, and developmental psychology, and organizational behavior, relating these theories to both the formal and informal developmental processes at West Point. Drawing from theories of authentic leadership development[2] and moral leadership,[3] we will then provide recommendations for accelerating cadets' moral development in the future. By *authentic*, we are describing the creation of lasting, positive change in these future officers so that their morality is internalized, and their moral decision-making and actions are natural manifestations of their *true self* rather than the result of social sanctions or expectations. Authentic moral development is thus intertwined with the development of leaders' human spirit and drive toward self-actualization. Specifically, as discussed in Chapter 2, a leader's worldview and character are at the center of his/her human spirit, and are reinforced through agency, self-awareness, social awareness, and faith. It is this core that provides leaders the independence to author their own values and belief systems. This form of development is part of

If leaders are not looking for truth, if situations are not framed as having moral implications in the first place, then these leaders make decisions based on other criteria alone, often with disturbing results. Moral sensitivity alone is not enough. Once leaders recognize that a moral problem exists, they then have to decide what is right. This requires moral judgment—discerning which action is most justifiable based on a set of ethical criteria. However, even moral sensitivity and judgments do not guarantee moral behavior . . . without the courage to take action.[1]

the larger leadership development process, entailing positive alteration of cadets' self-concepts, social perspectives, capacities for moral decision-making, and ultimately motivation and confidence for taking moral action—thus developing true leaders of character for the nation and the Army.

This chapter serves to advance our understanding of the scholarship behind the Cadet Leadership Development System (CLDS) described in Chapter 1 of this volume.[4] With a better understanding of how leaders are developed morally having been established in the present chapter, Chapter 5 will then discuss the full implications of this new understanding, revealing through research results from Operation Iraqi Freedom how these highly developed, authentic moral leaders positively influence their followers, teams, and organizations. We begin this chapter with an overview of what we call the "triad of moral capabilities" that we hold to be central to moral development: (1) *moral complexity,* (2) *moral agency, and* (3) *moral efficacy.* We then relate these three capabilities to the process of moral decision-making and behavior, showing how the leader's level of moral development enables the effective processing of moral dilemmas.

Authentic Moral Leadership Development and the West Point Experience

We propose that authentic moral development occurs in leaders through targeted developmental events, such as exposure to key moral/ethical experiences, coupled with coaching and periods of dedicated reflection. The English terms *ethics* and *morals* are derived from the Greek term *ethos* and the Latin term *mores,* respectively, which refer to the shared beliefs and practices of a people. The West Point experience is critical in this developmental process, because ethics are learned and practiced here as a part of living within a culture of professionals. Such organizations teach members the profession's ethics and values through the social learning processes. These processes are known to be particularly critical during the formative college years.[5]

A longitudinal study investigating the psychological development of West Point cadets over the four-year experience found that the majority (62.5 percent) by their senior year had transitioned upward one full stage of development, while the rest of the cadets were still in the process of this transition.[6] Most young adults enter college with a psychological perspective that is essentially selfish—it emphasizes personal gains and has a very limited ability to subordinate one's self-interest for the good of others, the group, or shared values. The study indicated that by senior year at the Academy, most cadets have developed a psychological perspective that allows them to internalize shared expectations (e.g., the Cadet Honor Code and principles of officership) and to start generating their own standards and principles for living in a professional community with others. This ability to internalize shared expectations provides cadets at this higher developmental level with the capacity to subordinate self-interests for the good of the group or others, which is necessary for developing teamwork and cohesion. However, a significant limitation to people in this stage remains—internalized, shared expectations that the perceptions of others significantly influence their own self-concept. This causes them to remain highly susceptible to social pressures such as group conformity and obedience.[7]

Moral development is, however, a lifelong journey; thus, an officer's commissioning from West Point should not be looked at as an end state. In fact the study found that officers in the rank of major averaging in excess of ten years of service were still developing morally, and that on average had not yet achieved the highest levels of moral development attainable.[8] These highest levels of moral development provide officers with the psychological autonomy to author their own system of values and standards. Such autonomy empowers them to make moral decisions and lead in a moral manner in the absence of social support and in situations involving competing expectations from others or their organizations. Therefore, the developmental objective at the Academy is to accelerate such moral development and to set the conditions for leaders to embrace their own self-directed and lifelong development plans to search for moral enlightenment. This search for meaning is central to individual moral development and, more specifically, to the spiritual domain of character development found in the CLDS.

Thus, to recapitulate, we believe that moral development of cadets should be largely focused on three key capabilities, namely: (1) *moral complexity,* (2) *moral agency,* and (3) *moral efficacy.* We propose that this triad of moral capabilities is at the heart of high-impact, moral leadership. Ultimately, leaders with these enhanced capabilities will bolster ownership and engagement in their moral experiences, increase the depth of contemplation during moral decision-making, and boost their personal confidence and courage to take the "right" actions in the face of adversity or social pressures. As we will discuss, many West Point experiences, such as reflection on the moral precepts contained in the Cadet Prayer, are influential in the development of this triad of capabilities and the creation of leaders of virtue and character.[9]

Making the "Right" Decisions

Nowhere are moral development and ethical enlightenment more critical than at America's national military academies. To lead in combat, young men and women must have developed a highly accurate moral compass in order to navigate the constant currents of tension between personal morality and their role as a member of the profession of arms—a profession that must manage violence on behalf of the greater good. The dilemmas faced by young military officers today are like those always faced in battle—morally ambiguous situations where leaders have to choose between imperfect solutions, all of which may have questionable moral overtones. Does a leader expose his soldiers to enemy fire to save an innocent young child? Does the leader order her soldiers to fire on a car filled with a civilian family that does not appear to be slowing for a traffic control checkpoint? In garrison situations, does a leader punish a soldier by reduction of pay knowing that his family already has financial problems? These examples should make clear that it is more important for the Academy to focus on how young leaders should think about and resolve such dilemmas than it is to focus on what the specific outcome should be. Although we will show how important the latter is, it is more critical to enable leaders to process such ambiguous dilemmas autonomously, without supervision, and to come up with the best moral and ethical solutions. This developmental philosophy is also evident in the Superintendent's introduction to the CLDS manual:

> CLDS introduces the concept of Officership and focuses primarily on the Be component of the [Army leadership doctrine's] Be-Know-Do paradigm. . . . Influencing the Be component is a significant challenge. It entails affecting an individual's core beliefs: what one stands for, how one views oneself, and how one views the world. It is an individual's character.[10]

It is precisely at this point that it becomes critical to address the importance of the human spirit in leader development. Inclusion of spirituality is a major dimension of character development in CLDS. Human spirituality, according to CLDS, is defined as one's drive to find personal meaning in life and to realize one's full potential.[11] It is in seeking an understanding of their evolving spirituality that all cadets will form and reinforce their self-identity, find their sense of purpose and meaning in life, form their own philosophy for viewing the world, and develop the standards that define for them what it means to live a good life. Regardless of one's approach to addressing spirituality, whether it is through religion, the study of philosophy or ethics, or other means, all leaders must establish clear core beliefs and values and uphold those beliefs with conviction to be a moral leader—a leader of character—a leader who brings meaning to his or her missions and organizations.

All major religions discussed in later chapters of this volume, regardless of any differences in their teachings, can serve as catalysts for spiritual development. They provide important structure and discipline in the process of spiritual growth for the members of their congregations, and offer as well increased opportunities for spiritual experiences, mentoring, and reflection. Some cadets are uninterested in adopting any particular religious faith, however, and the Academy of course makes no objection to such a personal choice. In either case, all cadets are encouraged to seek their own self-determined avenue for developing the human spirit as a centerpiece of their leadership development. Fortunately, at West Point both religious and nonreligious opportunities abound. We expressed in Chapter 2 the importance of the human spirit in human flourishing, and even more so in effective, principled leadership. Thus, as public institutions such as West Point continue to secularize, it is critical that they avoid the error of despiritualizing their developmental environments. Rather, we believe they must facilitate such personal searches for moral meaning by all cadets. Army officership is a professional calling, one that requires a sense of purpose and meaning and a sound view of how one relates to the larger group and society. By commissioning day, the Army's new officers must know that their moral compass is highly functional and guiding them along the path of character-based leadership.

Introduction to the Moral Development Model

We employ a model by James Rest proposing that moral reasoning occurs in four sequential stages and that ethical behavior will most often occur when an individual has progressed through all those stages in the following order: (1) *moral recognition,* (2) *moral judgment,* (3) *moral intention,* and (4) *moral behavior.*[12] Specifically, a leader must first recognize that a situation contains a moral issue, process that issue to form a moral decision, transfer that decision into an intention to act, and then carry that intention through to actual behavior. Due to their sequential nature, a failure to navigate any one of these steps may derail the leader from taking the right actions. As depicted in Figure 4-1, we will explain how leaders who are specifically developed and equipped to face the morally dynamic realm of military leadership will be better able to perceive and recognize the moral implications of issues, process the relevant factors to come up with better solutions, form intentions to act on those decisions, and, most importantly, summon the courage and conviction to act morally and do the right thing in the toughest of situations, such as combat. We turn now to a detailed discussion of our model for the development of authentic moral leaders. The heart of this model is the triad of moral capabilities: moral complexity, moral agency, and moral efficacy. We propose that these three moral capabilities are the foundation for moral development in authentic leaders.

Moral Complexity

The first element in the triad is *moral complexity,* the ability of the leader to attend to, store, retrieve, process, and, most important, make meaning of moral information. As the English philosopher John Locke noted, "No man's knowledge here can go beyond his experience." Our knowledge as a basis for contemplating moral issues is limited to our education and experiences. We must therefore first broaden our moral education and reflection. *Moral complexity,* as a capability, is based on high levels of cognitive development and one's ability to monitor moral thought processes, i.e., metacognition.

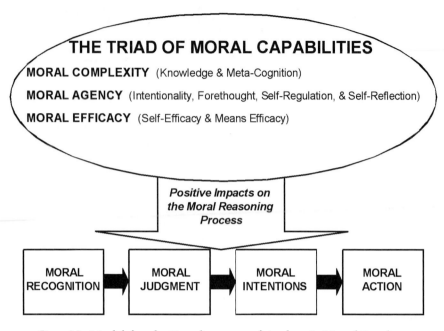

Figure 4-1. *Model for the Development of Authentic Moral Leaders.*

We propose that cognitive development and metacognition together provide the leader with a capacity for moral experiences and for translating experiences into knowledge through guided coaching and recognition and making judgments. We will later develop the idea that the motivation to conduct in-depth evaluations of moral dilemmas comes from the second of the triad of capabilities—*moral agency.*

Cognitive Moral Development

Theories of cognitive moral development by Lawrence Kohlberg[13] and Robert Kegan[14] propose that over their life span individuals develop cognitively through different levels. They begin with a focus on the self (ego) and gradually move toward an understanding of their interactions and interdependency with the social world in which they are embedded. Developmental growth often takes place when people are confronted with situations in which their current meaning-making systems are inadequate, such as a child made to recognize the harm of its actions to others, thus triggering a conflict with its own values and meaning-making system. These situations cause people to experience a state of cognitive disequilibrium, which prompts them to develop more complex meaning-making structures to restore this equilibrium (in the example of the child, perhaps by the child's better linking its behavior and the expected consequences with its value structures).

Jean Piaget, a famous developmental theorist, called this developmental process *accommodation*.[15] As people move towards the highest levels of development, they eventually transcend social expectations and constraints and begin to strive for universal values and principles in the decisions that they make. At what Kohlberg calls the *post-conventional* levels, and Kegan the *institutional and interindividual* levels, people achieve the capacity to go beyond the norms and authority of social groups and pursue virtue through their own moral regulatory processes and internal standards—i.e., what we have previously referred to as their internal moral compass. Thus, these internalized values of people define their character. Higher levels of cognitive moral development have been positively related to moral behavior in numerous studies.[16]

Scholars of ethics such as James Rest have argued that levels of cognitive moral development are related to the mental representations people hold in long-term memory.[17] These representations store and organize our knowledge and are formed through life experiences as people learn "how things work" (processes and structures), "what leads to what" (hypotheses about causality and consequences), "who we and others *are*" (self and person-concepts), and other similar mental representations that are central to processing moral dilemmas. These mental representations are critical, since they determine what people pay attention to in their lives, how they perceive and process information, the quality of their decisions, and ultimately their behavior.

Focusing developmental experiences on creating a capacity for robust moral complexity will enable cadets to conduct more comprehensive assessments of moral dilemmas and achieve more optimum solutions. Referring to Figure 4-1, we see that a leader's complexity is central to the stage of moral reasoning or processing known as *moral recognition*. Individuals attend to information that is relevant to and consistent with their existing knowledge, while ignoring or discounting incongruent information.[18] In essence, people find that consistency and predictability enhance their comfort zone. They have difficulty processing information when they cannot relate that information to existing cognitive frameworks.

Since people attend to consistent information, the more that cadets' cognitive frameworks are marked by moral complexity, the more likely they will be to recognize the moral components of leadership issues. This explains why one student may view copying another student's homework as cheating while an errant student sees it as "time-management," missing the moral component. Knowledge structures about one's self are also critical. Leaders who have worked hard to develop a self-identity marked by strength of character, and who accept responsibility for the moral aspects of their leadership's influence, will be more likely to attend to and process moral information and take action. In sum, as complex mental representations of a cadet's moral self are developed and integrated with representations of other people, their organizations, moral concepts, etc., they become the moral compass to guide the cadet's future cognitions and behaviors.

These complex mental representations are held in long-term memory, and thus can be developed through a broad range of life and educational experiences that serve as developmental trigger events, moments that create moral disequilibrium and force the accommodation of new information, as discussed earlier. It is critical that these experiences be coupled with dedicated reflection and coaching to make meaning of those experiences.[19]

Magnitude and Complexity of Moral Knowledge

All leaders, quite simply, are limited by the information they can retrieve from memory to make moral evaluations. Further refining the concept of moral complexity, we hold that leaders who have more complex mental structures can take in greater information from competing sides of an issue and create better linkages between different or perhaps conflicting information that may often characterize the moral dilemmas faced during combat. More cognitively complex individuals are also better able to acquire new knowledge, since they can more easily make meaning of and relate new information to what they already know. They also tend to spend more effort and time interpreting new information and resolving complex dilemmas.[20]

Leaders with a greater capacity for moral complexity also have fewer extreme or polar attitudes that can often lead to selective or biased information processing and resistance to change.[21] These leaders are less set in their ways—they take the blinders off and assess the full breadth of moral dilemmas using their greater complexity. Studies have directly tested and found that higher levels of moral knowledge were related to more frequent resort to moral reasoning and moral behavior. We are not saying that *any* kind of increased information leads to moral development. In fact, we will later take the position that leaders must negotiate the *right* trigger events to achieve heightened levels of cognitive *moral* development. We know that exposure to high levels of antisocial or immoral information can lead to grave consequences for a young person. Indeed, the primary goal of character development at West Point is to align the character of the individual cadet with the role and moral principles of officership. Thus, to return to our comments in the introduction, although we believe it is more important to teach cadets "how" to think morally, one should not underestimate the importance of instilling certain core character tenets in young leaders to provide the foundation and strength to make the right decision in ambiguous moral situations, especially when lives are at risk.

Beyond the amount of moral knowledge a leader must possess, the second component of moral complexity is *metacognitive ability,* that is, the ability to effectively access and process this robust knowledge. Metacognitive ability can be thought of as the capacity to "think about thinking," allowing leaders to effectively monitor and control moral processing and to regulate their own cognitive processes.[22] Metacognitive ability has been directly related to both more acute moral reasoning and greater moral content in actions.[23] Metacognitive processing is more than thinking about the specific aspects of a moral issue; it is assessing how one is thinking about and processing that information. During metacognitive processing, the leader may ask whether all relevant sources of information are being assessed, what information is missing, what personal emotional responses are influencing the assessment, and whether the leader is applying his or her core values and beliefs in the decision.

In summary, the components of moral complexity are mutually support-ing. Whereas high levels of cognitive moral development and the associated creation of rich and robust moral knowledge provide the database that lead-ers can access when faced with a moral dilemma, heightened metacognitive ability, or the ability to "think about moral thinking," is the human central processing unit that raises their ability to select from, access, and modify this database to drive conclusions for application to the moral dilemmas at hand. Thus coupled, the components of moral complexity truly transform the leader by providing greater capabilities for moral recognition and inquiry. Referring to the conceptualization presented in Chapter 2, these capabilities would bol-ster the human spirit by broadening leaders' worldview, capacity for self-awareness, and social awareness, and by increasing their ability to achieve coherence with their faith as they process moral dilemmas.

Development of Moral Complexity

We hold that it is only through the vast number and types of experiences cadets undergo at the Academy that they develop a higher level of cognitive moral complexity. These experiences may include for some their exposure to the moral precepts in the Cadet Prayer—e.g., to rise "above the common level of life," to discern the "whole truth" through the lens of their complex moral knowledge, and to weigh all options in electing the "harder right over the easier wrong."

We propose that there are at least five primary methods to develop such enhanced levels of moral complexity in West Point cadets: (1) guiding them through a series of moral experiences or trigger events with assisted reflection to enhance their interpretation and understanding of those experiences, (2) providing mentors and role models that personally model moral behavior, (3) placing cadets in situations that create cognitive disequilibrium, forcing them to challenge what they know in order to occasion deeper inquiry into moral dilemmas, (4) teaching specific moral decision-making skills and processes; and (5) having cadets live in a culture that requires and supports moral behavior.

Academy leaders such as instructors, coaches, and mentors, through deliberately planned trigger events, can expose cadets to moral dilemmas and assist them in their interpretation of such encounters through guided reflection. Cadets and their leaders must also be alert to the occurrence of unplanned trigger events, taking the opportunity to pause and engage in guided reflection. Such experiences do not necessarily have to be direct and personal; vicarious experience through observing others will also provide robust moral information for preservation in memory, thus to be called upon during the processing of future moral dilemmas.

Cadets must be exposed to moral conflicts in order to help trigger the development of heightened moral reasoning. We have stated that humans prefer consistency and therefore tend to discount or ignore occurrences that do not match their schemas. To alter and develop moral complexity, Academy instructors must expose cadets to opposed views and arguments that challenge their core perspectives, basic assumptions, and uncritical beliefs, thus assisting them to adopt an entirely new way of thinking about moral issues. This level of analysis and internal discovery requires facing the hard issues. After their first year or so at the Academy, cadets still tend to view moral issues such as lying, cheating, and stealing as black and white categories. Although there is value in discussing them to heighten sensitivity to those issues, such discussion does little to advance the ongoing transformation or development of cadets. The Academy must instead place cadets within a series of increasingly complex and ambiguous real or virtual situations that require hard decisions among less than perfect choices, decisions replicating what lieutenants face every day in Iraq such as during urban search-and-clear operations. These dilemma-laced decisions create cognitive disequilibrium, motivating cadets to reassess their knowledge and incorporate new information to restore balance.

The importance of role models and mentors in this process cannot be stressed too strongly. We know that leaders, as exemplars, can alter the value structures of followers. When individuals have moral discussions with mentors who have higher moral reasoning levels than their own, they are more likely to reflect on their values and beliefs and experience moral growth.[24] The more leaders are seen as role models by their followers, the more followers will identify with the leaders and be motivated to self-reflect on the examples they set. These role models show how things should be done, including the proper systems and processes. Some of the knowledge structures people hold are temporal—they have a sequence of events that unfolds through time, such as one's conceptualization of the proper steps in processing a prisoner of war. These structures, called *scripts*, are developed through experience, as one learns certain strategies when dealing with his or her environment. These strategies are recorded in memory, and subsequently reinforced over time.[25] Training and role modeling are critical in the development of effective moral scripts. Through observation, cadets essentially learn "what works and what is right" and tend to repeat the same sequence of events later, a process that becomes habituated over time. It should be clear by now that moral experiences, or trigger events coupled with periods of guided reflection, are central in attaining higher levels of moral development.

Education has also proven effective in the development of moral complexity so long as that education teaches methodologies for analyzing the merits of various competing moral choices. Again, we focus here not on inculcating in cadets *what* to think, but *how* to think. To be effective, ethics classes must not be lecture-oriented since cognitive growth is best stimulated using opportunities for role-playing, discussion, support, challenge, and guided reflection.[26] In a study reviewing 23 different ethics training programs, those using group discussions of moral dilemmas produced on average an astounding four and half times more positive effects on moral development than those without dedicated moral discussions.[27] West Point's ethics training programs could thus profit from focusing even more on guided processing of increasingly difficult and ambiguous moral issues.

Leaders must observe through multiple lenses as they reason to moral judgments in the dynamic and ambiguous context of military operations. Such an approach induces them to access and exercise their various moral mental structures and develop an inherent metacognitive ability to achieve maximum coherence in their decisions. Philosophical frameworks of morality that are discussed by Anthony Hartle in Chapter 6 of this volume can be used for this exercise. We propose that cadets be prompted to examine moral issues through three lenses or perspectives: (1) what is right by the laws, rules, norm, or duties *(deontological)*, (2) what produces the best consequences *(teleological)*, and (3) what is the most virtuous action *(areteological)*. Each one of these three lenses may produce a separate and distinct moral solution if viewed in isolation, so cadets must learn to simultaneously view moral dilemmas through all three lenses to understand the complete dynamics of an issue and determine the best course of action.

Rigidly employing only one lens is problematic when trying to resolve a moral dilemma. For instance, let us assume a soldier refuses to go on a combat patrol led by a squad leader who does not have the necessary training or experience to lead the patrol competently. If the commander views this situation only through the lens of "rules, regulations, duties, and laws" (deontological), he will most likely take action in accordance with the Uniform Code of Military Justice to punish the soldier's disobedience. However, the commander realizes that punishing a soldier who had compelling reasons for refusing to participate in an operation in which the institution had failed to properly develop the leader could have adverse effects on the unit's morale, cohesion, and trust in its leaders (teleological). Further, viewing this situation from the perspective of what would be the most virtuous action (areteological), the commander may place a competent leader in charge of the patrol to ensure all the soldiers are properly led, thus addressing the reluctant soldier's concerns and assuring that discipline and trust within the unit are maintained. As can be seen in this example, the three-lens approach provides leaders a systematic means for processing a moral dilemma in order to determine the best solution to resolve it. In sum, the Army needs leaders who can view moral issues from all three perspectives.[28]

Moral Agency

Having seen the critical importance of moral complexity in leaders of character, we turn now to a discussion of the second element in the triad of moral capabilities, *moral agency.*[29] Cognitive models of moral development, by themselves, are insufficient to explain moral behavior. To reason through complex moral dilemmas to a judgment and then take action on that judgment, cadets must have strong, directed motivation to be a moral actor. Moral agency concerns taking ownership of and assuming responsibility for one's own moral experiences. As the philosopher John Stuart Mill stated, "Over himself, over his own body and mind, the individual is sovereign." Such ownership by a leader of his/her moral experiences is a central element proposed in the conceptualization of the domain of the human spirit presented in Chapter 2.

Heightened moral agency provides the motivation for a leader to be more aware of moral issues and to explore more fully the span of complex information surrounding those issues. We all know, however, that people often do not take action on their moral inclinations. Although they may determine that something is wrong, leaders without high levels of moral agency will often fail to act. Moral agents, however, do take responsibility for the moral signature of their domain of influence and *do* the right thing. The Cadet Honor Code's injunction that cadets do not lie, cheat, or steal, *nor tolerate those that do,* is a clear expression of the moral agency cadets are expected to assume, not only over their own personal moral domain but also within their social environment.

Noted psychologist Albert Bandura states that agency is the capacity one holds to exercise control over both the nature and quality of one's life—it is, in fact, the essence of humanness.[30] Being producers as well as products of their environments, leaders cannot be passive; instead, they must own their own experiences and those of their followers and associates. As an active concept, moral agency includes both *refrainment power* (inhibition to keep from acting immorally) and *proactive power* (the power to intentionally behave morally). Bandura proposes that agency includes four major facets directly related to moral leadership: (1) intentionality—that one's actions are done intentionally; (2) forethought regarding consequences—that people anticipate the consequences of their actions and thereby select what they feel to be the best courses of action; (3) self-regulation—the ability to motivate and regulate one's self as a moral actor; and (4) self-reflection—the capacity to reflect upon the quality and impacts of one's thoughts and actions (see Figure 4-1). We propose that as the Academy focuses further on these four elements of agency, they will accelerate the development of morally-engaged junior officers who take command of their moral domain.

Moral agency is central to developing truly authentic leaders of character. When making moral judgments, followers tend to comply with what they deem to be the moral desires of their higher authority and thereby often eschew personal ownership and agency.[31] This phenomenon explains why under immoral leaders ethical disasters can plague organizations. We argue that a disengagement of moral agency by followers under immoral leaders was a contributing, if not the major factor, in the My Lai village massacre in Vietnam and in the Abu Ghraib prison abuses in Iraq. The Army needs to develop leaders who have the capacity (moral complexity) and ownership (moral agency) to challenge their organizations and their own leaders to greater levels of morality, and who have the internal fortitude to take charge and address ethical issues regardless of the will of their peers or superiors. The Army also needs to develop authentic leaders who invite dialogue openly and encourage their own followers to question the leaders' positions and decisions—a form of moral empowerment, allowing the leader, the follower, and the organization to grow morally.

We will next outline the critical role of moral agency in processing a moral dilemma through each of the four phases of moral reasoning that we introduced earlier in Figure 4-1 (moral recognition, moral judgment, moral intentions, and moral behavior). We will then explain how the four elements of moral agency (intentionality, forethought, self-regulation, and self-reflection) can be further developed in cadets.

Moral Agency—Impacts on Moral Recognition and Judgments

We start with the influence of moral agency on the first two stages of moral reasoning, i.e., moral recognition and moral judgment. When we presented earlier the first concept in the triad—*moral complexity*—we described it as providing an enhanced *ability* for a leader to both recognize and process moral dilemmas, but were silent as to the *motivation* for conducting such deep reasoning during those stages. We now state that it comes from agency. As suggested in Figure 4-1, authentically developed leaders with high levels of moral complexity and moral agency search for and are more likely to perceive moral issues within their environment. Moreover, they increase their depth of cognitive processing once they recognize an issue.

In Chapter 3 of this volume, Captain Erica Borggren and Colonel Donna Brazil discussed their personal experiences in internalizing West Point values and beliefs in their identity and self-concept. This is a critical step in moral development and the formation of agency. The likelihood of recognizing a dilemma as a moral issue is dependent upon the amount of issue-related thinking expended by the individual. People who have internalized moral values in their identity are more likely to process more penetratingly and with genuine metacognition those situations that have potential moral issues. This is so because their self-concepts—who they believe themselves to be and their core values—are actively involved.[32] In turn, these leaders who conduct deeper processing are then more likely both to recognize the complexities of the moral issues present and to process more effectively these complexities during the phase of moral judgment.[33]

Deep, controlled processing requires a significant investment of one's precious cognitive resources. Leaders' sense of agency, i.e., responsibility to behave morally, will motivate them to make this investment of energy and cognitive resources.[34] Although people seek validity in their decisions, they are generally "cognitive misers" who tend to use the lowest level of processing possible once initial hypotheses about a particular situation are confirmed.[35] In essence, once people have a sufficient level of information confirming what they already believe, they tend to accept those beliefs as true even when conflicting information may be present. Again, we emphasize that it is engaged leaders, those with higher degrees of moral agency, who take ownership over their domain, who will most thoroughly deal with the moral dilemmas officers' face.

Moral Agency—Impacts on Moral Intentions and Behaviors

By itself, mere cognitive processing is inadequate. To refer back to Figure 4-1, moral recognition and judgments must lead to the last two stages of the moral reasoning process: moral intentions and moral behavior. Military leaders must fully own their moral experiences. They do not have the option to determine that something is morally wrong and not take action to correct the problem. Such leaders must see it as their ultimate responsibility to act in a moral manner on behalf of a greater good within, and possibly even outside, their unit or organization. They must hold their own and the profession's virtues as part of their core self-concept.

Leaders with a highly developed sense of moral agency view themselves as moral actors, indeed exemplars, responsible for their moral environment and committed to maintaining and enhancing core values in their and their followers' self-concepts. The leader's self-concept is so critical to moral development because it is the largest and most elaborate of knowledge structures a person holds. Simply stated, as people constantly experience their "self," they gain and hold more information about their self than anything else in their environment. Although individuals may differ in the degree of accuracy of their self-knowledge—i.e., self-awareness—it is largely this knowledge that determines what tasks people engage in and how strongly they persist in those tasks.[36] The self-concept is also temporal—it changes across time. Leaders identify not just with their current self-concept *(current self)*, but also with a more distant image of a *possible self*, or who they want to become. It is this vision of a possible self that drives a leader's goals and development and is thus central to both moral development and action.[37] At West Point, it is through guided exercises to identify their current self through reflection, and then through additional exercises to envision a possible self (through such as the reflective essays required in the core leadership course), that cadets focus their development and internalize the four identities of officership as specified in CLDS: warrior, servant of the nation, member of a profession, and leader of character.

Developing Moral Agency

We turn now to a discussion of ways Academy leaders can better develop moral agency in future officers—authentic leaders of character who "own" their moral experiences and the honor of their institution. One way is by reflection on the moral precepts within the Cadet Prayer, e.g., "Help us to maintain the honor of the Corps untarnished and unsullied and to show forth in our lives the ideals of West Point in doing our duty to Thee and to our Country." This single tenet from the Cadet Prayer alone encapsulates much of the sense of moral agency. As noted earlier, moral agency has four components: *intentionality* and *forethought* in one's moral actions, and *self-regulation* and *self-reflection* with regard to one's moral thoughts and actions.

Much of the developmental effort at the Academy should continue to be devoted to inculcating core values in the self-concept of each cadet. The more mentors can focus cadets on the *self-reflection* aspect of agency—envisioning their possible self as a moral leader—the more cadets will be goal-driven and motivated to realize that possible self.[38] Mentor-cadet discussions should not be entirely abstract. They must go beyond the purely theoretical and compel serious personal empathy and engagement so as to uncover and then challenge the cadet's core values and beliefs. Academy leaders must guide cadets individually in their reflection on both their current and possible self, discover the "gaps" that exist between the two, and coach and mentor cadets to create a tailored developmental plan to fill or bridge these gaps. Aiding this process, there are currently in use 360-degree performance evaluations and personality measures that increase cadets' self-awareness and provide them developmental feedback. All cadets also compose self-reflection and leadership philosophy papers in their core psychology and leadership courses, which aid in identifying gaps and developing strategies to achieve their highest-potential selves.

Academy mentors can also employ another moral developmental tool, facilitating the inclusion of group values in cadets' self-concepts. The self-concept is multidimensional in that people conceptualize themselves at the individual, interpersonal, and collective levels.[39] In essence, all people have a concept of who they are; who they are in relation to others (e.g., who am I in my relationship with my platoon sergeant?); and who they are in various social groups (e.g., who am I/what is my role as a leader of my platoon?). Leaders can activate these various "levels" of the self in their followers to increase identification with facets of social morality. For example, the more leaders can inspire cadets to identify with the institution of West Point and internalize the values and beliefs of the institution, the more cadets will perceive their self-identity at the collective level. They come to see themselves not just as moral individuals, but as a responsible part of a larger moral community, first the Corps of Cadets and later the Army profession. They will then be more likely to internalize and act in accordance with these collective values (such as enforcing the Honor Code and the values of Duty, Honor, and Country) because the reputation of the organization increasingly becomes central to their own self-concept.

Imagine the inspiration and sense of identification felt by cadets when General Douglas MacArthur famously addressed the Corps on May 12, 1962, saying as he made his final departure from West Point that his "last thoughts will be of the Corps, and the Corps, and the Corps." Through such forms of inspirational motivation which link cadets' self-concepts at the collective level to the larger institution's moral identity, cadets come to accept their central role to lead with altruism and exemplary behavior within their organization.

Development of agency must also focus on building the capability for self-regulation. Self-regulation is the ability to control one's thoughts, emotions, and behaviors, with those having higher levels of this ability being better able to align their actions with their core beliefs. Those lacking in a capacity for self-regulation may practice moral disengagement, thus preventing their self-regulatory mechanisms from activating. They therefore forfeit agency and control over their impulse for immoral conduct (or fail to act when faced with a moral dilemma). It is through moral disengagement that people find excuses for their passivity, rationalizing that moral action is "not their job." For example, people conduct moral disengagement by dehumanizing the victims (e.g., calling their enemies demeaning names in times of war, such as "Gooks" in reference to North Vietnamese soldiers); using euphemisms and sanitizing language to discuss killing (e.g., "neutralize" the target versus "kill" the enemy); transferring responsibility (e.g., "I was just following orders" or "everyone else does it"); discounting the injurious effects (e.g., "only a few may suffer"); and blaming the victims (e.g., "they started it" or "they deserve it").[40] Resorting to these forms of disengagement allows leaders to protect their self-concept through self-delusion while conducting immoral acts or refusing to act to prevent moral transgressions by others.

In the current conflict in Iraq, for example, Iraqis are often called "Hajji" or "rag-head" by U.S. forces. Although such epithets may stem somewhat from anger, they are also used as mechanisms to allow soldiers to overlook the fact that these Iraqis are also husbands, wives, children, mothers, and fathers. It is a leader's role to determine when such coping mechanisms are dysfunctional to the extent that they rationalize or act as cover for immoral behaviors. Academy mentors should talk cadets through these human tendencies in the face of morally problematic stresses, raising cadets' awareness of and ability to control such impulses in themselves and in their future followers.

In addition to direct leader-on-follower developmental techniques such as mentoring, counseling, and inspiring, the organization's culture also plays a key role in developing agency and ensuring that members, especially leaders, do not disengage morally. The culture of the organization is the total aggregation of commonly held values and expectations regarding how members should think, feel, and behave.[41] Thus, the organization has tremendous influence over the behavior, values, and attitudes of its members, and the organization's leaders play a pivotal role in developing and maintaining culture. Disengagement by leaders is less likely to be found in organizations whose cultures value moral engagement and reject moral disengagement. For instance, the Academy's Honor Code has the non-toleration clause which, as a reinforcement of the culture, demands that cadets accept agency over their peers, morally engaging and reporting fellow cadets who violate the Code.

Leaders can also increase agency, and thus moral engagement, by highlighting the consequences—or what has been called the "moral intensity"—of leadership issues.[42] Among other methods, leaders can raise moral intensity by emphasizing (1) the degree of harm or benefit likely to result from an action, (2) the probability that the consequence will actually occur, (3) the short period it may be from the moment of their actions until the estimated consequences occur, and (4) how close the follower is to the victims or beneficiaries of his actions. In this case, "close" may refer to social, physical, or psychological distance rather than spatial. An extremely simplified example would be a leader who, during planning for an operation, states: "If we do not hold closely to the rules of engagement, we have a high probability of killing 30 or so combatants and up to five noncombatant civilians during the operation, and may displace many other civilians from their homes. These noncombatants are not sympathizers with the enemy, and we should view them as we would expect our enemies to view our own families." Statements from such a leader would trigger greater moral awareness, activate moral indignation toward inflicting collateral damage during the operation, and increase the propensity for subordinates to take greater ownership of their actions. This example also highlights that moral development may often occur more successfully when embedded in active field-training exercises, rather than in passive classroom settings that lack context and realism.

Over time, as Academy mentors and cultural influences expose cadets to analytical encounters with numerous moral dilemmas—particularly those involving elements of both moral engagement and moral disengagement—cadets will develop their own ability to perceive these facets themselves. In turn, their capacity for and inclination toward moral self-reflection and self-regulation will be increased.

Moral Efficacy

Saint Thomas Aquinas has declared: "The soul is known by its acts." It is true that the character of leaders will ultimately be reflected in their actions. Having outlined the processes of moral complexity and moral agency, we turn now to the third and last of the triad of capabilities shown in Figure 4-1—*moral efficacy* (confidence)—all three of which we hold are necessary to develop leaders of character. This third element is necessary since junior leaders can have increased ability for *moral complexity* (recognition and judgments), and even see it as their place to adopt *moral agency* (engagement and intending), but still fail to act because they lack the courage and resilience to see their intentions through to action. A central precept in the Cadet Prayer implores, "Make us to choose the harder right instead of the easier wrong." Often doing the "harder right" opens leaders to ostracism or alienation, or requires them to overcome strong social pressures. Leaders may even have to confront the moral indiscretions of their own superiors, "speaking truth to power." To spur such moral action, a leader needs a strong sense of moral confidence and courage.[43] Lawrence Kohlberg's theory of cognitive moral development alluded to earlier echoes our position that moral reasoning does not link *directly* to moral behavior, but rather is mediated through factors that increase or decrease the likelihood that the person will act on their own moral reasoning. These factors include the leader's felt confidence to realize moral ideals using his or her own intelligence and problem-solving capabilities.

Moral efficacy is essentially one's confidence in his or her capabilities to organize and mobilize the motivation and cognitive resources needed to attain desired moral ends while persisting in the face of moral adversity. This conceptualization includes not only one's confidence in his or her self, known as self-efficacy,[44] but also confidence in his or her *means*, known as *means-efficacy*.[45] *Self-efficacy* includes those facets of personal confidence that enable one to believe that he or she can succeed as a moral actor, i.e., that one has the interpersonal skills to interject himself or herself in a moral dilemma, overcome whatever resistance is present, and make a positive difference. Means efficacy, on the other hand, includes the belief that the environment will allow one to obtain that success. These external elements may include such factors as other people, policies, culture, or equipment. Means efficacy highlights the huge impact organizations have on the moral behaviors of their members. Organizations must generate cultures in which young leaders are immersed in a supportive, highly developed moral organization that encourages its members to be moral actors through such devices as rewards, positive reinforcement, empowerment, etc. Espousing given values within an organization is relatively easy, whereas creating a supportive, value-laden organizational climate is difficult and time-consuming, requiring authentic moral leadership at all levels.

Conversely, an organization that explicitly or implicitly punishes people who raise moral or ethical issues, thus "rocking the boat," or who challenge the morality of the actions of their leaders, will weaken the confidence of junior leaders to step forward. To develop and sustain moral leaders, organizations must solidify junior leaders' beliefs in both self- and means-efficacy—the type of moral efficacy displayed by the cadet who first stepped up to report the Military Academy's football team cheating scandal in 1951. Imbued with knowledge, principle, and confidence in both himself and his institution to face this issue and to maintain cherished ideals and virtues, this cadet put himself on the line and overcame enormous social pressure.

One's self-efficacy is not just a determination of the skills one has, it is rather a judgment of what one can do with those skills in specific contexts and tasks. For instance, one may feel that he or she can successfully intervene as a cadet platoon leader in the moral dilemmas existing in the platoon. When this cadet is on a summer detail out in the Army, however, he or she may lack the confidence to step forward and address a moral indiscretion of a noncommissioned officer/drill instructor. Once the cadet processes the drill sergeant's indiscretion through the first three phases of the moral reasoning process (moral recognition, judgment, and intention) as enabled by the cadet's cognitive complexity and moral agency, the cadet must decide whether and in what way to act. This decision will likely hinge on factors such as the cadet's self-perceptions of whether he or she has the interpersonal skills to reprimand and counsel a seasoned NCO, whether the cadet feels able to bring the issue to the chain of command and receive support on the matter, and whether the cadet's peers, other drill sergeants, or the chain of command will condemn or ostracize him or her for such actions. A morally confident leader will have the courage to go forward in the situation and the resiliency to face any resistance to achieve success.

As leaders experience moral dilemmas in varying situations and are successful in those experiences, they begin to establish a *domain* of moral efficacy across a broader spectrum of tasks and contexts. Over time these successes transform the leader into an increasingly confident moral actor in even more diverse situations. In sum, we propose that junior leaders with higher degrees of moral efficacy will be more likely to act on their beliefs and moral judgments and thus carry intentions through to actual behaviors. In essence, they become leaders who carry action through to do in the Army's leadership philosophy of Be-Know-Do.

Developing Moral Efficacy

Given the demands of combat, it is paramount that the Academy develop leaders who face moral adversity with courage, thus embodying the following precept suggested in the Cadet Prayer: "Endow us with courage that is born of loyalty to all that is noble and worthy, that scorns to compromise with vice and injustice and knows no fear when truth and right are in jeopardy." We now turn to a discussion of processes facilitating the development of such moral confidence in future leaders.

There are numerous ways to develop efficacy.[46] First, efficacy can best be built through enactive mastery experiences, i.e., hands-on encounters where cadets practice their moral leadership and succeed. These leaders will then be more likely to use such approaches to address future challenges of a nature similar to those already successfully employed. Not all experiences are the same, however. Leadership development experts Bruce Avolio and Fred Luthans opine that some experiences can be, as noted earlier, "triggering events" that jolt people out of their complacency and into a period of deep self-reflection, thus paving the way for exceptional individual development. Such an event might be, for example, having a roommate found guilty of an honor violation. Such a triggering event invokes the deep metacognitive processing outlined earlier, enhancing the likelihood that the person will reflect on the nature and adequacy of his or her own knowledge structures. Iteration of such events over time makes those structures more robust by incorporating the new experiences, increasing cognitive complexity.[47] Following this logic, as the Academy subjects cadets to a succession of moral jolts that are progressively more difficult to handle, cadets will achieve an ever-heightening level of success and strengthen their moral efficacy. The Academy's honor and ethics training programs can best be accomplished by providing such jump-starts for deeper moral reflection. So long as they are reinforced by a supp-ortive organization and guided in timely reflection by capable mentors, acquisition of confidence for moral thought and action will be accelerated.

It is critical that these trigger events allow for initial success and then be ratcheted up in their degree of difficulty at a pace such that cadets continue to succeed, thus avoiding the reduction of efficacy that can occur from failing. We know that moral efficacy can be raised through incremental goal-setting, since research shows that individuals will raise their level of motivation and persistence toward major goals of great difficulty if sub-goals along the way are seen as more obtainable.[48] Leaders can develop followers by assisting them in their moral goal-setting and illuminating realistic enabling pathways to their moral development. It is critical, however, that trigger events eventually begin to challenge the moral core of these emerging leaders and force deep reflec-tion.[49] Although ethics discussions in classrooms serve a useful function, they will not normally provide a sufficient level of challenge. Cadets must be immersed in experiences reflective of the real world, even if they are virtual or vicarious. Although some of these experiences can be brought into the classroom through well-planned, role-playing scenarios and similar formats, they are perhaps better embedded in other training, such as tactical training missions. Further, all trigger events do not have to be planned—leaders can seize upon fortuitous events cadets face as part of their normal life experience by assisting and coaching their reflections on those events. It is critical that leaders have an ability to recognize "moral moments" that have developmental potential. At that point, they can "pull up a chair" and talk cadets through the issue at hand. Fortunately, West Point has more than its fair share of such leader-developers in the rotating faculty (captains and majors with five to eight years of relevant leadership in the Army and then two years of graduate school just before joining the faculty) and staff.

Moral trigger events can also be vicarious experiences in which cadets view other leaders' actions and responses to moral dilemmas, with the stipulation of course that they be coupled with dedicated and guided reflection. These vicarious experiences are most effective when the actor being modeled is perceived by the cadet to be similar to himself. The more a cadet thinks "they are like me so I can do it too," the more effective the modeling will be. Efficacy can also be built through social persuasion, such as senior leaders inspiring junior leaders to believe that they are in fact moral actors and capable of uncommonly challenging moral action. Moral self-efficacy can be increased through psychological and physiological arousal—essentially "firing people up" about moral leadership and moral action. For instance, when leaders experience a strong emotional response to a moral dilemma, their strong feelings will evoke firmer determination toward addressing it, and their moral efficacy will accordingly be heightened. Thus one method leaders can use to fire up cadets is to show passion themselves toward moral issues and through framing those issues in moral terms. A leader's moral intensity begets moral intensity in his or her followers.

Finally, in developing moral efficacy in cadets it is essential that the Academy continue to articulate the quality and utility of means and support offered by the organization. This support cannot just be declared, it must actually be placed in use by the organization. A social fabric, a feeling of moral support, must permeate the culture in every nook and cranny. In essence, an organization must provide psychological safety to its members. Senior leaders must reinforce to cadets, through word and action, that the organization's leaders and members will support them in their moral initiatives. Leaders must ensure that existing organizational policies encourage, support, and protect those members who come forward to report potential moral improprieties. Supportive leaders will provide cadets with a sense of means efficacy needed for moral efficacy. Foremost, cadets must totally assimilate the value of creating a supportive culture so that they can replicate a supportive culture in their own units when they are leaders.

To Sum Up

Moral development is a vast and complex topic that requires integration of such sciences as moral decision-making; social, cognitive, and developmental psychology; positive psychology; organizational behavior; and leadership to form a holistic moral development plan for accelerating character development. This chapter has provided an overview of what we consider to be the three major elements of such a developmental plan, those we call the *triad of moral capabilities*, i.e., moral complexity, moral agency, and moral efficacy. We have focused here on authentic leadership development, which is evidenced by a true transformational change in the leader so as to enhance his or her self-sustaining capacity to be a moral actor in the absence of social sanctions or reinforcements. A recurring theme throughout this discussion has been the central role of robust moral trigger events, experiences that challenge the moral core of a young leader at ever-rising levels of difficulty. Coupled with mentored reflection and meaning-making sessions, these experiences will broaden and deepen the knowledge structures and cognitive abilities of these young leaders and enhance their levels of agency and confidence. Reinforced by a strong sense of agency, they will own their and their followers' moral experiences across their domain of influence, raising their orientation toward altruistic interpersonal behavior. Finally, an increased level of moral efficacy will provide confidence in the ability of young leaders to act and make a positive difference when faced with a moral dilemma—to do the "harder right instead of the easier wrong" as is so memorably expressed in the Cadet Prayer. If the foregoing factors are coupled with perceptions of supportive leaders in an organizational climate that values morality and provides the necessary means, the stage will be set for these leaders to engage fully as moral actors.

The objective of moral development at the Academy is to produce leaders who have internalized the Academy's and Army's values and the four roles of officership (leader of character, warrior, member of the profession of arms, and servant of the nation) in their self-concepts. It is being a leader of character that provides the foundation for the other three roles. With respect to the Army's Be-Know-Do leadership doctrine, we have tried to offer valid scientific underpinnings to the moral development aspects of this framework. The research findings offered in this chapter parallel this Army doctrine: moral agency (Be), moral complexity (Know), and moral efficacy (Do), which together support the development of leaders of character at West Point for the Army and the nation.

Notes

1. USMA Circular 1-101, *Cadet Leader Development System* (West Point, NY: Defense Printing, 2002), XX.
2. Adrian Chan, Sean T. Hannah, and William L. Gardner, "Veritable Authentic Leadership: Emergence, Functioning, and Impacts," in *Authentic Leadership Theory and Practice: Origins, Effects, and Development*, ed. William B. Gardner, Bruce J. Avolio, and Fred O. Walumbwa, Monographs in Leadership and Management, Vol. 3 (Oxford: Elsevier Ltd., 2005), 3-41; Bruce J. Avolio, William L. Gardner, Fred O. Walumbwa, and Douglas R. May, "Unlocking the Mask: A Look at the Process

by which Authentic Leaders Impact Follower Attitudes and Behaviors," *Leadership Quarterly* 15 (2004): 801-823.

3. Sean T. Hannah, Paul B. Lester, and Gretchen R.Vogelgesang, "Moral Leadership: Explicating the Moral Component of Authentic Leadership," in *Authentic Leadership Theory and Practice: Origins, Effects, and Development,* 43-81.

4. USMA Circular 1-101, 28-29.

5. Robert Kegan, *In Over Our Heads: The Mental Demands of Modern Life* (Cambridge, MA: Harvard University Press, 1994).

6. Philip Lewis et al., "Identity Development During the College Years: Findings from the West Point Longitudinal Study," *Journal of College Student Development* 46, no. 4 (2005): 357-373.

7. Ibid.

8. Ibid.

9. See chap. 1 of this volume for the Cadet Prayer with the moral precepts highlighted.

10. USMA Circular 1-101-1, *Cadet Leader Development System for Cadets* (West Point, NY: Defense Printing, 2005), 19.

11. Ibid., pp. 29-30.

12. James R. Rest, "Background, Theory, and Research," in *Moral Development: Advances in Theory and Research,* ed. James R. Rest and Darcia Narvaez (New York: Praeger, 1994), 59-88.

13. Lawrence Kohlberg, *The Philosophy of Moral Development* (San Francisco, CA: Harper Row, 1981).

14. Robert Kegan, *In Over Our Heads: The Mental Demands of Modern Life.*

15. Robert Kegan, *The Evolving Self* (Cambridge: Harvard University Press, 1992).

16. Rest, "Background, Theory, and Research."

17. James R. Rest et al., "A Neo-Kohlbergian Approach to Morality Research," *Journal of Moral Education* 29 (2000): 381-395.

18. Jane E. Dutton and Susan E. Jackson, "Categorizing Strategic Issues: Links to Organizational Action," *Academy of Management* 12 (1987): 76-90.

19. Bruce J. Avolio, *Leadership in Balance: Made/Born* (Hillsdale, NJ: Lawrence Erlbaum, 2005).

20. Gordon H. Bower and Ernest R. Hilgard, *Theories of Learning* (Saddle River, NJ: Prentice-Hall, 1981).

21. Alice A. Eagly and Shelly Chaiken, "Attitude Structure and Function," in *Handbook of Social Psychology,* 4th Edition, Vol. I, ed. Daniel T. Gilbert, Susan T. Fiske, and Gardner Lindzey (Boston: McGraw-Hill, 1998), 269-322.

22. Janet Metcalfe and Arthur P. Shimamura, *Metacognition: Knowing About Knowing* (Cambridge, MA: MIT Press, 1994).

23. H. Lee Swanson and George Hill. "Metacognitive Aspects of Moral Reasoning and Behavior," *Adolescence* 28 (1993): 711-735.

24. Marvin W. Berkowitz, John Gibbs, and John Broughton, "The Relation of Moral Judgment Disparity to Developmental Effects of Peer Dialogues," *Merrill-Palmer Quarterly* 26 (1980): 341-357; and Lawrence J. Walker, "Sources of Cognitive Conflict for Stage Transition in Moral Development," *Developmental Psychology* 19 (1983): 103-110.

25. Dennis A. Gioia and Peter P. Poole, "Scripts in Organizational Behavior," *Academy of Management Review* 9 (1984): 449-459.

26. Norman A. Sprinthall, "Counseling and Role-taking: Social Promoting Moral and Ego Development," in *Moral Development in the Professions: Psychology and Applied Ethics,* ed. James R. Rest and Darcia Narvaez (Hillsdale, NJ: Lawrence Erlbaum, 1994), 85-99.

27. James R. Rest and Stephen J. Thoma, "Education Programs and Interventions," in *Moral Development: Advances in Theory and Research,* ed. James R. Rest (New York: Praeger, 1986), 59-88.

28. David H. Petraeus, (untitled presentation given to the West Point faculty and staff members of the Department of Social Sciences, West Point, New York, February 4, 2006).

29. Albert Bandura. "Social Cognitive Theory of Moral Thought and Action," in *Handbook of Moral Behavior and Development,* Vol. 1, ed. W. M. Kurtines and J. L. Gewitz (Hillsdale, NJ: Erlbaum, 1991): 45-103.

30. Ibid.

31. Arthur P. Brief, Janet M. Dukerich, and L. I. Doran, "Resolving Ethical Dilemmas in Management: Experimental Investigations of Values, Accountability, and Choice," *Journal of Applied Social Psychology* 21 (1991): 380-396; and Philip E. Tetlock, "The Impact of Accountability on Judgment and Choice," *Research in Organizational Behavior* 7 (1992): 297-332.

32. Richard E. Petty and John T. Cacioppo, "The Elaboration Likelihood Model of Persuasion," in *Advances in Experimental Social Psychology,* ed. Leonard Berkowitz (New York: Academic Press, 1986), 123-205.

33. M. D. Street, "The Impact of Cognitive Elaboration on the Ethical Decision-Making Process: The Cognitive Elaboration Model," *Organizational Behavior and Human Decision Processes* 86 (2001): 256-277.

34. Shelley Chaiken, "Heuristic versus Systematic Information Processing and the Use of Source versus Message Cues in Persuasion," *Journal of Personality and Social Psychology* 39 (1980): 752.

35. Ibid.

36. John F. Kihlstrom, Jennifer S. Beer, and Stanley B. Klein, "Self and Identity as Memory," in *Handbook of Self and Identity,* ed. Mark J. Leary and June P. Tangney (New York: Guilford Press, 2003), 68-90.

37. Robert G. Lord and Douglas J. Brown, *Leadership Processes and Follower Self-identity* (Hillsdale, NJ: Erlbaum, 2004).

38. Ibid.

39. Ibid.

40. Albert Bandura, 45-103.

41. Edgar H. Schein, *Organizational Culture and Leadership* (San Francisco: Josey-Bass, 1992).

42. Thomas M. Jones, "Ethical Decision-making by Individuals in Organizations: An Issue-contingent Model," *Academy of Management Review* 16 (1991): 366-395.

43. Albert Bandura, 45-103; Albert Bandura, "Social Cognitive Theory in Cultural Context," *Journal of Applied Psychology: An International Review* 51 (2002): 269-290.

44. Albert Bandura, *Self-efficacy: The Exercise of Control* (New York: Freeman, 1997).

45. Dov Eden, "Means Efficacy: External Sources of General and Specific Subjective Efficacy," in *Work Motivation in the Context of a Globalizing Economy,* ed. Miriam Erez, Uwe Kleinbeck, and Henk Thierry (Hillsdale, NJ: Lawrence Erlbaum, 2001), 65-77.
46. Albert Bandura, *Self-efficacy.*
47. Bruce J. Avolio and Fred Luthans, *The High Impact Leader: Moments Matter in Accelerating Authentic Leadership Development* (New York: McGraw-Hill, 2006).
48. Albert Bandura and Dale Schunk, "Cultivating Competence, Self-efficacy, and Intrinsic Interest Through Proximal Self-motivation," *Journal of Personality and Social Psychology* 41 (1981): 586.
49. Albert Bandura, *Self-efficacy.*

5 | High-Impact Military Leadership: The Positive Effects of Authentic Moral Leadership on Followers

Patrick J. Sweeney and Sean T. Hannah

Introduction

For you as an Army leader, leadership in combat is your primary mission and most important challenge. To meet this challenge, you must develop character and competence while achieving excellence.
—FM 22-100, Army Leadership Manual[1]

The epigraph above, taken from the Army's leadership manual, clearly declares that character development plays a central role in preparing leaders to meet the challenges of leading in combat. In fact, character is one of the three pillars in the Army's Be-Know-Do leader development framework.[2] Character corresponds to the *Be* pillar of the framework, entailing the values and attributes which define a leader. The Know pillar pertains to the competencies (knowledge and skills) leaders must possess, while the *Do* pillar deals with the application of these competencies to leadership. Each pillar is necessary but not in itself sufficient to provide effective leadership of soldiers in battle. In the multidimensional and morally ambiguous realm of combat, the Army's young leaders must not just be tactically and technically skillful, knowledgeable of leadership skills, and able to use these abilities—they must be imbued with strong character in order to use these abilities in positively and ethically influencing their followers and organizations.

The Army leadership manual mandates that leaders must continuously develop all aspects of their physical, mental, moral, and professional repertoire to become competent leaders of character. A key aspect of this overall development is internalizing the Army's seven primary values: loyalty, duty, respect, selfless service, honor, integrity, and personal courage.[3] The Army values also reflect the values embodied in the U.S. Military Academy's motto of Duty, Honor, Country and the precepts of the Cadet Prayer. The Army and West Point believe that the internalization of these values would provide leaders with a solid character foundation essential for seeking the truth; applying values and principles in their decisions and actions; and displaying the courage, self-discipline, and commitment to do what is right in all situations.[4] Such self-aware and virtuous leaders are authentic leaders of character.

In Chapter 4, we introduced a framework for moral development and discussed how it advances understanding of the Cadet Leader Development System (CLDS). The focus was on the "how" of moral development. In this chapter, we focus on the "why" of moral development by highlighting the positive and synergistic impact that leaders of character have on their followers and organizations. The intent is to explain why the Army and West Point place such great emphasis on character development.

We start by exploring the impact of authentic moral leadership on followers' trust and leaders' ability to influence. The results from two studies conducted in the Iraqi combat zone are used to illuminate the positive impact of leaders' character on trust and leadership in combat. Next, we explore the impact that authentic moral leadership has on followers' moral development. As we specified in Chapter 4, an authentic leader is one who is morally developed and has internalized the Army and West Point's values as opposed to one who acts ethically merely to comply with social rules and norms or to avoid sanctions.[5] These authentic leaders are highly self-aware and able to regulate their behavior to stay true to themselves and exercise their core moral beliefs in the domain of leadership. Discussion will center on how moral leaders through modeling, persuasion, and organizational culture promote the moral development and moral actions of their followers. An example from Operation Desert Storm (1991) and recent examples from Operation Iraqi Freedom (2003–2005) are used to illustrate main points. We end the chapter with a discussion of the impact authentic moral leadership has on facilitating both the professional and personal growth of followers.

Authentic Moral Leadership's Impact on Trust and Influence

Leaders' character plays a central role in earning followers' trust.[6] For the purpose of this chapter, trust is defined as one's willingness to put life and limb at risk in the confident expectation that others—subordinates, peers, and leaders—can and will meet their end of the group's cooperative bargain.[7] How, then, does a leader's character impact the development of followers' trust? According to a trust development model based on interdependence theory, set forth in Figure 5-1, trust develops through a reciprocating cycle in which each person in a relationship acts to reduce the other's fear of exploitation and to show that the relationship will be mutually rewarding. A leader can reduce the followers' uncertainty about the relationship by taking action to show that he/she is dependable and has the ability to make the relationship rewarding. The leader earns his reputation for dependability by demonstrating his intentions to trust followers, his willingness to act out of concern for all involved in the relationship, the

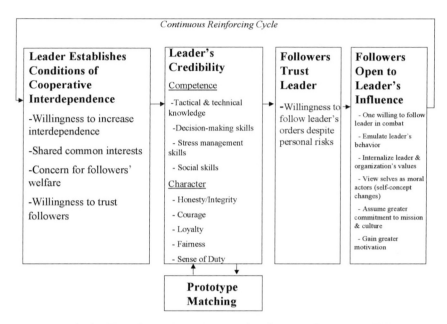

Figure 5-1. *An Interdependence Model for the Development of Trust.*

habitual sharing of common interests, and his willingness to depend on followers. These behaviors serve to establish cooperative interdependence in the leader-subordinate relationship.

Followers infer the leader's values and underlying character traits from the leader's demonstrated cooperative behavior. Thus, the leader's character influences perceptions of dependability. If soldiers think the leader's cooperative behavior is the result of sound and stable character traits, then the leader is perceived as dependable. A leader possessing good character is more likely to behave in a moral and ethical manner and not exploit the relationship. Further, followers' judgments concerning the leader's ability to make the relationship rewarding depend on an assessment of his or her skills, knowledge, and motivation to meet the responsibilities of the position. If soldiers believe that a leader's demonstrated competent behavior was due to authentic skills and knowledge, then they will be more likely to believe that the leader will most likely behave in a competent manner in the future.[8] Taken together, the perceptions of a leader's dependable character and competence form an overall evaluation of the leader's credibility. Credibility leads to the development of trust.[9] The model in Figure 5-1 further proposes that trust increases one's willingness to accept influence. Therefore, the processes of developing trust and influence are linked.

What follows is a discussion of how this model can be applied to understanding the development of trust and its positive impacts in a leader-subordinate relationship. To establish a cooperative interdependent relationship, leaders must trust their followers to do their jobs; genuinely care about their followers; emphasize how the accomplishment of organizational objectives is linked to the obtainment of followers' personal objectives as well; and willingly increase their dependence on their soldiers.[10] A cooperative and interdependent relationship helps provide group members with a sense of confidence that the relationship will be safer and more rewarding, that all members are working to ensure that everyone benefits from the relationship to the maximum degree, and that leaders trust and respect group members. Leaders who extend trust and respect, and demonstrate a willingness to work as a member of the team, prompt subordinates to reciprocate in kind. Followers will infer underlying character traits, such as loyalty, respect, and caring, from the leader's cooperative behavior. This is why the establishment of cooperative interdependence in leader-subordinate relations bolsters perceptions of the leader's credibility.[11]

To determine leaders' credibility, followers will assess both their character and competence. Leader competence entails technical and tactical knowledge, intelligence, decision-making skills, and interpersonal social skills.[12] A leader's character is the combination of values and attributes that define who the leader is as a person. Thus, leaders' characters will influence their interpretation of situations, their approach to leadership duties, their decisions, and most importantly how they behave as leaders.[13] Leaders who internalize the moral principles embodied in the Cadet Prayer—honesty, the courage and motivation to live with integrity, loyalty to higher moral causes, service to country, maintaining the honor of West Point and the Army by living their values—are more likely to behave in an ethical and reliable manner, especially in tough situations such as combat. Knowing in advance that their leaders will display reliable and ethical behavior in tough and dangerous situations is very important to soldiers because their lives depend on their leaders' ability to function effectively under the stresses of combat while protecting their welfare. Therefore, leaders will be perceived as credible if they possess good character and are competent in meeting the role requirements of their leadership position.

In summary, we propose that the strength of leaders' character (Be), the extent of their competence (Know), and the establishment of a cooperative and interdependent relationship with followers through leader behaviors (Do), combine to develop trust. As shown in Figure 5-1, the level of subordinates' trust in their leaders in turn determines the extent of leader influence the followers will willingly accept.[14] Followers are more willing to submit to the will of competent leaders of character because these leaders are more likely to fulfill all duties and accomplish all missions in an ethical manner, while at the same time protecting to the maximum degree the welfare of group members.

Importantly, subordinates will allow a trusted leader of character to influence their beliefs, values, attitudes, motivation, and behavior.

Thus, trusted leaders will not only have the ability to lead followers effectively in combat, they will also have the ability to change who the followers are as people, a central concept of transformational leadership theory.[15] Transformational leaders induce their followers to internalize their values, beliefs, and visions. Numerous studies have shown that these followers in turn excel beyond expectations.[16] In essence, followers will personally identify with such exemplary leaders and will over time internalize these leaders' values and ideals. This is the ultimate level of influence made possible by the establishment of trust, which is based on the leaders' good character and competence. Leaders who practice authentic moral leadership will earn their followers' trust, which provides them with the ability to exercise the high levels of influence necessary for leading effectively in combat.[17]

Illustrations from Studies Conducted in the Iraqi Combat Zone

Results from two studies conducted in the Iraqi combat zone provide new empirical support for the propositions that leaders who practice authentic moral leadership will earn their followers' trust and that this trust provides them a greater ability to exercise high-impact leadership. The studies were conducted by the first author in May 2003 after the end of major combat actions in Operation Iraqi Freedom. The first study tested the validity of an interdependence model for the development of trust, discussed above and outlined in Figure 5-1, using the responses from 315 Army soldiers. The results from this study indicated that the model provided a plausible explanation of how leaders earn their soldiers' trust in combat, that is, by establishing cooperative interdependent relationships, extending their own trust, demonstrating good character, and being competent. Followers' trust in their leader was highly predictive of their willingness to accept that leader's influence. The fact that findings from this study were based on data collected in a combat zone makes the results even more compelling.

This increased level of influence can be partially explained by prototype theory. Previous research had shown that through life experiences in general and through exposures to various leaders in particular, followers build their own implicit *leadership theory* (ILT) over time. An ILT is essentially a prototype of the skills, character, and other physical, emotional, and psychological attributes that followers determine a good leader must hold. This prototype is a form of schema, that is, a mental representation people form in long-term memory as we described in Chapter 4. Researchers have shown that a follower's ILT becomes the "lens" through which they view and judge any leader—as shown by the "prototype matching" box in Figure 5-1—and those leaders who best meet one's ILT prototype will be granted more influence.[18] Importantly, research has shown that the components of moral character are common across the vast majority of followers' implicit leadership theories as to what makes a good leader—Army leaders are expected to be highly morally developed and to lead pro-socially. Research has shown that immoral leaders are actually deemed *anti*-prototypical and will be greatly limited in their ability to influence followers.[19] It is also of interest that ethical character is not only a common factor in the prototypes of an ideal leader held by members of the American culture at large, but has been noticed in cross-cultural research to be a universally and internationally held expectation of leader character.[20] This suggests that highly ethical officers will also have greater influence over members of foreign militaries attached to or working with U.S. forces and over leaders of local civilian populations they must influence.

The effects of follower vision of the ideal leader were tested by the first author in a second study. Seventy-two Army soldiers voluntarily reported, in their own words, the attributes they look for in leaders who could be trusted in combat, discussed why each attribute influenced trust, and rated the relative importance of each attribute to the establishment of trust. They also shared their perceptions of how trust and leadership were related. The two main purposes of the study were to map the prototype of a leader who can be trusted in combat and to explore soldiers' perceptions regarding the relationship between trust and leadership.

The prototype of trusted combat leader that emerged from the study is outlined in Figure 5-2. Analysis of this prototype clearly indicates that leaders' competence and character are the foundations upon which trust is built. The individual character traits most frequently mentioned by soldiers as important for trust development in combat were loyalty and protectiveness with regard to subordinates' welfare; honesty/integrity in word and deed; physical and moral courage to do the right thing; and a sense of duty to fulfill responsibilities in the toughest situations.

---

1. Competence
2. Loyalty
3. Honesty/Integrity
4. Leadership by Example
5. Self-Control (Stress Management)
6. Confidence
7. Courage (Physical & Moral)
8. Practice of Sharing Information
9. Personal Connection with Subordinates
10. Sense of Duty

Figure 5-2. *Attributes of a Leader Who Can Be Trusted in Combat.*

Subordinates' views of the character trait of loyalty were very narrowly defined, focused on the leader's concern with and commitment to looking out for their welfare. Responses indicated that loyal leaders look out for their followers' welfare by planning, executing, and accomplishing combat mission objectives with the least possible risk to the lives of their soldiers. Also, loyal leaders genuinely care about their soldiers, support them, and place their soldiers' welfare before their own. These leaders look out for their subordinates' well-being even if it incurs risk or cost to themselves, which allows soldiers to proceed with their duties in the sure knowledge that their leaders will protect their best interests at all times, especially when the risks are great. It is thus an adaptive process for soldiers to trust leaders who are loyal to them, because it helps ensure their own survival in combat.

An episode related by an artillery lieutenant, serving as an Infantry Company Fire Support Officer, illustrates how his commander's willingness to defy a directive in order to protect his soldiers' welfare demonstrated loyalty and served to bolster trust. The company was conducting an attack in An Najaf while wearing full Nuclear, Biological, and Chemical (NBC) suits in conforming with the battalion commander's guidance. The NBC suits were very heavy and hot. The temperature during the attack was high, and the unit suffered two heat casualties early into the attack. If the unit continued to attack with the NBC suits on, the soldiers would suffer and combat effectiveness would decrease. In the artillery lieutenant's words,

> The Company Commander made the commonsense decision to wear just t-shirts and roll the pants to mid-shin. This may seem like an obvious decision, but it was going against command guidance, and the First Sergeant wanted to remain in uniform. However, it greatly increased the trust in the commander across the company because it was a decision that put the soldiers and mission first, and not the all-important image depicted through the attached news media.

In the situation describe above, the company commander made an adaptive decision based on the combat situation. His willingness to incur risk by defying command guidance to stay in chemical suits demonstrated loyalty to the soldiers' welfare and also enhanced the unit's combat effectiveness. The commander's willingness to hazard his personal standing with his commander in order to protect his soldiers' welfare boosted their trust in him. Research has repeatedly shown that leaders willing to take such personal risks or make self-sacrifices are seen as more charismatic by their followers, further increasing their influence and ability to be high-impact leaders.[21]

Soldiers tended to view leaders' truthfulness in word and deed as exemplifying the core character trait of honesty/integrity. Because soldiers had to take action and risk their lives based on information their leaders provided them, they demanded that leaders be absolutely honest in presenting information. A sergeant who served in an artillery unit provided a statement that captures the importance of leader honesty in combat: "Honesty in my opinion is what makes an effective leader. The Executive Officer of this unit kept us informed and never 'sugar-coated' anything. If we were headed for some rough times, he flat out told us. He always kept us informed and that is what soldiers need."

Leaders with such integrity provided soldiers with reassurance that in the extreme stress and chaos of combat, their welfare would be looked after and the mission accomplished according to the rules. A leader's integrity serves as a foundation for the moral and ethical execution of missions, which sustains his or her subordinates' moral justification for fighting and their will to win. Possessing a sound moral justification for fighting helps soldiers manage both the immediate and long-term psychological stress associated with killing.

Soldiers viewed the critical character trait of *moral courage* on the part of the leader (outlined in Chapter 4) as possessing the strength to act according to their values and beliefs (integrity), thus doing the right thing. Moral courage often entails taking risks by standing up to authority to protect soldiers' welfare or to defend the leader's decisions. Soldiers trusted leaders who had the moral fiber to take a stand for what they believed in and for the decisions they made, and who possessed knowledge of the proper way to conduct missions. As we also outlined in Chapter 4, authentic moral leaders have high levels of moral agency, that is, ownership of and acceptance of responsibility for their moral experiences. Those with high levels of moral agency value living with integrity more than they fear the consequences of taking a stand to fight for what they believe is the right course.

Moreover, authentic leaders also possess the physical courage to face the dangers and hardships of combat and still perform their duties. Leaders must be able to manage their fear—even the bravest will experience fear at times—without betraying it through their looks and manner. A leader's physical courage enhances subordinates' perception of credibility, which facilitates trust because soldiers can depend on courageous leaders to fulfill their responsibilities in the toughest of situations. An Artillery Battery Executive Officer in Mosul, Iraq, succinctly captured how physical courage influences the development of trust and subordinates' willingness to follow in combat: "I trust leaders who volunteer to share in any potential danger."

Authentic Moral Leadership at My Lai

Captain (USA, Ret.) Hugh Thompson's actions at My Lai epitomized moral agency, moral courage, and moral efficacy as described in Chapter 4. These three qualities drive an authentic moral leader in combat. On March 16, 1968, then Chief Warrant Officer Thompson witnessed American soldiers killing the civilians of the Vietnamese hamlet My Lai as he piloted a helicopter over the village. He became morally outraged at what he was seeing and landed his craft between the American soldiers and the villagers in an attempt to stop the atrocity and evacuate the wounded civilians. He ordered his gunner to open fire on the American soldiers if they continued to shoot the civilians. Thompson was aware that he was risking his own life, the lives of his crew, and a possible court-martial for ordering his gunner to fire on American soldiers in his effort to stop the killing of noncombatants, though he knew his action was the morally right thing.[22]

Further, Thompson had the moral courage to report the incident up the chain of command, to testify before Congressional and military inquiries, and to testify at the court-martial of Lieutenant William Calley. In the face of death threats and ostracism, he steadfastly voiced the truth to the Army and the American people about what happened at My Lai on that March morning.[23] Captain Thompson's action during the My Lai massacre and his subsequent quest to ensure that the truth about the tragic incident was heard, exemplified the principle of moral courage found in the following lines of the Cadet Prayer: "Make us to choose the harder right instead of the easier wrong, and never to be content with a half truth when the whole can be won. Endow us with courage that is born of loyalty to all that is noble and worthy, that scorns to compromise with vice and injustice and knows no fear when truth and right are in jeopardy."[24]

Captain Thompson's strong moral values and his courage to live by these values enabled him to exercise high-impact leadership at the hamlet of My Lai. More importantly, his authentic moral leadership set the example and served as the moral conscience for the Army at large when some members of the Army's leadership tried to cover up this sordid episode. He was truly an authentic moral leader.

The Link between Trust and Combat Leadership

The role of trust in combat cannot be overestimated. Leaders on a dynamic battlefield cannot do everything alone, so that functions need to be spread around and power shared. Effective leadership becomes a system of relationships across all levels of an organization, and these relationships must be sustained through trust, respect, and reciprocity. Leadership research prior to 1960s tended to view followers as being passive in the leader-follower relationship. Researchers focused more on leader traits or the "position powers" of the leader. These are the authorities they are assigned by virtue of their position, such as the various rewards and punishments that can be employed to influence their followers. More recent research, beginning with contingency models of leadership in the 1960s and continuing with current research on charismatic and transformational leadership, has increased attention on the active role of the follower in the leader-follower relationship.[25] This more active role of the follower focuses not on leader position powers, but on the "person powers" of the leader, i.e., those powers that must be "earned" by the leader such as referent and expert powers. Referent power exists when subordinates accept a leader's influence because they identify with the leader, use the leader as a role model, and seek the leader's approval.[26] It is the nature of these powers that they can be proffered by followers or denied entirely within their own discretion. We hold that it is these person powers that will have the greatest impact on followers, particularly in a life-threatening combat environment where the efficacy of incentives (reward power), threats of punishment (coercion power), or "because I am in charge and I told you so" (legitimate or formal power) may be seriously diluted. Major General John Schofield in his famous definition of discipline makes this point about as well as words can express:

> The discipline which makes the soldiers of a free country reliable in battle is not to be gained by harsh or tyrannical treatment. On the contrary, such treatment is far more likely to destroy than to make an army. It is possible to impart instruction and to give commands in such a manner and such a tone of voice as to inspire in the soldier no feeling but an intense desire to obey, while the opposite manner and tone of voice cannot fail to excite strong resentment and a desire to disobey. The one mode or the other of dealing with subordinates springs from a corresponding spirit in the breast of the commander. He who feels the respect which is due to others cannot fail to inspire in them regard for himself, while he who feels and hence manifests disrespect towards others, especially his inferiors, cannot fail to inspire in them hatred for himself.

The incidents involving "fragging" leaders in combat in the Vietnam conflict are extreme examples of the result when position powers are no longer recognized by followers in a combat environment.[27] In such extreme situations, followers will impute greater influence to leaders who have demonstrated high competence (and thus earned expert power) and have demonstrated the character and values that engender high levels of trust, in essence leaders who are credited by their followers with substantial referent power.

The role of referent power was evident in the second study conducted in Iraq. When asked to describe in their own words how trust was related to leadership, a majority (78 percent) of the respondents indicated that trust was necessary and essential for a leader to exercise influence in combat.[28] Or, to put it simply, subordinates' trust in their leaders determined their willingness to accept leader influence and to risk their lives to achieve the organization's objectives. This was a very powerful finding because the results suggested that in extreme situations, where the subordinates assume the greatest risks, trust is the psychological mechanism that persuades them to willingly accept leader influence, to downgrade their self-interests to a position secondary to the organization's interests, and to step into harm's way. As discussed earlier, competent leaders of character exercising authentic moral leadership will shine forth in their subordinates' eyes as role models, thus earning their followers' trust, which in turn enables them to exercise effective leadership in combat.

Below is a series of actual statements by subordinates that add up to a compelling story of how important trust was to their acceptance of leader influence in combat in Iraq:

> *I think trust is leadership. Leadership is the act of influencing soldiers to accomplish the mission by providing purpose, direction, and motivation. If soldiers don't know that they can trust you to feed them, let them rest, tell you what they are afraid of, then how in the hell are they going to follow you in any situation?*
>
> —Sergeant, Artillery Gunner, Mosul, Iraq

> *If you trust your leader, you are willing to go to hell and back if need be.*
> —Sergeant, Artillery Gunner, Tall Afar, Iraq

> *Soldiers first have to trust you to follow you. Following a leader and following orders are two different things. If they trust you and believe in you, there is nothing they won't do for you.*
> —Second Lieutenant, Infantry Company Fire Support Officer,
> Qayyarah West Airbase, Northern Iraq

> *Trust to me deals a lot with leadership. The more I trust a leader, the more I allow him/her to influence me.*
> —Specialist, Artillery Computer Operator, Mosul, Iraq

> *If you trust in your leaders, the soldiers will do more. On the other hand, if they do not trust their leaders, the soldiers will always second-guess their leaders before they do what they have to do.*
> —Sergeant, Mechanic, Mosul, Iraq

> *It is like a Field Manual. The Field Manual is the leader. If I do not trust it, I would not read it. I would not take information from it or apply it or risk any lives. Trust in a leader allows you to listen and do what is expected of you. And because you trust the leader, you know that he will not foolishly risk your life and that of your peers/subordinates.*
> —First Lieutenant, Platoon Leader, Mosul, Iraq

The responses above indicate that subordinates who did not trust their leaders would follow the leaders' directives only reluctantly, would question orders, and also would be unwilling to assume the risks of combat, all of which could put unit members' lives at risk and have a detrimental impact on organization effectiveness. The lack of trust in a leader would cause subordinates to fret about their personal safety and at the same time cause anxious doubts as to whether the leader's directives would result in accomplishment of the organization's objectives. This questioning of leader directives and focus on personal safety could result in subordinates' adopting a protective or timidly passive attitude, which would decrease their aggressiveness and the will to face the rigors of combat. Subordinates will look for ways to change or avoid a non-trusted leader's directive in an effort to minimize risks to their own safety, probably complying with his orders only as a last resort. In extreme cases, subordinates may even disobey orders of leaders they do not trust. The responses below illustrate how the lack of trust in a leader decreases subordinates' willingness to accept leader influence:

> *If you do not trust your leaders, it can be difficult to follow orders, especially if death or dismemberment is [a likely] result.*
> —Sergeant, Infantry Company Forward Observer
> Qayyarah West Airbase, Northern Iraq

> *If you cannot trust your leader, you are going to have doubts about your safety as well as the safety of your fellow soldiers. You will not perform at a 100 percent for your leader if there is not trust.*
> —Specialist, Artillery Gunner,
> Mosul, Iraq

> *If soldiers do not trust their leaders it leads to second-guessing and possible disobedience of orders.*
> —Staff Sergeant, Chief Fire Direction Computer,
> Mosul, Iraq

> *You can tell a man to fight as his leader. If he doesn't trust you, he will change the things you want. If he trusts you, he will do what you want.*
> —Sergeant, Supply Noncommissioned Officer,
> Qayyarah West Airbase, Northern Iraq

> *Trust is the most important thing that can relate to leadership. Because if I don't trust my leader, I will question every order in my head, which can make me hesitate and may get me killed.*
> —Specialist, Infantry Company Armor,
> Qayyarah West Airbase, Northern Iraq

> *The main foundation for leadership is trust. If you cannot trust the person or people who lead you, then basically you are lost. How can you be influenced to do something if you cannot trust the person telling you what to do?*
> —Sergeant, Artillery Gunner, Mosul, Iraq

> *A soldier who does not trust a leader will question decisions the leader makes and will not be willing to follow the leader into a dangerous situation.*
> —Staff Sergeant, Platoon Sergeant, Mosul, Iraq

As verified by the examples above and as portrayed in Figure 5-1, subordinates view trust in leaders as a necessary condition for their willingness to accept leader influence and the risks of combat. Subordinates in Iraq willingly followed the directives of leaders they trusted and seemed willing to put forth extra effort and assume a greater degree of risk to accomplish the mission—in essence these leaders were high-impact leaders. On the other hand, subordinates who did not trust their leaders did not willingly follow them, questioned orders, and seemed to take measures against orders to minimize the risk to their personal safety. The results clearly confirm that in order to lead effectively, especially in extreme situations such as combat, leaders must earn their subordinates' trust.

What is evident from this discussion is that higher trust will give leaders greater "negotiating latitude" with their followers under stress. Under the time constraints and dynamic nature of combat, leaders must often be very task-oriented and transactional in their leadership. Particularly during enemy engagements, there is rarely time for full explanations or mutual participation in decision-making. Followers must "blindly" follow their leaders under such situations and, as we have noted, unquestioningly put themselves in harm's way as ordered. The latitude that allows leaders to be directive in combat and still gain commitment of their followers must be built over time and prior to "game day" through the exercise of consistent and trust-evoking moral leadership. This type of leadership is an accurate reflection of the character of the leader.

Taken together, the results from the two studies conducted in Iraq provide empirical reinforcement for the proposition that authentic moral leadership has a positive impact on the development of trust with followers, and that this trust provides leaders with a greater ability to influence. As the epigraph opening this chapter asserts, and as we enlarged upon in Chapter 4, to meet the challenges of leading in combat, our young future leaders must continuously focus on developing their character and competence.

Authentic Moral Leadership's Impact on Followers' Moral Development

Authentic moral leaders bolster their followers' moral development through modeling, persuasion, and establishing a moral and ethical culture in the organization. In Chapter 4 we discussed the processes of moral development and the major outcomes of that process, such as *moral complexity* (extent of development), *moral agency* (acceptance of moral responsibility), and *moral efficacy* (confidence). Here we shall discuss the critical role that these highly developed leaders have on the development of their own followers and organizations. In fact, it is these leaders who in their turn lead others along the moral development processes.

As shown in Figure 5-1, followers who trust their leaders are more apt to identify with these leaders and use them as role models by emulating their behaviors. These leaders of character, who live the Army values, may serve as exemplars of an ideal military leader whom group members want to emulate. The ideal military leader is defined by the set of attributes, values, characteristics, and behaviors that reflect what the members of the organization or profession commonly believe makes such a leader.[29] The prototype of an ideal combat leader that emerged from the Iraqi studies, outlined in Figure 5-2, clearly established that a leader's competence and character form the basis of trust. Further, the results from these studies indicated that soldiers will trust and willingly follow leaders who are competent and possess the character attributes of loyalty, honesty, integrity, courage, and a sense of duty. Thus, the ability to lead, especially in combat, arises from a leader's competence and character.

Followers who view themselves as leaders or have the desire to become leaders are more likely to incorporate the profession's prototype of an ideal leader into their self-schema or future self-schema (their envisioned "possible self") because it pictures what they aspire to become. Once followers internalize the prototype of an ideal leader into their self-schemas, they will start to define themselves as moral-ethical leaders. This view of the self as moral-ethical leader causes followers to view situations in a different perspective, increases the salience of moral and ethic considerations in their decision-making, improves their behavior, makes them more attentive to the moral-ethical behavior of others, and provides them purpose and focus in their developmental journey to become authentic moral leaders.[30] Therefore, authentic moral leaders as exemplars serve as both sources of developmental information and motivation for followers.

Followers will use leaders of character as exemplars and sources of information to learn moral-ethical behavior, learn attitudes pertaining to morals and ethics, gain ideas on how to develop needed attributes, and, most importantly, form comparative standards for their development. Through focused observation, subordinates will learn moral-ethical behavior, attitudes, and decision-making skills from trusted leaders. By observing leaders who are in fact moral exemplars, followers learn to identify cues that frame a moral-ethical situation, infer decision criteria for measuring and comparing courses of action, and gain an appreciation for the first- and second-order effects of the decision both inside and outside the organization. Observational learning also provides followers with insights to the specific techniques and strategies that authentic leaders use to develop and maintain the attributes necessary to lead in a moral and ethical manner. Thus, by serving as role models, authentic moral leaders exercise an impact on the development of their followers' moral complexity and efficacy.[31] As discussed in Chapter 4, moral complexity refers to the extent of development of the followers' moral schemas (cognitive frameworks by means of which they make moral decisions) while moral efficacy pertains to the followers' degree of confidence and courage to engage in moral-ethical behavior.

This is why the military faculty at West Point, especially the rotating faculty, plays such an essential and pivotal role in the moral development of USMA cadets. They serve as exemplars of warriors who are leaders of character that cadets should strive to be like at the end of their four-year developmental journey towards officership. The military faculty engage cadets in moral and ethical discussions both in and outside the classroom. Besides teaching, the vast majority of military faculty members serve as cadet mentors, cadet sponsors, and officer representatives for cadet sports teams and clubs, and they attend cadet activities, all of which roles provide numerous opportunities for cadets and the military faculty to interact. These out-of-class interactions allow cadets to observe military faculty members behaving morally and ethically in all types of settings, provide opportunities to discuss the profession, and most importantly provide opportunities for military faculty to help cadets work through and/or make sense of moral and ethical issues. This extensive cadet engagement, both inside and outside of the classroom, by the military faculty plays an essential role in the development of cadets' moral schemas and efficacy.

Subordinates use authentic moral leaders as benchmarks to chart their developmental progress towards realizing their self-concept and becoming leaders of character through the process of social comparison. By comparing themselves against authentic moral leaders who possess the desired skills and attributes of an ideal Army leader, followers gain developmental insights.[32] They can use these insights to make adjustments to their developmental plan by shifting priorities and directing efforts to developing attributes or skills that are not up to the exemplar's standard. Serving as the comparison standard for followers' self-concepts is a high-impact effect of authentic moral leadership. Followers using exemplar leaders of character as the standard by which to modify their own self-concepts is one of the noblest forms of influence leaders can exercise.

Therefore, authentic moral leaders, whom followers use as comparison standards for their self-concepts, contribute to the development of their subordinates' moral complexity, moral agency, and moral efficacy through the social comparison process. Recall from the preceding chapter that moral agency refers to owning or accepting responsibility for one's moral experiences and having the self-discipline and resolve to become a moral-ethical person. Observational learning and the social comparison process not only provide group members with developmental information, they also serve as sources of motivation. Followers can gain inspiration by observing exemplary leaders being rewarded in terms of praise and respect for behaving in a moral-ethical manner. Observing a role model's moral-ethical behavior being rewarded increases the likelihood that one will learn and enact a similar behavior in the future. Subordinates' motivation to enact learned moral-ethical behavior rests with the perception that this behavior is rewarded by the organization for the right reasons.[33]

Thus, leaders can foster moral and ethical behavior in their organizations by ensuring that it is recognized and rewarded. For those followers who have a lower level of moral development, they have to see that behaving morally and ethically leads to external rewards such as recognition, praise, or promotions, etc. before they will learn and enact this type of behavior. On the other hand, followers who possess a higher level of moral development can experience vicariously and thus profit from the intrinsic rewards in the offing for leaders behaving in a moral and ethical manner. This vicarious experience alone might be sufficient to reinforce future moral-ethical behavior in followers with a high level of moral development.[34]

The social comparison process can also serve as a source of self-motivation for followers. Group members' developmental motivation will most likely increase when they compare themselves against an authentic moral leader and perceive progress. This perceived developmental progress or movement towards becoming one's *possible-self* as an authentic moral leader bolsters followers' motivation because it demonstrates growth and affirms their ability to reach their goals.[35] This is especially true if followers perceive that exemplary leaders are similar to them, because that similarity makes the example set by the exemplar appear more obtainable—it validates their self-concept, indicates a smaller developmental gap, and boosts their confidence that they may become an exemplary moral leader themselves.

Persuasion and Moral Development

Leaders of character can use persuasion to enhance their followers' moral development. Research in the area of persuasive communication has confirmed that credible communicators are far more persuasive than those who lack credibility. A credible communicator is a person perceived as honest or trustworthy and possessing expertise in the subject matter. People will listen to and trust information from credible sources and thus be more likely to be persuaded.[36] Authentic moral leaders are credible communicators when it comes to moral development and can better influence the development of their followers' moral complexity, agency, and efficacy.

Leaders of character should take the time to talk followers through their decision processes as they resolve, or after they resolve, a moral-ethical dilemma. This exercise would help group members gain insights into the thought processes needed to identify and successfully resolve moral and ethical issues. This in-depth exposure to the authentic leaders' thought processes in resolving a moral-ethical issue reinforces and enriches the information followers gain from observational learning, in the process promoting the development of the complexity of subordinates' moral schemas. From leaders sharing their moral-ethical decision processes, subordinates may gain useful new perspectives, e.g., for viewing or framing moral-ethical dilemmas, structuring a decision-making process, learning important criteria for evaluating possible solutions, acquiring techniques for implementing a moral-ethical decision, and gaining a greater appreciation for the implications of moral and ethical decisions. All these new perspectives serve to increase the subordinates' moral complexity.[37] Moreover, by providing followers with the insights and tools to analyze and successfully resolve problems in a moral-ethical manner, leaders are bolstering their followers' moral efficacy.

Similarly, subordinates will seek out authentic moral leaders to help them resolve personal moral-ethical issues. Leaders should help these followers by guiding them through a moral and ethical decision-making process to successfully resolve the issue. The salience of the personal issue, along with the follower's trust of the leader, would advance development of the group members' moral schemas.[38] Once an issue is thus resolved in a moral-ethical manner, leaders should encourage the subordinates who dealt with the problems to share their thoughts and decision-making process with the team if the issue is appropriate for outside discussion. Group members are more likely to attend to and learn from information presented by a peer.[39] Group sharing and discussion about moral-ethical issues promotes the moral development of all team members. The insights followers gain from these open discussions reinforce development of their moral schemas, and in seeing peers successfully resolve moral-ethical issues through such discussions, followers experience a further boost of their own moral efficacy.

Establishing a Moral and Ethical Culture

Beyond individual identification with the leader as a role model, at the collective level authentic moral leadership has a tremendous impact on the establishment of the moral and ethical culture in the organization. An organization's culture consists of a shared collection of implicit values and assumptions regarding the appropriate way members should perceive, think, feel, and behave in dealing with each other and in external functioning to reach goals. Thus, the organization's culture has a significant influence on the values, attitudes, beliefs, and behavior of each of its members.[40] The circular that explains the Cadet Leader Development System stresses the importance of organizational culture to the development of members' character: "Character is shaped in communities where members practice virtuous living and pass those virtues on to others."[41]

In addition to observing the behaviors of its members, one can assess an organization's culture by looking at the artifacts or observable objects associated with the organization, for example, the USMA Honor Monument cadets walk by on a daily basis at West Point. Leaders, who live the Army values and demand that followers do the same, establish the moral and ethical aspects of the culture in their organizations and reinforce values through consistent behaviors. Eventually, all members will understand that the organization and its members expect them to behave in a moral and ethical manner and perceive that it is correct to do so in all situations. Reinforced over time, these moral and ethical values and expectations will become incorporated into the organization's culture, which is passed on to new members of the group through socialization processes.[42] Authentic moral leaders can significantly influence the moral development of their subordinates by properly shaping the organization's culture.

We have spoken of the effects of the individual on the culture, but now let us discuss how, reciprocally, through creating a moral culture, leaders can in turn further build the moral aspects of individual organizational members' self-schemas through social identity processes. Organizational members gain much of their identity from the groups they belong to through such identity processes.[43] When people are asked to define themselves, they will normally include the main groups they are members of, such as American, female, infantryman, or Californian, and often various subgroups of attributes associated with a group (e.g., warrior as a subset of infantryman). Soldiers in particular, due to long work hours, the strong military culture and cohesion, and a shared common danger, interact and thus bond with their units more so than with any other social groups, sometimes including even their families, and are thus more likely to extract identity from their units. Social identity theory states that we identify with groups both to assist in categorizing ourselves and to gain esteem and psychological well-being. When one joins a prestigious country club or enters into a member of a profession (such as the profession of officership), he or she is able to assume the positive identity of that group and incorporate that identity into his/her self-schema.

Leaders that create a moral culture in their organization increase the likelihood that aspects of moral identity will be internalized by their followers.[44] For example, West Point is known throughout the world as a bastion of honor and integrity, bolstered by the Honor Code and other ameliorative cultural artifacts. Cadets, regardless of their level of moral fortitude prior to arrival at the Academy, are able to incorporate honor and integrity into their self-schema and almost immediately transform the way they look at themselves as leaders of stronger character. Moral improvement through identity with West Point becomes so central to cadets that they will strive to maintain the organization's codes in order to maintain their own self-schemas. Any stain on the code will be seen as a stain on their own identities.

In combat it is imperative that Army leaders exemplify the professional ethos and execute operations in accordance with the Rules of Engagement, the Laws of Land Warfare, and the Geneva Convention. By setting high ethical and moral standards for the unit, leaders reaffirm the organization's cultural values and clearly delineate the moral and ethical boundaries for subordinates to operate within. These boundaries are important for keeping the distinction between socially sanctioned and morally justified application of lethal violence, on one hand, and unlawful murder on the other. Leaders who ensure that their units conduct combat operations in a lawful manner uphold the sacred trust the citizens of this country have in the military profession and affirm the country's values and moral justification for fighting, all of which serve to sustain soldiers' will to fight.[45] The moral application of force also limits our enemy's ability to assail the integrity of our nation, our military, and our motives for engaging in the war. We have all seen how the moral failures of leaders at Abu Ghraib Prison in Iraq empowered our enemies to deride the United States in order to justify their own acts of terrorism and other atrocities, and to gain support of noncombatants against the U.S. and allied forces. Ethical lapses also demoralize our own soldiers. Soldiers' resolve to fight will remain strong as long as they believe that the cause is just and that combat operations are being executed in the most ethical manner possible.

Two examples will demonstrate the importance of highly developed moral leaders and how these leaders' actions clearly establish and reinforce the importance of adhering to the moral and ethical boundaries governing combat operations. As witnessed by the first author during V Corps' march to Baghdad during Operation Iraqi Freedom in 2003, the commanding general received intelligence that large formations of vehicles were moving from northern Iraq towards Baghdad. The conclusion from the intelligence analysis indicated that the Iraqi army was repositioning forces to reinforce Baghdad's defenses. At this time, the areas around Baghdad were experiencing major sand storms and the staff believed that the Iraqis were using this period of limited visibility to reposition military forces. Military units are most vulnerable to attack when they are moving in large formations on roads. The commander asked whether any element could physically observe these formations, which was a prerequisite for attack according to the Rules of Engagement (ROE) under which the Corps was operating. The storm prevented any friendly elements from confirming that the vehicle formations moving towards Baghdad were military. The commander was facing a stark dilemma: Should he adhere to the ROE, or should he direct an attack on these fleeting, lucrative targets without physical confirmation?

Prior to the start of this operation, planners estimated that the fight for Baghdad would result in heavy casualties and would be long drawn-out. If the formations moving south were military, they would strengthen the defenses of Baghdad, which would more than likely result in greater U.S. casualties. The commander had only a small window of opportunity to attack the formations. The commander was thus faced with a tough decision of exceptional moral content. He decided to adhere to the ROE and not to attack the formation of moving vehicles. His decision clearly communicated to his staff and subordinate units that the moral and ethical guidelines governing the Corps' conduct in combat were applicable and that the members of his unit could not violate them. The Corps battle staff was initially frustrated by not being able to engage such lucrative targets, but realized the commander did the right thing. The commander's strong moral leadership solidified the moral and ethical culture in the unit, which enhanced the probability that future combat operations would be conducted in a similarly ethical manner.

Another instance was experienced by the second author during the first Gulf War in 1991, when immediately after the end of hostilities his infantry battalion was moved to a position on the military demarcation line (MDL)— the line separating U.S. and Iraqi forces. The rules of the surrender agreement disallowed any hostile action across the MDL unless U.S. forces were directly fired upon. The Iraqis used this limitation to blatantly murder Iraqi civilians, primarily Shiites, who they claimed were "sympathizers" of U.S. forces. These executions, often in the direct view of U.S. forces and at times involving the murder of women and children, were atrocious and demoralizing to American soldiers. The battalion commander in this case talked to his junior leaders candidly about the moral aspects of this issue (thereby promoting the moral development of his junior leaders in the process) and formulated what he determined was the best moral solution given the less-than-perfect choices. He determined that the greater good is served by adhering to the ROE, but made best use of the maximum boundaries of the ROE by firing non-lethal illumination mortar rounds and at times staging feint attacks on Iraqi forces whenever executions were being commenced. These actions greatly reduced the overt executions while also reducing the psychological strain on U.S. troops and their need to take some humanitarian action. By staying within the limits of the ROE under such atrocious conditions, the commander balanced and reinforced both the rules of conduct and also the personal impulses of soldiers to take actions to stop these atrocities.[46]

In contrast to these two positive examples, we shall glance at an incident highlighting the consequences of a commander's decision to break ethical guidelines in an effort to prevent an upcoming attack against his unit. This incident from Operation Iraqi Freedom illustrates the significant impact a commander's behavior has on a unit's moral-ethical culture. In August of 2003, a battalion commander received intelligence that he was being targeted for assassination and that the guerrillas were going to ambush elements of his unit in a very short time. The intelligence also indicated that a local policeman was involved with the guerrilla forces. The commander had the local policeman arrested and brought to his headquarters for questioning.[47]

After the interrogators failed to get useful information from the policeman, the commander conducted his own interrogation. He had his soldiers physically rough up the policeman in an effort to get the information about the attack. When this failed, the commander decided to use his weapon for intimidation. The commander fired his pistol into a clearing barrel and then had the policeman placed next to the barrel. The commander then fired his pistol close to the policeman's head, frightening him so badly that he divulged information about the upcoming guerrilla attack, including names of those involved. With this information, the unit was able to capture the guerrillas and prevent the intended ambush. The commander thereupon informed his superior of his actions and was relieved of command after a formal investigation.[48]

The episode described above brings into bold relief the dilemma of how far a commander should go to protect the welfare of his soldiers in combat. The battalion commander used the threat of deadly force to persuade the prisoner to quickly reveal the information about the upcoming attack.[49] His interrogation technique was successful, the information obtained helped save soldiers' lives, and the prisoner, though terrorized, was unharmed. The foregoing scenario illustrates the tough situation commanders face when they have to ask their soldiers to assume more risk than would otherwise be necessary in order to hew to the moral and ethical path. The scenario also highlights the ramifications of the commander's actions when he or she takes a wrongful path. Unless one is embedded in the situation, he or she cannot fully appreciate the overpowering strength of the bonds of brotherhood that drive commanders to protect their soldiers. In tough, morally and ethically ambiguous situations, commanders are expected to consider all implications—immediate as well as long-term, direct as well as indirect, tactical as well as strategic—of their decisions.

In this case, the commander decided to break the moral and ethical rules to reduce a potential threat to his unit. His desire to protect the welfare of his soldiers was honorable; however, the means used to do it was not. The commander admitted that what he did was wrong, but he did it anyway to protect his soldiers.[50] By breaking ethical rules to get the information about the upcoming ambush, the commander blurred the moral and ethical boundaries for all soldiers in the unit. In addition, his behavior called into question the moral and ethical values of the organization's culture. The commander's actions during the interrogation put his unit on a very "slippery slope" that could lead to moral and ethical lapses in future combat operations. For instance, the next time his soldiers stopped suspected guerrillas and wanted information quickly, they might follow the example of the commander and threaten the use of deadly force. Since the commander's behavior blurred the moral and ethical boundaries pertaining to conduct in combat, soldiers in this unit could very easily have stepped over the line and committed an atrocity in pursuit of a laudable goal. Therefore, to negate the impact of the commander's unethical behavior on the unit's culture, he was properly relieved of command.

All of the foregoing examples highlight the concept of moral complexity covered in the previous chapter. A leader in the often morally ambiguous context of combat must be able to conduct moral reasoning through a set of multidimensional lenses that assesses the rules, outcomes, and also the inherent virtues associated with a moral dilemma. In the first two cases, drawn from the Iraqi wars, the leaders used multiple lenses in their reasoning, while in the case of the intimidation example, the leader was limited in his perspective to reasoning based on immediate outcomes, that is, justifying the means by the ends, at the expense of the other two lenses, which would have focused on the propriety of the means themselves.

Conducting combat in a moral-ethical manner also serves to protect the psychological well-being of the soldiers because it upholds the moral justification for killing and also serves to prevent atrocities. Moral justification for killing is important because it helps soldiers to deal with the psychological stress associated with taking another human's life. The act of killing can change a soldier forever. The soldier must now deal with guilt and stress associated with violating what most religions hold as a sacred moral preachment: Thou shalt not kill. Having moral justification for killing in combat may help soldiers come to terms with violating such a sacred value, thus alleviating some of the guilt and stress.[51] Leaders who encourage or allow soldiers to kill outside of the moral-ethical boundaries that govern combat strip away any moral justification for killing. The psychological trauma and stress associated with killing outside of the moral and ethical guidelines of combat could haunt these soldiers for the rest of their lives.[52] Authentic moral leadership that sets clear and firm moral and ethical boundaries for followers to operate within helps ensure that they will do the right thing in all situations and thus be protected from debilitating and dysfunctional emotions.

Conclusion

The moral values and principles contained in the Cadet Prayer, Cadet Honor Code, and Army values, if internalized by leaders, will lay the foundation for the development of their character. Leaders who live by these values and principles will have the ability to exercise authentic moral leadership. Results from the studies investigating trust and leadership in combat clearly indicate that leaders must have good character to lead effectively. Followers will trust competent and morally strong leaders and allow them a greater degree of influence and latitude under stress. Soldiers will willingly follow trusted leaders of character into the frightening, dangerous, and chaotic environment of combat. For they know that trusted leaders of character will accomplish the mission in an ethical manner and with the least risk to their lives.

Moreover, leaders' moral and ethical values and behaviors have a significant influence on the moral development of their followers by setting the example and establishing a positive moral and ethical culture in their units. The leader's character, coupled with a strong moral and ethical organizational culture, helps establish clear and firm boundaries for the conduct of operations in the brutal and corrosive environment of combat. Leaders serve as moral and ethical guardians to ensure that their units uphold the values of the nation and the Army, thus validating the moral justification for fighting, preserving soldiers' will to fight, protecting followers' psychological well-being, and maintaining the honor of the profession. These actions in turn maintain the American people's trust and respect for their military professionals. Character is the foundation for leadership.[53] This is why character development is so important to military leadership, and why West Point takes it so seriously.

Notes

1. Headquarters, Department of the Army, Field Manual 22-100, *Army Leadership* (Washington, DC: US Government Printing Office, 1999), 1-2.
2. Ibid., 2-1-2-28.
3. Field Manual 22-100, 2-3.
4. USMA Circular 1-101, *Cadet Leader Development System* (West Point, NY: Defense Printing, 2002), 28-29.
5. Adrian Chan, Sean T. Hannah, and William L. Gardner, "Veritable Authentic Leadership: Emergence, Functioning, and Impacts," in *Authentic Leadership Theory and Practice: Origins, Effects, and Development,* ed. William B. Gardner, Bruce J. Avolio, and Fred O. Walumbwa, Monographs in Leadership and Management, vol. 3 (Oxford: Elsevier Ltd., 2005), 3-41.
6. Omar Bradley, "On leadership," in *The Challenge of Military Leadership,* ed. Lloyd J. Matthews and Dale Brown (New York, NY: Pergamon-Brassey's International Defense Publisher, 1989), 8.
7. Harold Kelley and John Thibaut, *Interpersonal Relations: A Theory of Interdependence* (New York: Wiley, 1978), 232-235.
8. Kelley and Thibaut.
9. John J. Gabarro, "The Development of Trust, Influence, and Expectations," in *Interpersonal Behavior: Communication and Understanding in Relationships,* ed. Anthony G. Athos and John J. Gabarro (Englewood Cliffs, NJ: Prentice-Hall, 1978), 290-303.
10. Kelley and Thibaut.
11. Kelley and Thibaut, 232.
12. FM 22-100, 2-24 to 2-26.
13. USMA Circular 1-101, 16-17.
14. Gabarro.
15. Bernard M. Bass, *Leadership and Performance Beyond Expectations* (New York: Free Press, 1985).
16. Kevin Lowe, K. Galen Kroeck, and Nagaraj Sivasubramaniam, "Effectiveness Correlates of Transformation and Transactional Leadership: A Meta-analytic Review of the MLQ Literature," *Leadership Quarterly* 7 (1996): 385-425.
17. Walter F. Ulmer, "Introduction," in *The Challenge of Military Leadership,* ed. Lloyd J. Matthews and Dale E. Brown (New York, NY: Pergamon-Brassey's International Defense Publisher, 1989), xi-xviii.
18. Robert G. Lord and Karen Maher, "Leadership Perceptions and Leadership Performance: Two Distinct but Interdependent Processes," in *Advances in Applied Social Psychology: Business Settings,* vol. 4, ed. J. Carrol (Hillsdale, NJ: Erlbaum, 1990), 129-154.
19. Olga Epitropaki and R. Martin, "Implicit Leadership Theories in Applied Settings: Factor Structure, Generalizeability, and Stability Over Time, *Journal of Applied Psychology* 89, 2 (2004): 293-310.

20. Bernard Bass, "Does the Transactional-Transformational Leadership Paradigm Transcend Organizational and National Boundaries?" *American Psychologist* 52, 2 (1997): 130-139.

21. Jay A. Conger and Rabindra Kanungo, "Toward a Behavioral Theory of Charismatic Leadership in Organizational Settings," *Academy of Management Review* 12 (1987): 637-647.

22. Hugh Thompson, "My Lai" (Talk given to United States Military Academy Cadets enrolled in General Psychology for Leaders Course, West Point, New York, in March 2002).

23. Ibid.

24. United States Military Academy, *The Cadet Prayer*. West Point, NY.

25. Edwin P. Hollander and Lynn R. Offermann, "Power and Leadership in Organizations: Relationships in Transition," *American Psychologist* 45, 2 (1990): 179-189.

26. Gary Yukl, *Leadership in Organizations*, 4th ed. (Upper Saddle River, NJ: Prentice Hall, 1998), 178.

27. Fragging is the term used when a leader is killed by his or her own soldiers.

28. Patrick J. Sweeney, *"Trust in Combat"* (A paper presented at the Academy of Management Annual Conference in New Orleans, August 10-12, 2003).

29. Nancy Cantor, "A Cognitive-social Approach to Personality," in *Personality, Cognition, and Social Interaction,* ed. Nancy Cantor and John F. Kihlstrom (Hillsdale, NJ: Erlbaum, 1981).

30. Shelly E. Taylor, Letitia A. Peplau, and David O. Sears, *Social Psychology,* 11th ed. (Upper Saddle River, NJ: Prentice-Hall), 99-124.

31. Sean T. Hannah, Paul B. Lester, and Gretchen R. Vogelgesang, "Moral Leadership: Explicating the Moral Component of Authentic leadership," in *Authentic Leadership Theory and Practice: Origins, Effects, and Development,* ed. William B. Gardner, Bruce J. Avolio, and Fred O. Walumbwa, Monographs in Leadership and Management, vol. 3 (Oxford: Elsevier Ltd., 2005), 43-81.

32. George R. Goethals and John M. Darley, "Social Comparison Theory: Self-evaluation and Group Life," in *Theories of Group Behavior,* ed. B. Mullen and G. R. Goethals (New York: Springer-Verlag, 1987), 21-48.

33. Albert Bandura, *Social Learning Theory* (Englewood Cliffs, NJ: Prentice-Hall, 1977).

34. Ibid.

35. Goethals and Darley.

36. R. Glen Hass, "Effects of Source Characteristics on Cognitive Responses and Persuasion," in *Cognitive Response in Persuasion,* ed. Richard E. Petty, Thomas M. Ostrom, and Timothy C. Brock (Hillsdale, NJ: Lawrence Erlbaum Associates, 1981), 141-172.

37. Hannah, Lester, and Vogelgesang.

38. Ibid.

39. Hass.

40. Edgar H. Schein, *Organizational Culture and Leadership* (San Francisco: Josey-Bass, 1992).

41. USMA Circular 1-101-1, *Cadet Leader Development System for Cadets* (West Point, NY: Defense Printing, 2005), 19.

42. Ibid.

43. Michael A. Hogg, "A Social Identity Theory of Leadership," *Personality and Social Psychology Review* 5 (2001): 184-200.
44. Hannah, Lester, and Vogelgesang.
45. John Mattox, "The Ties That Bind: The Army Officer's Moral Obligations," in *The Future of the Army Profession,* project directors Don M. Snider and Gayle L. Watkins, ed. Lloyd J. Matthews (New York: McGraw-Hill, 2002), 293-312.
46. Note in Chapter 1 of the present book, in the experiences of General Donald Bennett, that such occurrences, sadly, have been observed by other Americans in combat.
47. Rowan Scarborough, "Army Files Charge in Combat Tactic," *Washington Times,* October 29, 2003, p. 1.
48. Ibid.
49. Ibid.
50. Scarborough.
51. David Grossman, *On Killing: The Psychological Cost of Learning to Kill in War and Society* (Boston, MA: Little, Brown, and Company, 1995), 262-264.
52. Grossman, 87-93.
53. Matthew Ridgway, "Leadership," in *Military leadership,* ed. Robert L. Taylor and William E. Rosenbach (Boulder, CO: Westview Press, 1992), 43-52.

6 | Moral Principles and Moral Reasoning in the Ethics of the Military Profession

Anthony E. Hartle

Why We Teach Ethics

Although a country's armed forces serve many purposes, to include disaster relief, maintaining domestic law and order, and deterrence in national security strategy, the first priority has always been combat. The Military Academy designed the Cadet Leader Development System (CLDS) to develop officers; in that endeavor CLDS clearly recognizes that "officers develop and maintain the expertise to apply lethal violence to fight and win our Nation's wars."[1] That ultimate mission for the Army fundamentally focuses on warfare, which shapes the nature of military activity. Combat challenges every participant—physically, mentally, psychologically, and morally. In our discussion here, the moral challenges are of particular concern. Maintaining a moral compass in the conduct of warfare demands the very best of military leaders and their soldiers.

In this chapter we will examine the moral guidelines for members of the United States armed forces, with emphasis on the professional ethic that guides the United States Army. That military ethic provides structure and content for the education, training, and inspiration of future Army leaders at West Point. To become mature officers, cadets must first examine their own personal beliefs and then they must recognize the Army's expectations of professional leaders. Doing so is part of a process of education and development in which cadets reconcile the institution's requirements and the demands imposed by their personal values. Chapter 4 examined the process of individual moral development at the Military Academy. This chapter focuses on the history and content of the set of standards to which the Academy and the Army expect the commitment of every officer upon commissioning.

Without exception, war erodes humanity. The professional ethic, which emphasizes competence and discipline, provides a defense against brutalization, though professional conduct has other, more obvious purposes. In this discussion, we will consider how the features of the moral compass for military professionals have come into being and what guidance that compass provides today. Because the decisions of those in uniform so often have life and death consequences, the military services emphasize the criteria for making those difficult decisions, the training of individual leaders, and the professional values that should frame their decision-making. These emphases provide insights concerning the moral foundation for the conduct of members of the military profession in the United States. Accordingly, at West Point, they help to identify objectives for the development of future officers.

General Sir John Hackett once claimed that good soldiers must first of all be good people.[2] His argument for that claim is compelling and one that the Military Academy fully accepts. The further question for a developmental institution like West Point focuses on what it means to be a good person. Over the last 20 years I have had the opportunity to work with the staff and faculty at the Military Academy in pursuing that question as well as the issue of what the Academy should teach cadets to help them become good men and women as well as good soldiers.

When I was a cadet learning about the values of the Academy and of the profession I aspired to enter, all cadets attended chapel on Sundays. Each cadet could choose which religious service to attend, but all participated.[3] One common element of our lives on Sunday was the Cadet Prayer. I remember reflecting at the time that the virtues identified in the Prayer had a fundamental appeal that easily crossed faith and denominational boundaries—the Prayer expressed what it means to be a good person from a religious perspective, indeed, but it also presented a prescription that held in almost any context. That congruence with our society's views explains to a degree why the Cadet Prayer is consistent with the ethic of the military profession as well. In this discussion, I will argue that the Prayer's description of what it means to be a good person applies directly to General Hackett's statement that good soldiers are first of all good persons.

The Cadet Prayer rendered in Chapter 1 presents the following exhortations, among others:

Admire honest dealing and clean thinking.

Do not tolerate hypocrisy or pretense.

Live above the common level of life.

Choose the harder right instead of the easier wrong.

Do not be content with a half truth.

Be loyal to all that is noble and worthy.

Scorn to compromise with vice and injustice.

Reject fear when truth and right are in jeopardy.

Keep honor untarnished and unsullied.

Manifest the ideals of West Point.

These expectations provide useful insight concerning the character of a good person in terms of development at West Point. As I examine the ethics of the military profession in what follows, you will see that the strictures of the Cadet Prayer, the traditions of the military, and the requirements of the military ethic have much in common.

With those thoughts in mind, I will examine the emergence of military service as a profession in order to emphasize the broad moral principles that structure the military ethic and the moral reasoning that characterizes sound decision-making by military leaders. The Academy has long followed this approach and keeps it constantly in mind. History plays a major role in cadet education. I will also trace the work of the Academy staff and faculty in recent years as they studied the content and application of the professional military ethic that guides the actions of leaders in our military services. I will present the conclusions that now structure the development of future officers at West Point. The conclusions have direct implications for both character development (what kind of persons leaders should be) and behavior (how leaders should act).

What We Teach

Foundations of the Military Profession

Much of what we teach at West Point comes from history and tradition. To understand the substance and depth of the military ethic, one needs to know how it evolved. A part of that understanding comes from knowing how military service developed as a profession.[4] When we look at the historical record, we find that professional military forces emerged during the last two centuries, although a long history of warriors and armies leads up to their emergence.[5] Military institutions have evolved into complex organizations that serve the purposes of their political masters, and military culture has become bound by both custom and law. In that culture, professional and moral guidelines limit permissible action by those who exercise military force in the name of the state. In educating cadets at West Point, the faculty has carefully studied the history of the profession and the standards for professional conduct of members of the military that have evolved over time. Understanding that history, which I will sketch very briefly in what follows, makes clear that the standards are firmly grounded in both tradition and principle.

Warriors and Soldiers

Historical records show that armed warriors have played a central role in the life of almost all societies, and evidence indicates that was true long before written records appeared. Besides to hunt more effectively, human beings have taken up arms to defend themselves, their families, and their communities from a variety of external threats that often included other people.

Over 4,000 years ago, however, events triggered a momentous change that altered the nature of conflict prevailing in primitive societies. More structured governing organizations, agricultural development that stabilized populations and made land highly prized, and other factors in combination led to the widespread establishment of armies. Expanding societies turned from ritualized combat between warriors to the pursuit of conquest by large, organized military forces. In disciplined, trained military formations, the warriors became soldiers, and over the centuries between 9,000 B.C. and 3,000 B.C., civilization and politics introduced systematic warfare.

The State

The emergence of the state brought the genesis of armies, which only the state could support. At the same time, the army was essential to the existence of the state. The Roman legions provide a striking example. Historians consider Rome the "mother house of modern armies."[6] Beginning in the fifth century B.C., the Roman Empire began to expand, subsequently using the fierce discipline and merciless efficiency of the legions in an ever-widening circle of conquest. In the view of John Keegan, "The Roman centurions, long-service unit-leaders drawn from the best of the enlisted ranks, formed the first body of professional fighting officers known to history."[7] At its height during the second century A.D., the Empire, through the legions, controlled provinces stretching from Gibraltar to Hadrian's Wall on the Scottish border, encompassing most of modern Europe and the Middle East, and then extending across all of northern Africa to Morocco. The purposes to which Rome put her professional soldiers may well be questioned, but few question the dedication and sacrifices of the legions.

The "centurionate," the professional core of the legions, provided the great strength of an army that dominated the known world for century after century. The higher-ranking leadership came from the upper levels of Roman society and came in good supply since service as a tribune (a military commander associated with the lower classes) was a prerequisite for political service leading to the ruling consulate and imperial power.[8] Contemporary military forces whose members take pride in their traditions and successes pale in achievement when we consider the record of the legions of Rome over nearly six centuries.

The role the military played in the evolution of Roman society also proved notable. John Keegan emphasizes its centrality: "Rome, unlike classical Greece, was a civilization of law and physical achievement, not of speculative ideas and artistic creativity. The imposition of its laws and the relentless extension of its extraordinary physical infrastructure demanded not so much intellectual effort as unstinted energy and moral discipline. It was of these qualities that the army was the ultimate source. . . ."[9]

While no one makes so strong a claim for the military services in America today, the military remains a repository of some of the primary values that have formed our society and its institutions. John Keegan says of the legionnaire that "[h]is values were those by which his fellows in the modern age continue to live: pride in a distinctive (and distinctively masculine) way of life, concern to enjoy the good opinion of comrades, satisfaction in the largely symbolic tokens of professional success, hope of promotion, expectation of a comfortable and honourable retirement."[10] And throughout, of course, the life of the legionnaire demanded iron discipline and extraordinary loyalty.

From Roman Legionnaires to Modern Military Professionals

Feudalism

Five centuries after the barbarians sacked Rome, men still fought in the same manner, though not nearly as efficiently as had the legions. The swarming horse cavalry of the steppes and the Arab world were ferociously successful, but their contributions to military development were tactical rather than formative. With the fall of Rome, the disciplined Roman armies disappeared. Standing military organizations serving the state did not reappear for almost a thousand years. Throughout the medieval centuries, the feudal system, in which the mounted man-at-arms was the central figure, dominated Europe. During this period, and especially after the 11th century, chivalry became a dominating feature of Western military culture. While overlaying the brutality of the Crusades with the ideals of chivalry appears suspect at first glance, the influence of the Church and the founding of knightly orders led to refinements in the outlook and conduct of fighting men that remain with us to this day. Enemies in battle (other than heretics, unbelievers, and peasants who failed to adhere to their appropriate class roles, of course) were to be accorded respect and treated in accordance with an elaborate code of honor. Such attitudes provide the moral foundation for the modern international laws of war. To the indispensable virtue of loyalty and the courtesies owed to fellow members of the knightly class, the religious knightly orders such as the Templars and the Hospitallers added the characteristics of discipline in personal affairs as well as in battle and service to a higher cause. Loyalty and service to a higher cause became lasting features of the military culture of the West, though the example of the mercenary soldier obscured that picture for some time.

Regulars: Professional Beginnings

The Roman tradition had relied upon the idea of a citizen army, an arm of the state, and that concept gradually reentered Western institutions, coming to full flower under Gustavus Adolphus of Sweden in the 17th century in the midst of European powers that still relied upon mercenary forces (mercenaries dominated conflict for more than a century). Gustavus Adolphus "successfully developed and applied [the Roman model] on the battlefield, and the system he evolved persisted in its essentials well into the twentieth century."[11] That system involved conscripted soldiers, generally linear formations, smaller units (though larger armies), and more junior leaders who had to exercise some initiative.[12] The Swedish commanders endlessly drilled infantry units in precise formations, prepared them for specific tactical maneuvers, and used cavalry elements for shock action. Sweden's great success was a factor leading to the development of standing armies.

In the Europe of the 17th and 18th centuries, in the midst of the Enlightenment and the flourishing of science and human progress, each state believed that it could ensure its survival only by developing military forces and alliances sufficient to defend against other states pursuing their own interests at the expense of their neighbors. We can find features of the professional military, as we understand that term today, in the European armies of the mid-1700s, even though the professional officer corps came into its own only after the Napoleonic wars. The officer ranks had begun to develop the characteristics described by Samuel Huntington in his penetrating study of military sociology: corporate unity, career structure, and specialized training.[13] Army and navy officers were about to become not just masters of their trade, as many undoubtedly had been over the centuries, but members of a profession, a distinction that requires some explanation and one that illuminates the status of the military ethic.

Many developments revealed the need for professional skills in managing armed forces, but the enormous increase in logistical requirements in the 19th century provides an obvious one. Large, technologically advanced armies called for professional military logisticians. Amateur soldiers could not meet the demands of the campaigns that followed the Napoleonic era, as the following historical note illustrates:

> Napoleon's artillery at Waterloo [1815] . . . numbered 246 guns which fired about a hundred rounds each during the battle; in 1870 at Sedan, one of the most noted battles of the nineteenth century, the Prussian Army fired 33,134 rounds; in the week before the opening of the battle of the Somme [in World War I], British artillery fired 1,000,000 rounds, a total weight of some 20,000 tons of metal and explosive.[14]

As a result of these and other requirements of combat operations, the military evolved into a profession, if by profession we mean an occupation with "a distinguishable corpus of specific technical knowledge and doctrine, a more or less exclusive group coherence, a complex of institutions peculiar to itself, an educational pattern adapted to its own needs and a distinct place in the society which has brought it forth."[15] In order to develop a well-rounded picture of the profession of arms today, we will consider below other aspects of military professionalism, adding characteristics such as self-regulation and commitment to society, but the definition above certainly conveys some of the most essential aspects of the professional military establishment. We will also see that the historical features of military service in the West are still reflected in the guidance for members of the military today.

To become professional, the officer corps of military organizations had to make competence a foundation. Leaders had to be selected on the basis of competence and ability rather than political influence or class prerogatives if military organizations were to assume the characteristics noted above. The Prussians led the way toward professional forces by lowering class barriers for officer appointments, establishing entry standards that officer candidates had to meet, and beginning an educational system for career officers that came to fruition in 1810 with General Gerhard von Scharnhorst's establishment of the famous *Kriegsakademie* in Berlin. Comprehensive examinations for officers seeking promotion ensured a new level of competence.[16] Other European countries emulated Prussia's success in the decades that followed.

The United States began with an abiding distrust of standing armies and "the man on horseback" that delayed the development of its military as a profession. That distrust was probably the legacy of our experience with the British and the background of European history, with its Caesars, Cromwells, and Napoleons. Thus, not too surprisingly, military professionalism developed later in America than in Europe. Instantly following the resolution of foreign crises requiring the raising and commitment of armed forces, the nation's military invariably declined in strength and readiness, with a corresponding decrease in the prestige and attention accorded the officer corps.

Despite the Revolutionary War against the British, the American military largely adopted the traditions of the British officer corps: an officer is a gentleman, a man of courage and unquestioned integrity. Those who led our forces, after all, had grown up as British citizens. Morris Janowitz claims that the American military inherited four central elements from the British military tradition: gentlemanly conduct, personal fealty, self-evaluating brotherhood, and the pursuit of glory.[17] If by glory we understand not self-aggrandizement but esteem for patriotism, for leadership in combat, and for public service, and if we recognize that 200 years have removed the aristocratic tenor of honor from American officership, Janowitz's observation appears accurate. For the century that followed the establishment of the United States, however, the characteristics of a profession emerged only slowly. During much of the 19th century, America's best educated military officers were graduates of West Point but were better known as engineers than as battlefield leaders. Although the Civil War, 1861–1865, changed that, after the war the Army became little more than a constabulary force in the west, fighting and policing the Native American tribes. Not until the turn of the century did the military profession as we know it today in the United States assume maturity. During that period the Army and Navy established permanent schools for advanced military education and began to develop systematic processes for educating and training career professionals.[18]

Relationship to the Parent Society

Characteristics of the Profession Today

One indelible characteristic of the American military that emerged from its first century of development remains foundational: *the military is entirely subordinate to and responsive to the civilian leadership of the nation*. That feature receives little attention when we consider our own military forces because it is so deeply ingrained in our society's consciousness. In Latin America, however, and in the Middle East, Asia, and elsewhere, such subordination is decidedly not the rule, and to note that military cultures differ markedly from one society to another raises few questions because the statement is so obviously true. In a number of countries we can mention, the military is the government. Until recently, the military dominated life in Haiti, Brazil, and Argentina, as it still does in Thailand, Pakistan, and a number of African countries. If we are to understand the military profession, we need to understand why military establishments differ in these obvious ways—and why they nonetheless share so many features. When we recognize the major formative influences on military organizations, we can more readily focus on moral principles and moral reasoning.

Factors Shaping the Military Ethic

The nature and structure of any military organization result in large part from the basic exigencies of warfare. If the military organization is to be effective, both leaders and subordinates must possess competence in the use of weapons, the application of effective tactics, and the provision of support necessary to sustain combat. Such skills represent one of the essential characteristics of any profession: a set of abilities acquired as a result of prolonged training and education that enable the professional to render a specialized service considered essential to society.[19] The weapons, the tactics, and the organizational structures of military establishments may differ radically as a result of different circumstances, but certain commonalities will always exist. Such commonalities are those aspects of the institution unique to the military function. They shape the nature of any professional military group and, in particular, they shape the culture and ethos that together provide direction, purpose, and guidance for the conduct of military affairs.

In what follows, we will examine the factors producing the military ethic that in turn forms the core of the professional culture. These factors will provide further insight concerning the historical development we have considered. Figure 6-1 shows the three primary factors that shape the military ethic of every country's armed forces today.[20]

Figure 6-1. *Factors Shaping the Military Ethic.*

Warfighting Imperatives

The imperatives of effective combat operations constitute the most obvious shaping influence. Though functional necessities vary greatly in detail over time and in differing circumstances, the general nature of such requirements remains constant. In broad terms, we recognize that any consistently successful military organization must have members who possess physical courage; soldiers who flee the battlefield will not win. Soldiers and sailors must be courageous and physically strong if they are to prevail. Military organizations must also be sufficiently disciplined, with a recognized hierarchy of authority, to ensure that orders are carried out consistently and reliably. Individual soldiers must possess the skills necessary to employ weapons and equipment in the accomplishment of tactical missions, and commanders must possess both character and the tactical skills required to pursue military objectives successfully without excessive losses. These broadly described functional requirements involved in the systematic application of force will be essentially constant from one society to another. Professor Samuel Huntington observed of the military profession—with emphasis on profession—that it

> exists to serve the state. To render the highest possible service the entire profession and the military force which it leads must be constituted as an effective instrument of state policy. Since political direction only comes from the top, this means that the profession has to be organized into a hierarchy of obedience. For the profession to perform its function, each level within it must be able to command the instantaneous and loyal obedience of subordinate levels. Without those relationships, military professionalism is impossible. Consequently, loyalty and obedience are the highest military virtues.[21]

Without disciplined organization, military units cannot maintain obedience. Huntington and others have shown us that the requirements of the military profession demand loyalty, obedience, and discipline no matter what particular nation or society may be involved. As we have noted, the values of technical competence and physical courage also arise directly from the nature of military activity. In some form, over time, such functional requirements will become institutionalized as standards of conduct for members of the armed forces. In the U.S. Army, physical fitness provides a clear example of a functional imperative. Individual soldiers and the institution both recognize that successful armies must be composed of those who are physically fit. Within our military culture, physical fitness has become admirable and expected as well as necessary for Americans in uniform. Functional requirements thus emerge as one of the major factors shaping the ethic of any military organization.

The Laws of War

A second factor that shapes a military ethic, the international laws of war, has become progressively more prominent in the last 60 years. With essentially all countries now being signatories to the most important international treaties and conventions governing the conduct of war, all military organizations are affected by the existing laws, and particularly those with a Western heritage. The degree to which a specific military ethic has incorporated the principles manifested in the laws of war may vary considerably, but those existing laws exert a persistent influence that cannot be ignored. Moral principles ground the international laws of warfare as they now exist; to the extent that a military ethic recognizes and incorporates the provisions of the laws of war, it incorporates two underlying humanitarian principles:

1. Individual persons deserve respect as such.
2. Human suffering ought to be minimized.[22]

Both of these principles have become fundamental to the ethics of the military profession in the United States, in part because they also manifest basic values in American society.

Values of Society

The third and most complex factor that influences the ethic of the military profession, one that further circumscribes and limits the other two, emerges from the dominant values of the society that creates and sustains the military institution. In all societies, the purposes, concerns, and interests of the people involved in an institution give it life and mold its character. And because its members are drawn from the society served, their own society, those members reflect the society's basic cultural values and infuse these into the organization's culture Military institutions reflect this same pattern of cultural influence—from society to its individual citizens and on to the military institution. But, because societies differ in these cultural values, the military cultures that develop within them will differ as well, despite the common professional exigencies. We can thus understand why subordination to civilian authority, such a dominant feature of the American military, does not characterize the military forces of some other nations. General Eric Shinseki, former Chief of Staff of the Army, observes that the values of the U.S. Army are not just war-related. He notes that "[t]they are deeper, more universal values. And most importantly, they accord with values we are taught in our families, our schools, our churches, synagogues, and mosques. Only in this way can they be deeply felt, made congruent...."[23] General Shinseki's observation thus reinforces the explanation of the military ethic that we are exploring.

From the values of American society arise enduring principles that characterize the nation's armed forces as well. Americans have long held that human beings have an inherent right to freedom. That principle and others are specified in the foundational document of American society, the Constitution. The fundamental values manifested in the Constitution directly affect the ethic of the military profession through the oath that officers take upon commissioning. That oath makes the commitment of officers clear:

> I do solemnly swear (or affirm) that I will support and defend the Constitution of the United States against all enemies, foreign and domestic; that I will bear true faith and allegiance to the same, and that I take this obligation fully, without any mental reservation or purpose of evasion; and that I will well and faithfully discharge the duties of the office on which I am about to enter. So help me God.

The officer's primary loyalty is to the Constitution, not to an organization or to an individual. We thus turn to the Constitution to identify the most important values that our society imposes on the members of the military services. Preeminent among those values are the following:

1. The principle of individual rights, which states that individuals have certain rights that are not to be denied by the government itself nor by the desires of the majority.
2. The rule of law, which establishes that no person is above the law of the land and that the law applies equally to all. Law secures individual rights.
3. The principle of constitutional authority, which establishes the Constitution as the abiding and foundational structure for the content of law in the United States.

The third principle makes clear why the officer's oath focuses on the Constitution. The other two help explain why the status of the individual takes a central place in the ethic of the military profession and why adherence to law governs military behavior. Within the context of a hierarchical military organization, the principle of individual rights holds that individual soldiers have value because they are human beings and deserve to be treated with respect within the context of military organization and discipline. A further principle enshrined in American institutions because of our constitutional foundation is the moral and legal equality of all American citizens. All members of our society have equal status in these realms until their own transgressions lead to abridgment. That principle also finds expression in the requirement of leaders to protect the welfare of subordinates within the military institution.

As is the case with respect to several moral principles that structure the activity of the American military, the soldier's commitment to defend her society's values as well as its people and institutions generates a multi-level moral obligation. Not only must the nation be protected, but it must be protected in a manner consistent with the society's fundamental values. Failure to adhere to the values is a failure to fulfill the oath. The obligation to protect a set of values creates the potential for difficult choices. A military leader has an obligation to treat members of her command as autonomous individuals deserving respect in their own right, but she also has an obligation to perform with maximum competence in her role as a military professional. The two requirements may lead to situations in which a leader must decide to choose an action that protects her subordinates or to choose a different action that satisfies tactical requirements. She also has an obligation to adhere to the professional standards of her organization. Cases will arise in which she must give a particular professional requirement priority over another. Given such multiple levels of moral obligation, leaders must exercise moral reasoning. Later, I will discuss the nature of that reasoning in more detail.

Specialized Education and Training

Despite a few skeptical views of the military's professional status, which include concerns about "a trade devoted to slaughter" and the view that a career soldier is a "paid jack-of-all-trades,"[24] the profession of arms exemplifies the general pattern of specialized education and training that leads to a profession-peculiar body of expert knowledge and associated expertise. Following a diversified basic education, career members of the American military undergo a systematic program of education that extends over a period of 20 years. The officer corps of the services, from which the senior military leadership is ultimately drawn, provides the most obvious example of this aspect of the American military profession.

Junior officers in the Army, following a pattern found in all the services, undergo initial training that includes preparation for service in their branch (infantry, field artillery, signal corps, etc.). They learn fundamental skills, leadership techniques, and small-unit tactics, among many other subjects. During a full career, each officer attends further courses of instruction in preparation for higher command and increased responsibilities. In addition, the majority of the officers in our armed forces earn graduate degrees during the last half of their careers.

Thus a senior professional military officer is one in whom the nation has made a major investment. He or she has an expert knowledge of a complex intellectual discipline that results only from extensive training and education, wide experience, and long application. The commander of an aircraft carrier group or a similar naval command must understand the relationships between tactical alternatives and organizational capabilities, the technological abilities and limitations established by highly complex equipment, and the variety of interpersonal and leadership skills necessary to motivate and lead others. The mastery of complex staff procedures and the competent command of large military formations require capabilities normally achieved only after progression through years of professional preparation and experience.

During the Cold War, Professor Roger Nye of West Point's Department of History observed: "The clear consensus of the American people, whose elected representatives have created and maintained the authorization for" military forces, is that a professional officer corps remains indispensable.[25] That observation remains true today. Recent operations in Afghanistan and Iraq have made the competence of our military leadership a subject of intense public interest. Occasional failures in the conduct and character of military leaders cause great concern, if not alarm, and public demands for corrective measures invariably follow.[26] Two considerations obviously at work are the military's role as the ultimate defenders of freedom and rights and the military's responsibility for the lives and welfare of the sons and daughters of America who serve in military organizations. Those considerations alone establish competence in military duties as a moral imperative for leaders at all levels.[27] Incompetence can result in disaster for serving members of the military and danger to national security. In view of such possibilities, the military's continuous concern about individual skills and performance and the profession's competence in general follow logically. The military services' extensive systems of schooling and focus on professional development reflect such concern.

Corporateness and Autonomy

As Professor Huntington observed decades ago, fulfillment of the functional imperatives over time give rise to complex vocational institutions that mold officer corps into autonomous social units possessing a collective awareness of their corporateness. Entrance into such a unit is restricted to those with the requisite education and training, and new members usually begin at the lowest ranks. The corporate structure of the officer corps includes not just the official bureaucracy but also societies, associations, schools, journals, customs, and traditions.[28]

Corporateness thus involves characteristics that make a group providing a specialized service to society a distinctive and relatively autonomous entity.

By "autonomous" I mean that the group establishes its own criteria for certification of candidates for membership and for the development and application of its expert knowledge, evaluates and judges the conduct and competence of its members, and imposes its own sanctions for failures to meet the professional standards set by the group. Members of the group are the only ones ultimately competent to judge the professional abilities of individual officers. Officers can be judged in terms of the results they achieve, just as medical doctors can be judged by the success of their treatment of patients, but as with the case of doctors this is best done only by other doctors who can accurately judge the technical performance of a member of the medical profession. Thus, the officer corps is a largely self-regulating body that determines the standards of competence and conduct for its members. Such internal standards reflect the institution's relative autonomy and constitute an important aspect of its corporateness.

Another facet of corporateness emerges from the individual's sense of identity with the institution and its values, which we will discuss in more detail shortly, and from the feeling of obligation to further the institution's purposes. Individual members thus share responsibility for maintaining the standards of the corporate group with respect to the performance of other members, and a variety of institutional procedures and mechanisms help safeguard and perpetuate the standards.

In addition to structural indications of corporateness, the military exhibits a strong sense of group identity that is strengthened by and in turn supports the value of loyalty in the professional ethic. This feature reflects the historical significance of loyalty discussed earlier. One sociologist describes the contemporary sense of loyalty for the American military in these terms:

> Loyalty is the quintessential military virtue: loyalty to the country, the Constitution, and the president as commander-in-chief . . . to the [military] itself and its standards and traditions; to the unit in which a soldier serves, and to peers, superiors, and subordinates. In theory the most important of these loyalties is to the United States Constitution; in practice the most important—to a soldier's morale and to his or her willingness to obey orders and assume responsibility—is to comrades.[29]

Loyalty strengthens the sense of identity with the professional calling and the willingness to subordinate one's own interests to the interests of the institution and the client the institution serves. Both developments enhance the corporate nature of the activity.

Moral Principles

The preceding discussion of loyalty leads directly to the American military ethic, the core of professionalism for members of the Army, Air Force, Navy, Marine Corps, and Coast Guard. When Academy officials studied the content of the ethic at West Point,[30] we recognized that the American military and the individual services had no formally published code of ethics as such (all we have formally common to all is the *Uniform Code of Military Justice* that establishes military law, which admittedly governs behavior but in an exclusively proscriptive legal fashion). Nonetheless, the military services do have standards of conduct passed on through the education systems previously described and the process of professional socialization. In the view of one outside observer, it appears that "loyalty to this code and to the people with whom it is shared is the essential military quality."[31]

In considering loyalty to one's superiors, many have turned to the classic statement in Shakespeare's *Henry V*. On the eve of the historic battle of Agincourt, where the English under King Henry won an improbable victory, the disguised monarch walks among his soldiers to assess their temper. Henry hopes to prompt a supportive response by declaring, "Methinks I could not die anywhere so contented as in the king's company, his cause being just and his quarrel honorable." When one soldier rejects that view by replying, "That's more than we know," another describes the view long held to both justify and excuse the actions of soldiers necessary in war: "Ay, or more than we should seek after, for we know enough if we know we are the king's subjects. If his cause be wrong, our obedience to the king wipes the crime of it out of us."[32] Because the information available to common soldiers had always been so limited, the principle of superior orders held that so long as one was obeying the orders of one's superiors in the military chain of command, one could not be held accountable for those actions.

More recent history in the form of the Nuremberg Trials after World War II, however, has modified this tenet in important ways. In fact, published guidance in military manuals today repeats in emphatic terms the requirement for members of the military to refuse to obey illegal orders. The U.S. Army's *The Law of Land Warfare* presents an uncompromising position on this point, one that we felt must be emphasized in cadet education: "The fact that the law of war has been violated pursuant to an order of a superior authority, whether military or civil, does not deprive the act in question of its character as a war crime, nor does it constitute a defense in the trial of an accused . . . ."[33] As I noted previously, the international laws of war have strongly influenced the guidance for conduct of members of the military-ethical guidance as well as legal.

As we studied the military ethic, we clarified the elements that guide the conduct of all members of the American military by reconsidering in more detail the three formative influences we discussed earlier (again, see Figure 6-1). The first and most ubiquitous of these is that set of functional requirements arising directly from the nature of warfare. Courage, competence, and discipline (obedience) were the foremost elements of the ethic we identified in this category. Secondly, because they are sworn to uphold and defend the Constitution, soldiers are constrained by Article 6, Clause 2, of that document, which states that international treaties signed by the United States become the law of the land. As *The Commander's Handbook on the Law of Naval Operations* states, "Pursuant to the Constitution of the United States, treaties to which the United States is a party constitute a part of the supreme law of the land with a force equal to that of laws enacted by Congress."[34] Among such treaties are the Hague Conventions and the Geneva Conventions. Despite ambiguities that arose from the American response to the terrorist attacks of September 11, 2001, and from the subsequent American experience in Afghanistan and Iraq, when an American serviceman or servicewoman swears to uphold and defend the Constitution, he or she swears to uphold the international laws of war. Any deviation from that obligation will have to have legal justification for modifying what appears to be a constitutional requirement. This second set of constraints on permissible conduct further delineates the officer's commitment to the military ethic, especially when we recognize that commitment to uphold the laws of war logically entails commitment to the two previously cited humanitarian principles that underlie those laws of war, which we repeat here for emphasis:

1. Individual persons deserve respect as such.
2. Human suffering ought to be minimized.

Mission requirements impose duties and dictate actions, but those requirements must always be consistent with the recognition of and respect for these two overarching moral principles.

Our review of the basic elements of the military ethic identified the third major influence on the ethic as the set of fundamental and unique values of American society. We recognized that tension may arise at times between the requirements of military activity (accomplishing the mission most effectively and efficiently) and our fundamental social values. When such conflicts occur in our system and society, the fundamental values of society, respect for the individual as a person, the rule of law, and the authority of the Constitution, provide boundaries on permissible action.[35] While translating those values into specific guidelines may take different forms, the values ultimately do establish the final moral constraints on acceptable behavior by members of the American military.

These three major influences that shape the contents of the American military ethic provide no simple equation for identifying permissible actions, even after we specify the structure and the broad content of the ethic. Recognizing the nature and relationship of the influencing factors merely provides a framework for considered judgment by the individual officer or soldier. Having identified such factors, however, we can more convincingly summarize the central tenets of the American military ethic that has emerged, and continues to do so, from the interaction of these formative influences.

First and foremost, military officers are expected to be loyal to their organization and their country. During the Korean Conflict, for example, under brutal duress numerous American POWs collaborated with the enemy or performed actions demanded of them that were impermissible under military regulations. Our national dismay at such conduct by captured soldiers and a determination to minimize future recurrences led President Eisenhower to promulgate *The Code of Conduct for Members of the Armed Forces of the United States* in Executive Order 10631, August 17, 1955, which President Reagan revised in a 1988 executive order.[36] Standards established in that document, reproduced below, grow out of the basic value of loyalty.

CODE OF CONDUCT

1. I am an American, fighting in the forces which guard my country and our way of life. I am prepared to give my life in their defense.

2. I will never surrender of my own free will. If in command, I will never surrender the members of my command while they still have the means to resist.

3. If I am captured, I will continue to resist by all means available. I will make every effort to escape and aid others to escape. I will accept neither parole nor special favors from the enemy.

4. If I become a prisoner of war, I will keep faith with my fellow prisoners. I will give no information or take part in any action which might be harmful to my comrades. If I am senior, I will take command. If not, I will obey the lawful orders of those appointed over me and will back them up in every way.

5. When questioned, should I become a prisoner of war, I am required to give name, rank, service number, and date of birth. I will evade answering questions to the utmost of my ability. I will make no oral or written statements disloyal to my country or its allies or harmful to their cause.

6. I will never forget that I am an American, fighting for freedom, responsible for my actions, and dedicated to the principle which made my country free. I will trust in my God and in the United States of America.[37]

A second fundamental element of the military ethic, selfless service, implicit in *The Code of Conduct*, follows necessarily from the ultimate liability of combat: loss of life. The same principle applies in many contexts, albeit to a lesser degree, in which the military institution often expects the individual to subordinate personal interests to the requirements of military duty. In paying tribute to the heroes of D-Day in World War II, General Gordon Sullivan, then Army Chief of Staff, emphasized selfless service:

> I think these soldiers—the Eisenhowers, the Summers, and the Pinders and all the rest whose names are known only to buddies, loved ones, or God alone— did their duties and made their sacrifices for each other and for us. They epitomized the ethics of *selfless service*, the core value of American soldiers and, indeed, everyone in the country's armed forces.[38] [Emphasis added.]

The value of obedience provides a third element in the foundation of the military ethic. In the military context, it follows from commitment to the profession and its purposes. In contrast, obedience that results from fear cannot be relied upon in crisis situations when immediate dangers might otherwise overwhelm the threat of sanctions. Obedience in all circumstances relates directly to loyalty, selfless service, and the overarching emphasis on mission accomplishment (the duty concept). Thus the central place of duty in military values suggested earlier by the passage from Shakespeare also holds today, within clear limits emplaced by law and our fundamental social values. In the Academy's study of the military ethic, we found that all versions of moral guidance for American soldiers include in some form the duty concept, which usually obligates subordination of personal interest and, indeed, personal safety to the fulfillment of professional obligations.

Those four values—loyalty, selfless service, obedience, duty—all basic elements of the American professional military ethic, result from the functional requirements of military service, just as do courage and integrity. Courage needs no further elaboration. Unless subordinates can rely on the honesty and sincerity of their leaders, the basic components of integrity, trust will be elusive. Without trust in the unit's leadership, no combat organization will be nearly as effective as it must be to succeed consistently in combat. For example, without accuracy in reports from subordinate headquarters, no commander can make timely, informed decisions that will maximize opportunities for success in battle. The importance of integrity appears undeniable and uncontroversial as well. At the Military Academy, the principle of integrity finds application in the Cadet Honor Code. Not only are cadets expected to live up to the standards established by the Honor Code, but they are also expected to make those standards part of their own belief systems and to help their comrades do the same by not tolerating their violations of those standards. Only then will they be able to manifest the character necessary for leadership of American forces.

While military organizations have long recognized commitment to the welfare of one's fellows and one's subordinates as a practical benefit, serving as a multiplier of combat effectiveness, such commitment also flows from respect for the integrity and the fundamental rights of individual persons. In the American military, the functional aspect of respect receives strong reinforcement from the core American social value of individualism. In American culture, the worth of the individual has shaped all of our primary social institutions. The religious tradition that posits an immortal soul, the idea of equality before the law, and the principle of protecting individual rights from the power of the state all contribute to the value imputed to individual soldiers, a value that has become fundamental to the American military culture. That tradition buttresses the appreciation of initiative in the American soldier, sailor, and airman. Initiative and independent action, which superficially appear to be directly contrary to the expectations of a hierarchical, authoritarian institution, actually have great practical value. Initiative, innovative thinking, and adaptability contribute greatly to success on the battlefield, as we see today in operations in Afghanistan and Iraq.

Principles of Officership

The preceding discussion summarizes what the Military Academy has concluded concerning the influences on and the basic moral content of the Army's professional ethic. While remembering that any specific articulation of the Army's or the American military ethic will be problematic in view of the penumbra of values that inform the ethic and the complexity of the moral concepts that provide its structure, the staff and faculty at West Point did identify a set of principles for officers to live by, principles intended to guide them as they live out their shared professional identity of being an officer. We believe these principles capture the central features of the military ethic, the values of the military profession, and the underlying moral foundation necessary for an effective Army. "The Principles of Officership," now a fundamental aspect of CLDS, are here reproduced in their entirety (see also Chapter 1, Appendix 1–A):

The Principles of Officership

(1) Duty. Professional officers always do their duty, subordinating personal interests to the requirements of the professional function. They are prepared, if necessary, to lay down their own lives and the lives of their soldiers in the Nation's interest. When an officer is assigned a mission or task, its successful execution is first priority, above all else, with officers accepting full responsibility for their actions and orders in accomplishing it—and accomplishing it in the right way. The officer's duty is not confined, however, to explicit orders or tasks; it extends to any circumstance involving allegiance to the commissioning oath.

(2) Honor. An officer's honor is of paramount importance, derived historically from demonstrated courage in combat. It includes the virtues of integrity and honesty. Integrity is the personal honor of the individual officer, manifested in all roles. In peace,

an officer's honor is reflected in consistent acts of moral courage. An officer's word is an officer's bond.

(3) Loyalty. Military officers serve in a public vocation; their loyalty extends upward through the chain-of-command to the President as Commander-in-Chief and downward to all subordinates. Officers take care of their soldiers and families. This loyalty is central to the trust that binds together the military profession for its public servant role.

(4) Service to Country. An officer's motivations are noble and intrinsic: a love for the technical and human aspects of providing the Nation's security and an awareness of the moral obligation to use that expertise self-sacrificially for the benefit of society. The officer has no legacy except for the quality of his or her years of service.

(5) Competence. The serious obligations of officership—and the enormous consequences of professional failure—establish professional competence as a moral imperative. More than proficiency in the skills and abilities of the military art, professional competence in this sense includes attributes of worldliness, creativity, and confidence. Called to their profession and motivated by their pursuit of its expertise, officers commit themselves to a career of continuous study and learning.

(6) Teamwork. Officers model civility and respect for others. They understand that soldiers of a democracy value the worth and abilities of the individual, both at home and abroad. But because of the moral obligation accepted and the mortal means employed to carry out an officer's duty, the officer also emphasizes the importance of the group as against the individual. Success in war requires the subordination of the will of the individual to the task of the group. The military ethic is cooperative and cohesive in spirit, meritocratic, and fundamentally anti-individualistic and anti-careerist.

(7) Subordination. Officers strictly observe the principle that the military is subject to civilian authority and do not involve themselves or their subordinates in domestic politics or policy beyond the exercise of the basic rights of citizenship. Military officers render candid and forthright professional judgments and advice and eschew the public advocate's role.

(8) Leadership. Officers lead by example always, maintain the personal attributes of spiritual, physical, and intellectual fitness that are requisite to the demands of their profession and that serve as examples to be emulated.[39]

Moral Reasoning

One task remains, that of explaining how we believe officers develop the ability to apply the ethic we have been discussing. As mentioned earlier, obviously there are no formulas for the moral reasoning required. Even the "rules of engagement" carefully developed for each military operation cannot foresee all situations that leaders will face in combat. If, as one scholar has noted, the professional practice of Army officers is the "repetitive exercise of discretionary judgment while making decisions and taking actions that fulfill their responsibilities under the Commission," how does West Point foster the type of moral reasoning needed for such demands?[40] The first step is to ensure that cadets understand the forms of moral reasoning available. Education in the processes of moral reasoning occurs within the academic curriculum, in the practical lessons presented during the values education program, and in living under the Honor System.

In the classroom, cadets learn the difference between consequentialist systems and non-consequentialist systems of moral reasoning. Moral reasoning and analysis usually take one of these two forms. Consequentialist systems base moral decisions on the anticipated results of the actions under consideration. For example, utilitarian moral reasoning, one of the consequentialist systems, begins with the assumption that the right action is the one that will produce "the greatest good for the greatest number." The best known non-consequentialist systems are rule-based, or deontological, to apply the label used in moral philosophy. In that form of moral reasoning, an action is right if it conforms to a specific moral rule or principle. Cadets study various processes for resolving moral questions. They examine numerous case studies in academic courses and in the values education program, often case studies that generate debate and differing opinions. Cadets learn that under the military ethic, consequentialist reasoning has limited application.

In a well-publicized case in Iraq during Operation Enduring Freedom, an officer chose to mistreat a prisoner to extract information about a planned ambush of the officer's unit.[41] Although he was prosecuted and convicted, the officer declared that he had to choose the welfare of his soldiers over the constraints imposed by regulations and policies concerning the treatment of prisoners. His criterion for decision was to choose the action that best served the interests of his soldiers. Even though objective analysis suggests immediately that we would not expect a military leader to apply such a standard to all cases, widespread discussion of the case demonstrated that many people, including soldiers, did not understand the guidance established by the military ethic. They found it difficult to accept that the ends do not justify the means, a principle that the officer in Iraq apparently applied. Cadets examine many such case studies and apply the military ethic in the process of analyzing the moral reasoning process. Ideally, they come to recognize the relationships among the various constraints on the actions of military professionals that we discussed earlier.

On reflection, we can see that the American military ethic is rule-based. The actions of those bound by the American military ethic are first constrained by the functional exigencies of military operations, further constrained by the laws of war, and finally by the enduring values of American society—the values that soldiers defend. In addition to regulations and rules established by the profession, the laws of war and the values of American society both limit actions permissible in accomplishing assigned missions. Classroom studies and sessions in the values education program, spread over the entire four-year baccalaureate experience, further cadet understanding in these areas.

Living under the Cadet Honor System also strengthens understanding of and commitment to a set of values that does not justify action solely in terms of results or consequences. The emphasis falls on rules. The Honor Code does not recognize conditions under which violation of the prohibitions against lying, cheating, and stealing are acceptable in the lives of cadets. Although sanctions for violations of the Code have changed over time, the guidance for conduct has remained clear and consistent. The Academy and the Corps expect cadets to be men and women of integrity. In Aristotelian terms, acting with integrity over time builds integrity. Doing strengthens being. Thus the Honor System, which encourages truthfulness, fairness, respect for the property of others, and commitment to professionalism, contributes to the process of character development and moral understanding. Cadets and graduates alike participate in that process through adhering to the duty concept, which establishes limits by applying the active boundary conditions supplied by the Principles of Officership and the military ethic. The strengthening of character must continue throughout an officer's professional life if he or she is to meet the demands of senior leadership.

Under the American military ethic, consequentialist reasoning does not provide final answers, however tempting that formula may be in difficult situations. Extreme circumstances may be the basis for morally excusing some actions, but they do not justify transgressions. Considerations arising from the American value system limit morally permissible actions under the American military ethic. The moral reasoning involved is at bottom non-consequentialist in nature. The military ethic clearly functions under a moral teleology, but the purpose of the ethic is to guide the actions of the military in the effort to maintain the nation under the Constitution. The purpose is to uphold a matrix of institutional values. During their four years at West Point, cadets learn not only the nature of the military ethic and the reasoning involved in applying its mandates, but also the reasons for the limitations on professional conduct. That is why they need to understand the history of the development of the American military ethic and the factors that have shaped it over time. They need to understand the central role that the Constitution plays in both law and morality. When they do, they are much better prepared to apply the military ethic in situations in which grave issues hang in the balance and they as leaders must choose a course of action.

A Concluding Note

The laws of war will change over time, slowly, and the core values of our society will evolve, even more slowly, eventually bringing about changes in our military ethic, but the central features of the code of professional military ethics identified here will guide the conduct of members of the American military profession for the foreseeable future. The critical point to recognize is that stable, enduring standards of conduct do exist. The "Principles of Officership" incorporate them. Those standards of conduct are part of our military heritage, and they can be and have been passed on from one generation of military leaders to another. The processes of professional socialization in all the military services are designed to foster in the officer corps a deep commitment to professional values and to strengthen such values among all members of the armed forces. Americans can depend upon the military institution to carry out its responsibilities largely because of the ethic of the military profession and the institutional commitment to professional military values. At West Point, that commitment takes tangible form in the Cadet Leader Development System.

Many have questioned the efficacy of the military ethic in the face of blatant violations of its tenets. The recent events at Abu Ghraib Prison and at Haditha in Iraq during Operation Iraqi Freedom provide well known examples. At a 2006 presentation in Austin, Texas, however, by Brigadier General (Retired) Howard Prince to a military audience on the subject of Abu Ghraib, discussion suggested that the ethic remains strong. General Prince asked whether any members of the audience had served in Iraq. Two volunteered that they had served there as junior officers, and in fact were there when the Abu Ghraib revelations of prisoner mistreatment and torture became public. General Prince asked about their reactions to the disclosures. Both related that they were dismayed and ashamed that fellow soldiers in uniform had so egregiously violated the laws of war and Army regulations. The two former officers saw the actions of the prison staff as betrayals of the trust that Americans place in their military services. Although the investigation proceeded at a deliberate, careful pace, the Army did eventually try eleven military personnel for their actions, to include the officer commanding the prison. The harsh, demanding environment of combat generates the full spectrum of human reaction, from compassion and heroism to brutality and viciousness. The issue central to the moral status of the military profession is the reaction of the institution when violations of the ethic occur. The disposition thus far of Abu Ghraib and other instances of unacceptable behavior indicates that the military ethic described here remains firmly in place and central to the development of leaders of character.

Discussions in this chapter make clear that we can identify, explain, and justify the moral guidelines for members of the armed forces; nonetheless, the demand remains for officers to make discretionary judgments, often in the heat of battle, and not all moral decisions will be straightforward. What a specific leader should do in a particular situation, and what we should be willing to excuse should the prohibitions established by law or by the ethic be violated, remain difficult questions. That reality explains the need to develop in cadets an understanding of the capabilities discussed in Chapter 4: an appreciation for moral complexity, a recognition of moral responsibility, and confidence in one's own beliefs. The Army expects and requires moral reasoning based on moral principles established by the military ethic. The moral landscape of the soldier has always been difficult, perhaps more so now than ever before when we consider that in the long war against Islamic radicals using the techniques of terror among urban populations, situations of moral ambiguity abound. The actions of individual soldiers can affect both subsequent policy decisions and public support for security operations. Chapter 5 emphasizes the impact on followers of a leader's character and actions. The American interventions in Afghanistan and Iraq reinforced that conclusion in the context of counterinsurgency and terrorism following initial combat operations. Military losses can often be overcome; however, moral failings constitute greater obstacles to national success, and leadership is the only effective answer to such challenges. The battle against terrorists that now spans the globe highlights not only the important role of the profession of arms but also the military ethic under which it functions. The inculcation of that ethic has become the foundation of developmental systems at West Point.

Notes

1. United States Military Academy, USMA Circular 1-101, *Cadet Leader Development System* (West Point, NY: June 2002), 15.
2. General Sir John Hackett, "The Military in the Service of the State," in *War, Morality, and the Military Profession,* 2d ed., ed. Malham Wakin (Boulder, CO: Westview Press, 1986), 119. For a discussion of Hackett's claim, see Anthony Hartle, "Do Good People Make Better Warriors?" Army 42, no. 8 (1992), 20-23.
3. A variety of religious services were available, to include Protestant, Catholic, and Jewish. The Academy no longer requires attendance, though many cadets voluntarily participate.
4. A number of books provide detailed discussions of the military as a profession, to include Samuel Huntington, *The Soldier and the State* (New York: Vintage Books, 1964); General Sir John Hackett, *The Profession of Arms* (New York: Macmillan, 1983); William Skelton, *An American Profession of Arms* (Lawrence, KS: University Press of Kansas, 1992); several books by Morris Janowitz; and Don Snider, project director, and Lloyd J. Matthews, ed., *The Future of the Army Profession,* 2nd ed. (Boston: McGraw-Hill, 2005).
5. Professional armies are not a development peculiar to the modern world. In all probability, ancient Egypt in certain periods maintained well-trained, highly experienced armies of men who made careers of fighting wars, but in the period that we know well, from 900 A.D. to the present, professional armies came into being only during the last two centuries.
6. John Keegan, *A History of Warfare* (New York: Alfred A. Knopf, 1993), 263-81.
7. Keegan, 268.

8. Keegan, 268.

9. Keegan, 283.

10. Keegan, 270.

11. Hackett, *The Profession of Arms,* 58.

12. Ibid.

13. Huntington, 37-39.

14. Julian Thompson, *The Lifeblood of War: The Logistics of Armed Conflict* (London: Brasseys, 1991), 38, as quoted in William T. Divale, *War in Primitive Societies: A Bibliography* (Santa Barbara, CA: ABC-Clio, 1973), xxi.

15. Hackett, *The Profession of Arms,* 9.

16. Ibid., 103.

17. Morris Janowitz, *The Professional Soldier: A Social and Political Portrait* (Glencoe, IL: Free Press, 1960), 218.

18. For an examination of the nature and the difficulty of that transformation, see Matthew Moten, "Root, Miles, and Carter: Political-Cultural Expertise and an Earlier Army Transformation," in *The Future of the Army Profession,* 2d ed., project director Don Snider and ed. Lloyd J. Matthews (Boston: McGraw-Hill: 2005), 723-748.

19. Janowitz, 5.

20. For a more detailed discussion, see Anthony E. Hartle, *Moral Issues in Military Decision Making,* 2d edition (Lawrence, KS: University Press of Kansas, 2004), Ch. 3.

21. Huntington, 73.

22. Hartle, Ch. 5.

23. General Eric Shinseki and Frances Hesselbein, *Be-Know-Do: Leadership The Army Way* (San Francisco, CA: Jossey-Bass, 2004), 26.

24. Lloyd J. Matthews, "Is the Military Profession Legitimate?" *Army* 44, no. 1 (1994), 16.

25. Roger Nye, *The Challenge of Command* (Wayne, NJ: Avery; 1986), 12-13.

26. The transgressions of individual soldiers, particularly against noncombatants, cause public concern, but the greatest unease always focuses on the leadership that either fails to prevent war crimes or fails to take swift corrective action.

27. See Lewis S. Sorley III, "Competence as an Ethical Imperative," *Army* 34, no. 8 (1982), 42-48.

28. Huntington, 16.

29. Kim Hays, *Practicing Virtues: Moral Traditions at Quaker and Military Boarding Schools* (Berkeley, CA: University of California Press, 1994), 54.

30. Chapter 1 of the present anthology discusses the studies that led to the revised version of the Cadet Leader Development System (2002).

31. Hays, 43.

32. William Shakespeare, *The Life of King Henry the Fifth,* IV, i, 123-6.

33. U.S. Department of the Army, FM 27-10, *The Law of Land Warfare* (Washington, DC: GPO, 1956), 182.

34. U.S. Department of the Navy, NWP 9, *The Commander's Handbook on the Law of Naval Operations* (Washington, DC: Department of the Navy, July 1987), 6-1.

35. The fundamental values of society and thus the moral constraints for the military normally change and evolve slowly. In any individual's career, they will appear to be constant. The application of those principles may change more noticeably. Thus, the military's treatment of racial issues, the role of women, and the status of

homosexuals has evolved relatively rapidly over the past several decades as a result of social practice and legal interpretation.

36. U.S. Department of Defense, *The U.S. Fighting Man's Code,* DoD Pamphlet 1-16 (Washington, DC: GPO, 6 August 1959); U.S. Department of Defense, DoD GEN 36-A, *The Armed Forces Officer* (Washington, DC: GPO, 1988), 74.

37. The Code of Conduct clearly applies to members of the military today, though it is supplemented by statements such as the Soldier's Creed, the Warrior Ethos, and other publications that receive focused attention upon distribution and subsequently play a significant role in training.

38. General Gordon R. Sullivan, "D-Day Plus Fifty Years," *Army* 44, no. 6 (1994): 26.

39. I note that this set of principles is fully consistent with written guidance within the Army today, to include the most recent guidance specifically designed for conduct in the War on Terror featuring urban counterinsurgency operations: "The Soldier's Rules," published in 2006 in Army Regulation 350-1.

40. Don M Snider, "The Multiple Identities of the Professional Army Officer," in *The Future of the Army Profession,* 2nd ed., Chap 6.

41. The case centered on the actions of LTC Allen B. West on August 20, 2003 in Taji, Iraq. LTC West was a battalion commander in the 4th Infantry Division.

III

Moral Guidance for Military Leaders from the Cadet Prayer: Interfaith Perspectives

7 The Cadet Prayer: A Catholic Perspective

Edson J. Wood

Introduction

> Along with the armor of the body, put on the surer and stronger armor of the spirit.
>
> —St. Augustine[1]

As the Roman Empire in the West was entering its inevitable twilight, there lived in the North African city of Hippo Regius a man who, because of his complete dedication to the pursuit of truth and his prodigious literary output, is more familiar than any other figure in classical Roman history. Author, theologian, philosopher, orator, and Roman Catholic bishop, St. Augustine of Hippo provided his civilization with "seeds of thought" that have grown and blossomed over the centuries . . . and which, 1,600 or so years later, still resonate, strong and vibrant, wherever civilized discourse is valued.

One of his "seeds" was what has become the Just War Tradition, his attempt to soften the warrior culture of his day by applying the principles of Catholic Christianity to the harsh and inevitable human reality of war. His resulting criteria for what constitutes a "just war" (i.e., just cause, legitimate authority, right intention, etc.) became a foundation upon which later thinkers built a system of societal norms which governed so much of the social thought of successive generations on the topic.

What is less known, however, is that while he never wrote a moral manual for soldiers, thoughts from his correspondence with a notable military officer of the day show that he had a pretty specific idea about what the character of a soldier should be. Writing to his sometime friend, the Roman general Boniface, military leader of the Roman army in North Africa at the time (427 A.D.), he made some specific observations about warfare and a soldier's behavior. In subduing Saharan tribes that were making troublesome incursions over the borders of the Empire, Boniface's troops had proved themselves rapacious and interested in plunder; they were attacking civilians and were neglecting the military foe. Augustine was pointed in his advice to Boniface:

> Even in waging war, cherish the spirit of a peacemaker. . . . Let necessity, therefore, and not your own will slay the enemy who fights against you. As violence is used towards him who rebels and resists, so mercy is due to the vanquished and the captive.[2]

Moral precepts all, because character is about moral precepts. Then as now, the godly moral character of an officer was the sine qua non upon which his moral authority and credibility, as well as that of his cause, rose or fell. And this is what the Cadet Prayer is all about: the godly moral character required of a leader.

It is not such a long leap from the recommendations of Augustine for his friend, the general Boniface, to the moral precepts of the Cadet Prayer, or from Catholic moral tradition to the description of a leader of character found in the Academy's Cadet Leader Development System ("CLDS" as it is known and was detailed by Professor Don Snider in Chapter 1). A Catholic cadet is very much at home here. For a Catholic, behavior cannot occur in a vacuum. Behavior is engendered by belief, and the Cadet Prayer offers a view of human life that is in perfect consonance with Catholic views about prayer and morality.

The measured cadences of the Prayer begin with God and end with God, the Ultimate Mystery, the reason why moral precepts are valid in the first place and why human character matters. These cadences rise and fall with timeless moral principles that have always constituted the basis for the whole Catholic moral tradition. They provide a picture of the ideal human being, the man whom the Roman poet Horace once described as "integer vitae" or "a person complete and wholesome in life."[3] And they also lay out for every cadet the goals of West Point and its program to develop leaders of character for the nation, leaders who can "discover the truth, decide what is right, and demonstrate the courage to act accordingly, always."[4]

What follows is a brief tour of the Cadet Prayer as a Catholic would make that tour: first, a general picture of West Point's view of spirituality and the moral life; next, the moral precepts of the Cadet Prayer as they would be interpreted by a Catholic cadet; and finally, an opportunity to hear from Catholic cadets themselves, discussing how they look at this scenario of their own moral development.

Spirituality and the Moral Life at West Point

The following sentiment of St. Augustine, expressed to his listeners so long ago, is, in a nutshell, what West Point is all about:

> Make progress, my brothers; examine yourselves honestly, again and again. Put yourselves to the test. Do not be content with what you are if you want to become what you are not yet. Always add something more, keep moving forward, and always make progress.[5]

As described in Chapter 1, the mission of West Point is "to educate, train, and inspire the Corps of Cadets so that each graduate is a *commissioned leader of character*." Further, the Cadet Leader Development System defines character as "those moral qualities that constitute the nature of a leader and shape his or her decisions and actions." A leader of character "seeks to discover the truth, decide what is right, and demonstrate the courage to act accordingly, always.[6] Again, hearkening back to Professor Snider in Chapter 1, in laying the groundwork to produce such leaders of character, West Point recognizes that cadets experience growth in six areas or domains of their humanness: intellectual, military, physical, spiritual, ethical, and social. The casual visitor to West Point can easily note the time and effort spent to ensure that cadets are intellectually developed, militarily proficient, and physically fit. Indeed, endless hours are spent training cadets to be well above average in these three domains.

What might not be so quickly recognized, however, is that these are only three targets in the Academy's plan for cadet development. The other three domains of character—the spiritual, ethical, and social—can be easily assumed and perhaps taken for granted by a casual visitor. These domains can be very private, very internal elements of the cadet's human personality, but they are equally crucial in the Academy's developmental design because competence is not always a barometer of character, and the basic thrust of West Point is, after all, character. As quoted in the CLDS manual, General of the Army George C. Marshall wrote: "The soldier's heart, the soldier's spirit, the soldier's soul are everything." Using other words, West Point captures Marshall's thought when it speaks of a cadet's spirituality as:

> that vital energizing force or essence at the core of each person's self [which] serves as a well-spring of individual identity, as the core of personal values and ethics, and provides meaning to an evolving worldview.[7]

Such spirituality is, first and foremost, about the meaning of an individual life. A cadet's spirituality—whether faith-based or not—is the core of personhood, and in the course of individual growth, it fuels the individual to view the world in a certain and precise way. This, in turn, is the foundation upon which a human being justifies his or her reasons to act in one way as opposed to another, to decide what is virtue and what is vice, to embrace truth and eschew falsehood. In short, a person's spirituality provides the building blocks of character from which the attitudes, the worldview, the actions, and, indeed, the professional and personal life of the future Army officer will be assembled.

It is only natural, then, that West Point, without propounding any particular way of cultivating spirituality (whether it be specifically "religious" or not), views this "domain" as described above. One might interpret the spiritual component as the root, and the other five developmental areas as the plant. To aid the cultivation of this very critical foundation of life at West Point, there is available an impressive array of opportunities. Cadets can deepen their "spiritual sense" in the academic setting (e.g., philosophy, psychology, military ethics), in the military setting (e.g., instruction in honor, respect, and officership), and naturally in the specifically religious settings (e.g., diverse opportunities for cadets to explore or to deepen their personal religious faiths through the Corps Chaplains).

A Catholic Looks at The Cadet Prayer

Each year on the second night before their graduation, Catholic Firsties (seniors) gather with their families at the Chapel of the Most Holy Trinity to celebrate the annual Baccalaureate Mass. It is a solemn recapitulation before God of their four years at West Point and a pointed dedication of their lives to continual service to the nation. In the hushed setting of that night, one of the graduates leads the assembled officers-to-be in a recitation of the Cadet Prayer, the cadences of the text quietly echoing through that sacred space where Roman Catholic members of the Long Gray Line have gathered for over 100 years to offer prayer, whether public or private. The Prayer thus becomes a map for these soon-to-be graduates, detailing their past and charting their future.

Perhaps remembering the dictum of St. John of Damascus (d. 750 A.D.)—that "prayer is the raising of one's mind and heart to God or the requesting of good things from God,"—a Catholic cadet can find in this venerable West Point text a true "prayer" in every sense of the word.[8] It is at once a surge of the heart toward a welcoming Creator, a desire of the mind for union with that Creator, and a commitment of the soul to develop one's life in moral agreement with the Creator's life-plan for human excellence. Such profound statements recall the ancient words of King David:

> O God, you are my God whom I seek; for you, my flesh pines and my soul thirsts like the earth, parched, lifeless and without water. My soul clings fast to you; your right hand upholds me.[9]

For a Catholic, the first sentence of the Cadet Prayer reverberates with tones that ring true to human longing as the simple words recognize the nature of God. They speak of God as the "searcher of human hearts," a timeless image of a God Who takes the initiative, a God Whose action was very familiar to St. Augustine and so many believers, as one can read in the *Confessions:*

> You cried to me and broke open my deafness; You sent forth Your beams and chased away my blindness; I tasted You, and now I hunger and thirst for You; You touched me, and I have burned for Your peace.[10]

A second image immediately follows that of the "searcher of human hearts." It is a plea that the speaker be united with this Source of life, "drawing near. . . in sincerity and truth," akin to an ancient image of human yearning which provided an apt springboard for St. Augustine in considering his own human nature, while speaking to humans of every age: "You have made us for yourself, and our heart is restless until it rests in you.[11]

And then there follows the quintessence of the Cadet Prayer, a chain of supplications for moral rectitude, for good conduct, for excellence of life. The Prayer literally becomes a guide for moral excellence, a vade mecum that can serve any cadet, whether a believer or not. Its timeless maxims paint a picture of desired moral character:

> Strengthen and increase our admiration for honest dealing and clean thinking. . . . Encourage us in our endeavor to live above the common level of life. . . . Make us to choose the harder right instead of the easier wrong. . . . Endow us with courage that is born of loyalty to all that is noble and worthy.

One can think of St. Paul writing to the Philippians:

> Finally, brothers, whatever is true, whatever is honorable, whatever is just, whatever is pure, whatever is lovely, whatever is gracious, if there is any excellence, and if there is anything worthy of praise, think about these things.[12]

This is the domain of moral character, pure and simple!

Catholic moral tradition begins with the following expression of belief, voiced by the 2nd Vatican Council:

> Deep within his conscience man discovers a law which he has not laid upon himself but which he must obey. Its voice, ever calling him to love and to do what is good and to avoid evil, sounds in his heart at the right moment. For man has in his heart a law inscribed by God. His conscience is man's most secret core and his sanctuary. There he is alone with God whose voice echoes in his depths.[13]

And this "law in the heart" propels the attentive listener to a life of doing good and avoiding evil, in other words, to a life of virtue (the word comes from the Latin *virtus*, which means "strength" or "courage"). For a Catholic, the map to such a life is found initially in such basic biblical maxims as the Ten Commandments, in the ethical precepts of the Mosaic Law, and then ultimately in the sayings and example of Jesus of Nazareth, whose radical ethic formed the basis for Catholic development of what morality is all about. This is evident most specifically in Jesus' Sermon on the Mount as found in the Gospel of Matthew, Chapters 6–8. Consider the technique of Jesus in teaching and developing moral precepts for his listeners, as Matthew tells the story in his Gospel:

> You have heard that it was said to your ancestors, "You shall not kill; and whoever kills will be liable to judgment." But I say to you, whoever is angry with his brother will be liable to judgment.[14]

> You have heard that it was said: "You shall not commit adultery." But I
> say to you, anyone who looks at a woman with lust has already committed
> adultery with her in his heart.[15]
>
> Again, you have heard that it was said to your ancestors: "Do not take a
> false oath, but make good to the Lord all that you vow." But I say to you, do
> not swear at all, Let your "Yes" mean "Yes," and your "No" mean "No."[16]

Thus Jesus deals not only with the actions of a human being but with the
intention or the "interior disposition" of the human being, laying out for his
followers the logical "life choices," implicit in him and following from their
belief in him. His approach formed the initial stages of the Catholic interpretation of the moral life of a human being.

The whole long moral tradition of Catholicism followed, each successive
generation laying out the choices for the believer. Note the introduction to and
random maxims from an early Catholic writing, *The Didache,* c. 100 A.D.:

> There are two ways, one of life and one of death, but a great difference
> between the two ways. The way of life, then, is this: First, you shall love God
> who made you; second, love your neighbor as yourself, and do not do to
> another what you would not want done to you.[17]

And, elaborating on what it means to "not do to another what you would not
want done to you," The Didache—sounding very much like the Cadet Prayer—
offers specifics: "You shall not bear false witness; you shall not speak evil; you
shall not be double-minded or double-tongued; your speech shall not be false,
nor empty, but fulfilled by deed; be not a liar."[18] This is the gist of the Cadet
Prayer: a plea to God to help the suppliant develop character, to lead a life of
virtue.

In many ways, Catholic discussion of virtue can begin with The Ethics of
Aristotle, where he defines virtue in the following way: "The disposition which
makes a man good and causes him to do his own work well."[19] For Aristotle,
the goal and result of virtue is *eudaimonia,* meaning blessedness or happiness.
And in a way, the Catholic tradition "baptized" the thought of Aristotle and
expanded it. Note what the Catechism of the Catholic Church has to say
about virtue quite a few hundreds of years later:

> Human virtues are firm attitudes, stable dispositions, and habitual perfections
> of intellect and will that govern our actions, order our passions, and guide our
> conduct according to reason and faith. They make possible ease, self-mastery,
> and joy in leading a morally good life. The virtuous man is he who freely prac-
> tices the good.[20]

From the beginning, Catholic development spoke of three theological
"virtues" or "spiritual habits that fit a person for eternal life." These are faith,
hope, and love, as grouped together by St. Paul in I Corinthians 13:13: "So

faith, hope, love remain, these three, but the greatest of these is love." Note that their immediate and proper object is God. But the tradition remembered not only the Greeks, but also the Jewish Book of Wisdom:

> If anyone loves righteousness, the fruits of her works are virtues; for she teaches temperance and prudence, justice and fortitude, and nothing in life is more useful for men than these.[21]

Thus there entered into the Catholic conception of virtue those habits of life which came to be called the four "cardinal virtues": prudence, justice, fortitude, and temperance. They are called "cardinal" from the Latin root *cardo* meaning "a hinge." These are four stable dispositions that touch every area of natural and supernatural human life, dispositions to which every other good habit is "hinged."

For the Catholic cadet seeking such dispositions, a closer examination of these virtues as found in The Cadet Prayer is beneficial. Before all else, it needs to be remembered that in its ideal state, virtue is never practiced to enhance one's personal reputation. On the contrary, it is practiced to more closely align one's life with the intent of the Creator regarding each human personality. If it is practiced solely for self-aggrandizement, then that motive vitiates and ultimately destroys any value in the virtuous life.

In his lengthy consideration of the reasons that the Roman Empire collapsed, St. Augustine opined that it was precisely because the Roman culture practiced virtue solely to further its own political interest and not for any deeper motive. Note his train of thought:

> It is most improper that the Virtues...should be the servants of Glory. For then Prudence would exercise no foresight, Justice make no dispensations, Fortitude show no endurance, Temperance impose no moderation, except so far as to win human approval, and to serve the ends of Glory and her inflated conceit.[22]

An insight into Augustine's intent is offered by an Augustinian scholar:

> In other words, it would (and did) become a virtue NOT to rise above opinion. Augustine claims that ultimately Rome failed because it had become a society closed in on itself, unable to rise above the prevailing opinion on what was just, temperate, courageous, and prudent behavior. In its fixation on its own virtue precisely as its own, that is, precisely as a pattern of behavior and accomplishment meriting praise, it in the end squelched its own imagination by rendering it unable to allow for self-criticism.[23]

Thus, consideration of motive needs to envelop virtue right from the start (whether on the corporate or the individual level), and, consonant with the Catholic view, the Cadet Prayer founds its moral maxims in the eternal reality of God, not on the exaltation of the ego. It reminds the prayerful one that any motive for attaining virtue—other than conforming oneself constantly to the ideal in the mind of God—essentially dooms any quest for true moral character.

Seen in this light, then, the cardinal virtues are not practiced to bring about mere self-mastery or self-possession; they are practiced to orient people outward toward God and others through loving self-giving. As opposed to becoming one's personal "possessions," these virtues are rather aspects of a unified quest for a life of openness to God and to others. And it is certainly true that "orienting oneself outward toward others through self-giving" defines the kind of moral character that West Point seeks to develop in its future officers.

Although the Cadet Prayer does not use the term "cardinal virtues" nor does it mention any of the four by name, the moral picture it paints about character is precisely that of a man or woman who is in essence prudent and just and temperate and filled with fortitude. Upon what other human habits can the moral precepts of the Cadet Prayer be founded? To honestly ask that God "make us choose the harder right instead of the easier wrong and never to be content with a half truth when the whole can be won" (and all the consequences implied therein) presumes a moral view which is the natural consequence of a decision to live one's life prudently, justly, fortitudinously, and temperately.

A brief consideration of each of these "hinges" might now prove valuable. Among medieval moralists, prudence was called *auriga virtutum* or "the chariot of the virtues." It is the "know how" virtue of the practical intellect, entailing the capacity to translate general principles and ideals into practice. A simple definition that works as well as any might be that of Augustine (Eighty-three Questions, #61), as quoted by St. Thomas Aquinas. Augustine observed: "Prudence is the knowledge of what to seek and what to avoid."[24] Catholic tradition sees this virtue as the one that guides the other three by setting rule and measure and by immediately guiding the judgment of conscience. Although sometimes wrongly confused with timidity or fear or even with duplicity and dissimulation, it is instead the power to apply moral principles to particular cases without error and overcome doubts about the good to achieve and the evil to avoid.[25] Defined thus as the ability to perceive what is right and to figure out the best way to do it with maximum effect, one might easily say that the entire Cadet Prayer is, in fact, a prayer for prudence.

As a relevant aside, St. Thomas Aquinas (whose treatment of the cardinal virtues in his massive *Summa Theologica* is among the most detailed in Catholic moral history) even speaks of the fittingness of what he terms "Military Prudence," noting among other points that "the execution of military service belongs to fortitude, but the direction, insofar as it concerns the Commander-in-Chief, belongs to prudence"[26]

And if prudence is the ability to know what needs to be done, then justice (the second of these virtues) is doing what needs to be done in the way it needs to be done. Prudence discerns; justice enacts. Aquinas defines justice as "a habit whereby a man renders to each one his due by a constant and perpetual will."[27] He thus affirmed what St. Ambrose had said some 600 years earlier in

De *officiis ministrorum* (I, 24): "It is justice that renders to each one what is his and claims not another's property; it disregards its own profit in order to preserve the common equity"[28] Thus, justice is the virtue which disposes a person to respect the rights of every other person and to establish in human relationships the harmony that promotes equity with regard to persons and to the common good. As the Catechism of the Catholic Church points out: "The just man . . . is distinguished by habitual right thinking and the uprightness of his conduct toward his neighbor."[29]

Understanding that this virtue governs relationships between people, both on the individual and communal level, one can easily identify the concept of justice within the Cadet Prayer:

> Strengthen and increase our admiration for honest dealing. . . . Endow us with courage. . . . That scorns to compromise with vice and injustice. . . . Soften our hearts with sympathy for those who sorrow and suffer. . . .

These, and each similar sentiment in the Prayer, seek to invest the leader of character with the predominating conviction that each person is important, that each person has rights (as well as duties), and that a true leader treats everyone equitably, responding to the needs of each just as God responds to the needs of each.

Of the four cardinal virtues, the third—fortitude—would seem perfectly apt for a military setting. It means the strength of mind enabling one to confront pain, adversity, or danger with courage. Or, as defined similarly by Aquinas (who used Cicero's definition), it is the "deliberate facing of dangers and bearing of toils."[30] Traditionally, the Catholic moral interpretation does not limit the meaning simply to the courage of a soldier on the battlefield, but understands this virtue also as a moral stance that holds its ground in spite of adversity and opposition, and it does this precisely to preserve goodness and right. In the Academy's developmental plan this is what a leader of character is all about.

Aquinas approvingly notes other words from St. Ambrose's *De officiis*: "Fortitude . . . wages an inexorable war on all vice, undeterred by toil, brave in face of dangers, steeled against pleasures, unyielding to lusts, avoiding covetousness as a deformity that weakens virtue.[31] Considered carefully, Ambrose's depiction can be read as ascribing to fortitude two principal characteristics: attack and endurance. Attack would be the aspect of fortitude that does not hesitate to pounce on evil and bar its progression, while endurance holds steadfastly to the good while refusing to yield to fear or pain. Both attack and endurance play a key part in the Cadet Prayer, especially when the petitioner asks the Creator to:

> Endow us with courage that is born of loyalty to all that is noble and worthy, that scorns to compromise with vice and injustice and knows no fear when truth and right are in jeopardy.

Finally, there is the fourth cardinal virtue, temperance, the virtue that "tempers." Catholic moral tradition has considered the focus of temperance to be the human emotions, which, in extreme form, can stand squarely in the way of the development of virtue. This happens in one of two ways: the emotions can grow so powerful that they can make a person rash or careless, or they can cause a person to feel so enervated as to lack the will to act at all. Temperance "tempers" the emotions, either up or down, shaping them into their most appropriate expression. St. Ambrose, in the aforementioned *De officiis* (I, 43), made an observation about temperance which Aquinas cited in one of his arguments: "What we observe and seek most in temperance is the safeguarding of what is honorable, and the regard for what is beautiful."[32]

Catholic tradition consistently holds to the belief that what most strongly debases virtue is "emotion to run amok"; and thus the mission of temperance is to permit one's reason to control and to moderate the powerful emotions that are a part of human nature. Aquinas holds that this important virtue has two parts: shame and honor (or beauty). Regarding shame, he observes: "Intemperance is shameful . . . for it debases a man and makes him dim. He grovels in pleasures well-described as slavish . . . and he sinks from his high rank."[33] In "sinking from his high rank," a person would in turn wound his "honor," thus diminishing his "beauty" as a human being.

In Aquinas' consideration, therefore, temperance is an effective conduit to moral excellence, producing a person of honor: "Now honor . . . is due to excellence, and the excellence of a man is gauged chiefly according to his virtue."[34] Aquinas equates the person of honor with the person of spiritual beauty: "In like manner, spiritual beauty consists in a man's conduct or actions being well proportioned in respect of the spiritual clarity of reason."[35] So temperance becomes a "cardinal virtue" because it seeks to bring the emotions (or "passions") under the rule of the reasoning power in a human being. It does this through a sense of shame in the person and the desire in the human heart to become an example of honor or spiritual beauty for others.

As noted by a commentator in the *New Dictionary of Catholic Spirituality:*

> Temperance shapes behavior into a proper balance of intelligence and passion. With temperance, every moral act is a thing of beauty; even the simplest act of kindness is something beautiful when done with style and grace.[36]

Using a somewhat different approach, one could say that the virtue of temperance is a virtue of balance, acknowledging the ebb and flow of human emotion in the personality and striving to control that ebb and flow within reason and proper bounds. It looks to increase or decrease passion, to add to or subtract from its intensity, to be concerned with amounts and checks and balances in the soul—all with a view to permitting the development of a human personality that reflects honor and spiritual beauty. It is worthwhile to pause and inspect the verbs used in the Cadet Prayer because several of them implicitly suggest this capacity of the human heart for "movement" and the need to regulate that same movement.

Verbs such as "strengthen" and "increase" and "kindle" and "soften" imply the capacity and need of a human being to balance the affections, to recognize the ebb and flow of spirit, to measure one's own performance against the rhythm of God's ideal, and then to change what needs to be changed. Such is the conceptual foundation of the virtue of temperance.

In sum, the Cadet Prayer speaks loudly and clearly—although without naming or explaining them in terms of Catholic moral teaching—of the four cardinal virtues, so dear to the hearts of generations of Catholic moralists. It nonetheless charts the details of "the good life" and "the moral life" as Catholics have understood them for centuries. Moreover, the Prayer challenges the reader, regardless of faith, to consider not simply the acquisition of virtue but also the far-reaching consequences of choosing not to embrace virtue. Consider a cadet First Classman who returns to the Barracks inebriated after an evening of socializing. It goes without saying that he or she has violated the virtue of temperance on a personal plane, but the action also needs to be considered on a social plane. Since a Firstie functions as a leadership model for his or her subordinates, this particular Firstie would have violated not just the concept of temperance but also the other cardinal virtues: prudence (in failing to consider the consequences of inebriation itself), justice (in failing to provide the example that is due to every subordinate), and fortitude (in failing to muster the courage to place the legitimate needs and expectations of the subordinate above his or her personal preferences).

The Cadet Prayer thus proclaims for every reader its basic message of character, the desired character of a man or woman who strives after spiritual beauty and, in particular, who sincerely commits his or her future identity to the stated purpose of West Point: developing commissioned leaders of character. At the same time, the Prayer embodies the whole moral understanding of the purpose of a human life, so central to the Roman Catholic moral tradition. Yes, a Catholic cadet at West Point feels perfectly comfortable in the moral cadences and content of the Cadet Prayer.

Musings of Catholic Cadets

There is no more appropriate source for insights of Catholic cadets concerning the moral precepts of the Cadet Prayer than the cadets themselves. This chapter closes with the anonymous reactions of several of these future officers. They form a powerful and fitting conclusion to this meditation. Additionally, more eloquently than any words of the author, they demonstrate the goal to which West Point calls its Corps of Cadets.

From a Second Class Cadet (junior):

> The Cadet Prayer has a great significance to all of us, because it puts into words what we do day in and day out, finding the strength—physically,

mentally, spiritually and morally—to do the right thing, even when we think nobody is watching. The bottom line is that life is full of temptations, and at West Point, just because we have the Honor Code doesn't mean that temptations aren't present. Both our religion and our future profession call upon us to be honest and forthcoming with the truth . . . both because it is necessary and because it is the right thing to do. I know no matter how low I score on a test, no matter how poorly I perform a task, that I always have my honor and integrity, and nothing can take that away from me.

From a First Class Cadet (senior):

I have reflected on the Cadet Prayer often, and the line "never to be content with a half-truth when the whole can be won" has become important to me in my Christian walk and search for a better Christian life. Searching for truth goes well beyond "he said, she said" on this earth; it means searching for God's truth and seeking His guidance through the Bible. It has convinced me to seek Jesus as a guide and to know what He had to say about my beliefs.

And from another First Class Cadet:

"Living above the common level of life" has really helped me to get through my time at West Point. I feel like this is synonymous with the phrase "Do the right thing even when no one is looking." I feel that any success that I've ever had at West Point has come from doing my duty to the best of my ability so that I can be a good example to other cadets and do the best for them. For example, with any task that you are asked to complete at West Point there is always some sort of shortcut that, while it would make the task easier, would detract from the quality of the product. I feel that fulfilling your responsibilities to the best of your ability not only helps others, but it sets an example for others to do the same. "Doing the right thing even when no one is looking" is one of the most important phrases that have kept me on the straight and narrow through my four years at West Point.

Concluding Thoughts

Catholics are a "Communion of Saints" kind of people. The saints of Catholic tradition serve as models of behavior and faith, strong friends—from beyond the grave—in the journey of life, and serve as heavenly intercessors at the Throne of Grace for all who still endure this mortal coil, facing the challenges of daily life.

At the Chapel of the Most Holy Trinity at West Point, the stained-glass windows are replete with images of these celestial companions, the great "soldier-saints" of the Roman Catholic heritage. St. Michael the Archangel is there, patron of airborne soldiers. St. Barbara is there, patron of the field artillery. St. George is there, patron of armor. St. Martin of Tours and St. Sebastian are there as well, patrons of soldiers in general from ancient times, plus a host of others including Joan of Arc, Stephen of Hungary, Maurice—all soldiers of their own times and saints for all time.

They surround each worshiping congregation, mute but powerful testimony to the eternal connection that has uplifted, inspired, and strengthened Catholic soldiers from time immemorial. And each year, as he presides over the Baccalaureate Mass before graduation, this writer finds his gaze wandering, again and again, first to the windows, then to the gathered First Classmen, then again to the windows, and back to the assembled officers-to-be. His predominating thought in such moments is that in this particular congregation, there may well be a saint-to-be, whose image at some future time might well grace a similar window in a future military chapel.

And if that were to transpire, the underlying reason would be easy enough to understand: the West Point graduate in question would have been one whose whole life was founded on the practice of extraordinary virtue, a life in which prudence, justice, temperance, and fortitude were among the major and necessary themes, a life, in fact, which was consistently defined by the moral precepts of the Cadet Prayer. He or she would have thought as St. Augustine thought: "The soul grounded in piety prays not to inform God, but to conform self."[37]

Of course, West Point's mission is not to graduate "saints" as such, but in a broader sense the Cadet Prayer does indeed provide a moral blueprint by which a Catholic cadet (or any cadet) can see and understand what kind of a life is necessary for moral excellence. It is the consistent thrust of spirit that considers the needs of others to be paramount in every setting, the moral dedication that puts the personal ego in second place and the sacredness of the "other" in first place.

And this is how a leader of character is formed. It is to this end that prudence, justice, fortitude and temperance are all directed. It is to this end that the four years of training at West Point are uncompromisingly aimed. It is with this end in mind that the Cadet Prayer states for all time the unchanging pattern of moral excellence in a leader of character.

These are the reasons that the recitation of the Cadet Prayer by Catholic First Classmen at the annual Baccalaureate Mass is so dramatic and timely: it recapitulates, before God, their four years at West Point; it pointedly dedicates their lives to continual service to the nation by laying ego aside to serve the nation's sons and daughters; and it states publicly, powerfully, and forever their willingness to live their lives as leaders of character and paragons of moral excellence.

Notes

1. *The Fathers of the Church* (New York: The Fathers of the Church, Inc., 1956), vol. 32, 104.
2. Ibid., vol. 30, 269-70.
3. Charles Anthon, trans., *The Works of Horace* (New York: Harper and Brothers, 1854), 20.

4. USMA Circular 1-101, *The Cadet Leader Development System* (CLDS) (New York: Office of the Superintendent, U.S. Military Academy, June 2002), 16.

5. This quotation is taken from an unpublished manuscript, an internal document of the Augustinian Order, in the possession of the author.

6. CLDS, 15.

7. Ibid., 28.

8. *The Fathers of the Church,* vol. 37, 328.

9. *The New American Bible* (Wichita, KS: Catholic Bible Publishers, 1990), 581.

10. Edward B. Pusey, trans., *The Confessions of St. Augustine* (New York: Random House, Inc., 1949), 221.

11. Ibid., 3

12. *The New American Bible,* 1291.

13. Walter M. Abbott, ed., *The Documents of Vatican II* (New York: American Press, 1966), 213.

14. *The New American Bible,* 1015.

15. Ibid., 1016.

16. Ibid.

17. Roberts-Donaldson, trans., *The Didache,* available at: http://earlychristianwritings. com/text/didache-roberts.html. Accessed by author on February 1, 2006.

18. Ibid., Chapters 3 and 4.

19. *The Westminster Dictionary of Christian Theology* (Philadelphia, PA: Westminster Press, 1983), 600.

20. United States Catholic Conference, *The Catechism of the Catholic Church,* 2nd ed. (Libreria Editrice Vaticana, 1997), 1804.

21. *The New American Bible,* 686.

22. John Cavadini, "Jesus' Death is Real: An Augustinian Spirituality of the Cross," in *The Cross in Christian Tradition,* ed. Elizabeth A. Dreyer (Mahwah, NJ: Paulist Press, 2000), 182-3.

23. Ibid.

24. *The 'Summa Theologica' of St. Thomas Aquinas, Part II* (London: Burns, Oates & Washburn, Ltd. 1929), vol. 10, 2.

25. *The Catechism of the Catholic Church,* 1806.

26. *Summa Theologica,* vol. 10, 52.

27. Ibid.

28. Ibid., 133.

29. *The Catechism of the Catholic Church,* 1807.

30. *Summa Theologica,* vol. 12, 177.

31. Ibid., 196.

32. Ibid., vol. 13, 16.

33. Ibid., 26.

34. Ibid., 43.

35. Ibid., 45.

36. P. J. Waddell, "Virtue," in *The New Dictionary of Catholic Spirituality,* ed. Michael Downey (Collegeville, MI: 1993), 1007.

37. *The Fathers of the Church,* vol. 20, 119.

8 | Prayer and Leadership in the Tradition of Moses Our Teacher, Peace Be Upon Him[1]

Carlos C. Huerta

Introduction

In our individual distant pasts, while we were in our mother's womb, a day came when we consciously became aware of something not us. The first thing might have been the womb itself, the pressure of our mother's or father's hand rubbing mommy's belly, or the sounds of life coming from the outside through the abdominal wall imping on our newly formed ears.

Regardless of the what or when, the fact is that we became aware of something outside of ourselves, we became aware of the Other, we became aware of the place we lived in while still in our mother's womb. We may not have been aware of what that Other was, or how it might affect us, or what our relationship to it was or should be, but we sensed there were other things in this place that we would one day call the Universe.

When we were born, our senses were bombarded with the lights and sounds of the birthing process and the people around helping it to happen, all in some fashion taking care of the mother and baby. There were faces, hands, and bodies that touched us in ways we never had felt before, and we cried. We were reaching out to let that Other know we were uncomfortable, scared, and suddenly very cold and hungry.

That is when we uttered our first prayer, our cry. Instinctively we knew how to pray in those first moments of life with a dedication and devotion of soul that we have tried to attain again and again all our lives. That prayer was our purest and most profound, the one that went straight to the ears of G-d.[2]

Towards a Definition and Purpose of Prayer

The purpose of this anthology is to talk about character and leadership development in terms of officership, and in particular how the moral precepts expressed in the Cadet Prayer can be viewed as a guide for that development. The first question that needs to be asked is, What is prayer and what is the purpose of prayer? A priori, we know that one cannot talk about a cadet prayer, or any prayer, without some sort of definition of what prayer is, or what people who pray seek to accomplish. Prayer seems to be one of those words many think they understand but often have a difficult time verbalizing.

Many people take their own personal experience of what prayer is and extrapolate from it to prayer as experienced in other faiths, cultures, and traditions, with unfortunate effects. Prayer for the Christian is not the same as prayer for the Jew, Muslim, Hindu, or Buddhist. While it may have many overlapping features among the various faiths, how it is performed is profoundly different. One can quickly experience this reality by the level of discomfort felt if he or she is a Christian attending a Jewish service, or is Jewish attending a Muslim service. Why do we feel so naked attending the prayers of other faiths if prayer is the same for all? Are we not all addressing the same Greater Being? Prayer may seek to achieve similar ends for all, but its significance is as diverse as the diversity of souls G-d has created on this planet.[3]

In the prayers of Judaism, reason alone leads to several underlying assumptions. Prayer assumes the existence of G-d. It assumes certain characteristics of that Supreme Being and His/Her relationship with us. It assumes, due to the nature of the Supreme Being, a certain order and purpose in this universe. It assumes that the purpose of man is to seek to understand this order and to fulfill this purpose of our Supreme Being. Because of these assumptions, the concept of leadership in Judaism is firmly planted in the purpose and definition of prayer. One can even argue plausibly that to formalize the concept of leadership outside the medium of prayer and belief in G-d will be as empty and destructive as trying to formalize a sexual relationship without the bonds of love and marriage.

So how does Judaism view prayer? The Rambam[4] states in his opus "The Mishneh Torah":

מצות עשה להתפלל בכל יום, שנאמר: ועבדתם את יי אלקכם. מפי
השמועה למדו, שעבודה זו היא תפלה, שנאמר: ולעבדו בכל לבבכם –
אמרו חכמים: אי זו היא עבודה שבלב? זו תפלה.

[A positive commandment is to pray every day as it is said, "And you shall serve the L-rd your G-d" (Exodus 23:2). From tradition we learn that this service is prayer. As it is said, "And serve Him with all your heart" (Deuteronomy 11:13). Our wise men say, "What is this service of the heart? This is prayer."[5]]

Clearly, and quite profoundly, Judaism equates prayer with service to G-d, and it calls this act a service of the heart. Judaism sees prayer as a way to experience G-d and seek out His/Her will so that we can serve it on this earth. This service to G-d has no room for selfish desire, personal aggrandizement, or personal gain. For students of leadership ethics, this may sound very familiar. A critical point to note here is that this service to G-d, an understanding of which comes through prayer, is a service to carry out His/Her will on Earth.[6]

In assuming a leadership role, a person of faith clearly understands he/she has been given power and means not for the purpose of performing one's will or achieving one's desire. Rather, the sole purpose of this power is to perform the sought-out will of the Infinite. Many of our great American leaders understood this. President John F. Kennedy expressed this idea explicitly in his inaugural address on January 20, 1961: "With a good conscience our only sure reward, with history the final judge of our deeds, let us go forth to lead the land we love, asking His blessing and His help, but knowing that here on earth God's work must truly be our own."[7]

The question can plausibly be asked, With what spirit does one perform this service of the heart, this prayer, this basis of leadership? The kernel of Jewish belief is tied up in a prayer all Jews know as "The Shema." The prayer in a standard prayer book reads as follows:

שמע ישראל, יקוק אלקינו, יקוק אחד.
ואהבת את יקוק אלקיך בכל לבבך,ובכל נפשך ובכל מאדך.

[Hear O Yisrael, the L-rd our G-d, the L-rd is One.
And you shall love the L-rd your G-d
with all your heart,
And all your soul and all your might.][8]

In its use of the word love as a function of the heart, the passage reminds of similar images in the Rambam. Upon recognizing the unity of G-d, we are to show this unity in our lives through service. This service, the beginning and ending point of all prayer, action, and leadership, is best performed and described by the clause, "and you shall love." All prayer, all service to G-d and man, must be centered on the word love. Christian readers cannot help noticing that this concept of service is very similar to their own. As Paul wrote to the Corinthians, "But now abide faith, hope, and love, these three: but the greatest of these is love."[9] Our Muslim brothers and sisters also note that this concept is the very basis of their service to Allah. In a Hadith of the Prophet Muhammad (pbuh), he reports the following words of Allah: "My love belongs to those who love each other in Me, who experience intimacy in Me, who shower each other with goodness for My Sake, and who visit each other joyfully for My Sake."[10]

What we have in terms of a definition and purpose of prayer is service, service to G-d. This service to G-d will in turn lead us to true selfless service to mankind. This service that we learn through prayer can be carried out only through love, a love of the Other that begins with a love of G-d. This true service is one that can be properly performed only with a total commitment that involves, as it says in Deuteronomy, all our heart, all our soul, and all the strength of our existence. This is a total commitment to service that can best be described as selfless service.

Prayer and Leadership

If, as we asserted earlier, leadership has no foundation without prayer and a belief in G-d, then at the very heart of this assertion, and therefore at the very heart of leadership, must be the concept of love. It is inconceivable in Judaism, Christianity, Islam, Hinduism, Buddhism, or any great faith that any concept of true leadership is possible without love. This love must center around G-d, and thus be extended to the people leadership chooses to involve.

One may think that this love, so required in prayer and in any concept of leadership by a person of faith, has no place in a military setting. Thus one may think that when chaplains bring this subject to the table in discussing military leadership with soldiers, the ears of those at the table grow deaf at the mention of the word love in such a martial context. Such thinking would be wrong. One of the outstanding military leaders and heroes of this generation, Army Chief of Staff General Eric Shinseki, said at his retirement ceremony on June 11, 2003:

> Command is about authority, about an appointment to position—a set of orders granting title. Effective leadership is different. It must be learned and practiced in order for it to rise to the level of art. It has to do with values internalized and the willingness to sacrifice or subordinate all other concerns—advancement, personal well-being, safety—for others. So [such] men of iron invested tremendous time, energy, and intellect in leader develop-ment to ensure that those who are privileged to be selected for command approach their duties with a sense of reverence, trust, and the willingness to sacrifice all, if necessary, for those they lead. *You must love those you lead* before you can be an effective leader.[11]

To a military leader like General Shinseki, it would be inconceivable to even consider leadership without love. Love can be considered the glue that holds all other leadership values together. Without love, the values deducible from the General's statement—values like loyalty, duty, respect, selfless service, honor, integrity, and personal courage—have no meaning.

Of course, one can find the denotative meaning of these words in a dictionary, but they have no transcendent significance apart from their incorporation in love itself. As we all know from our experience watching politics and business, words can be defined and interpreted in whatever way best satisfies a person's personal agenda. How often in the arenas of business and politics is achievement measured by the size of one's salary, or career success gauged by holding the "right" positions?

Here we run into the difficult task of trying to differentiate between the objective and subjective meanings of leadership. There were and are genera-tions of people who, subjectively, would point to Stalin, Hitler, or Sadaam Hussein as models of leadership despite the fact that they destroyed the nations they led. A sound objective definition of leadership would shun such subjective considerations, emphasizing instead those concrete values associated with love as discussed above, values that Stalin and the like so sorely lacked. Did they have a selfless value system? No. Did they love those they led? No. Did they show respect for all humanity, even those not under their leadership? No. Were they leaders of moral character? Emphatically, no.

A person of faith understands that to find meaning in the enduring values of leadership, one must introduce the Infinite into the picture. This cannot be done without prayer. The author of the Cadet Prayer understood that the acquisition of such important attitudes and values as an increased admiration for honest dealing, or the willingness to choose the harder right instead of the easier wrong, all began with the words, "Oh God."

When we try to understand such concepts as selfless service, we cannot understand the subjection of self to something outside the self without understanding what that "something outside" is. So often we try to define selfless service in terms of the needs of others, or in terms of the needs of the Army or our nation. How inappropriate and misguided this can be. Without a value system that is subordinated to G-d's will and design, we at best are groping in the dark. Given this darkness, we can never appreciate what selfless service is, or what the harder right is or what the sacred things in life are.

This truth can best be exemplified in the life of Moshe Rabbeinu, **ע"ה** (Moses Our Teacher, Peace Be upon Him). Here was a man raised in the palace of one the most powerful men in the world. He was given every possible privilege and honor, all aimed at producing in him the god reincarnate on earth—Pharaoh—in accordance with Egyptian religious beliefs. However, rather than fulfill this human destiny, leadership at the helm of the world's greatest nation at the time, he chose a more humble path. Because of his encounter with the Infinite through prayer, Moses was inspired to lead a ragtag band of insignificant slaves through a desert, to an uncertain place, wandering for 40 years.

How easily one could argue that the path of selfless service for Moses was to remain in Egypt. One might construe the harder right for him as sitting on Pharaoh's throne, dealing with all the machinations of internal politics and international diplomacy that such an exalted position demanded. Similarly, one can argue that "the courage . . . born of loyalty" for him should have been the courage to show loyalty to the Egyptian family that adopted him as an infant, raised and educated him, met all his needs until he came to manhood, and groomed him for the royal house as Pharaoh. All these arguments, logical as they seem on the surface, fall to the wayside when weighed against the Infinite, as they did for Moses, in his encounter with the burning bush.

This encounter with the Infinite changed his perception of what he needed to do with his life. The encounter truly gave him an understanding of what were the harder right, the whole truth, and the sacred. While he was standing in the presence of the Infinite, even Moses failed to grasp how to "guard against flippancy and irreverence in the sacred things of life." He had to encounter the Infinite through prayer to be taught what Holy ground was and that he was standing on it.

Judaism sees all efforts to understand the meaning of leadership apart from the Infinite touchstone as a futile gesture in intellectual gamesmanship, as simply chasing the will-'o-the-wisp. In fact, Judaism would argue that unless the values of leadership are defined in terms of the Infinite, we are truly being flippant and irreverent with the sacred things of life. In his quotation above, General Shinseki makes it very clear that he views leadership as a sacred and reverent trust. The Cadet Prayer, along with the exemplum from the life of Moses, affirms that this sacred trust cannot be properly defined without reference to the Infinite.

As General Shinseki points out, subordinating all other concerns to concern for the led is critical in military leadership. For the person of faith, such subordination is impossible without belief in an omnipotent Infinite. More specifically, with regard to achieving this subordination of self that the General speaks about, it can be done only through contact with the divine through prayer. As Father Thomas Merton once pointed out,

> In meditative prayer, one thinks and speaks not only with his mind and lips, but in a certain sense with his whole being. Prayer is then not just a formula of words, or a series of desires springing from the heart—it is the orientation of the whole body, mind, and spirit to G-d in silence, attention, and adoration. All good meditative prayer is a conversion of our entire self to G-d.[12]

This total conversion of self that Father Merton mentions is the very same thing that General Shinseki alludes to when he talks about the willingness to sacrifice all. The conversion of self to G-d is a conversion that subordinates the self, seeks no personal advancement except the advancement of the Divine will, wishes no gain except the gain of the whole truth, and embraces every new opportunity for service. This conversion of self is none other than as set forth in the words of the Torah: ". . . and you shall love the L-rd your G-d with all your heart, with all your soul, and with all your might. . . ."[13]

Up to this point, we have talked about such diverse topics as prayer, leadership, and experience with the Infinite. What we hope to do in the next section is to locate these topics in an appropriate framework enabling us to better understand the Jewish concept of leadership.

A Jewish View of Leadership

Jewish literature extends into the past for over 3,000 years. It is one of the most ancient forms of world literature still being added to today. Because of its antiquity, there are very few, if any, topics that this chronicle of the Jewish odyssey on the planet Earth does not touch. Within this vast storehouse of human thought are extensive ethical commentaries touching all areas of human endeavor. It is almost impossible to study medical ethics, for example, and not come across 1,000-year-old Jewish sources that are very relevant and applicable today.[14]

It would only seem natural that these ancient sources would have something to say on the subject of leadership. Despite the existence of contemporary books on the subject of leadership within a Jewish context,[15] it is remarkable that these ancient sources are silent on the topic of leadership as an isolated concept. It is not that these ancient sources have not developed a concept of leadership and grappled with its meaning, but rather that this concept is so completely intertwined with the concept of G-d and contact with the Infinite.

For Jewish scholars, one of the quintessential leaders of all time would of course be the prophet Moses. Not only are there many sterling traits embodied in his leadership style, but around him forms the fundamental Judaistic view of what leadership is all about. There are other great leaders before and after him, like the prophet Abraham and King David, but it was Moses alone who was assigned the transcendently important task of leading the Jewish people out of the land of Egypt, breaking the bonds of slavery and oppression, forging them into a nation, and bringing them to the Promised Land.

The most significant, and probably most difficult, task he was required to perform was to change the habits and attitudes of a group bent to the custom of slavery and prepare them for life as a free people in a free land. It was during those 40 years of wandering in the desert that Moses changed attitudes, developed traits of loyalty and duty, organized the tribes under their own banners, assigned tasks of defense to each, developed teamwork and subordination through the building of the Sanctuary and its Service, and taught honor and service through receipt of the Law on Mount Sinai. After 40 years of observing his leadership, guided through constant contact with the Infinite, the people eventually developed their own competency in performing their tasks and assuming leadership responsibilities on their own.

Through studying the example of Moses, we can fashion a specifically Jewish model of leadership. This model consists of three parts: the Situation, the Results, and the leader's Action that transforms the Situation into the desired Results (see Fig. 8-1).

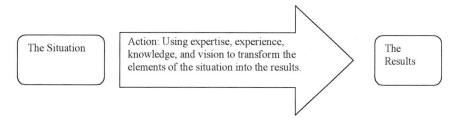

The Situation

Action: Using expertise, experience, knowledge, and vision to transform the elements of the situation into the results.

The Results

Figure 8-1. *Jewish Leadership Model.*

We can derive from this model a Jewish view of leadership that incorporates many of the concepts we have addressed earlier. A leader is called to take elements of an existing Situation and Act on them in such a way as to transform them into desired Results, thus producing a new Situation, if you will. The leader's Action, if it is to be sufficient, must reflect three components: (1) competencies, (2) character, and (3) authority. Leader competencies, as we will discuss later, are connected to the concepts of leaderly knowledge, expertise, and experience. Let us discuss now the Situation, the leftmost element of the Jewish Leadership Model.

An important problem of leadership, in the Jewish view, comes in identifying the specific aspects of the Situation that require action by the leader. Not only does one have to identify what is to be acted on, but also to what end. The Jewish view of leadership holds that it is critical to understand exactly what one is acting on as a leader and where one is going. This requires a full understanding of the elements one is acting on and the range of possibilities resulting from one's Actions. Anything less than this full knowledge of the Situation, the people led, and all other elements needed to accomplish the mission—including a right vision of the final outcome expected of the leader's Action—will produce ineffective leadership.

This is something Moses of course came to realize. When he was living in the Pharaoh's house and assumed the role of a leader, killing the Egyptian who was beating the Hebrew slave, he was later rebuked and rejected by the subjected people he was trying to help.[16] His life of privilege and ease did not give him the knowledge and understanding of who he or his people were; they needed to envision the possibilities of how this insignificant nation of slaves could later impact the world. Moreover, Moses had no understanding of their or his spiritual needs that, as is always the case, must take precedence over such worldly needs as physical freedom or leadership. He was able to gain such large understandings only by dent of the humility he learned as a lone shepherd in the desert for many years and his contact with the Infinite at the burning bush.

It was his time in the desert and the burning bush experience that together served as a message from G-d the Infinite, giving Moses the vision and understanding of the means of leadership he was called to follow. How often this part of leadership is misunderstood and how very difficult it is to teach. How does one impart the fire of the burning bush to the hearts of future leaders of character? How does one take young people, who have not yet tasted of the vastness of the Universe, and help them to understand the infinite possibilities to be chosen from while treading the path of leadership?

The Cadet Prayer, in the moral character petitioned there, seeks to bring cadets to their own burning bush in the desert so that they too can gain understanding and perceive the value of those led. The Cadet Prayer shows cadets the possibilities of what their selfless, loving leadership can do. This burning bush can turn on their inner fire and inspire them to pursue the education and training they require in developing the character prerequisite for leadership. It is only when they assimilate their own burning bush, coming to "guard against flippancy and irreverence in the sacred things of life," that they will be removing the sandals from their feet as a sign of respect. For after all, the place on which they are standing, the ground on which they learn to lead America's sons and daughters in battle, is holy ground.[17]

Unless their own burning bush is experienced and its edifying vision imparted, they will never be the leaders of character we hope for. We should make no mistake about it: for a person of faith, this experience at the burning bush can happen only through prayer and communication with the Holy One. Judaism tells us that anything less than this experience is a false substitute that will leave one lacking in attempting to deal with the real problems that leadership is often required to solve. Going it alone without the humbling experience with the Infinite will only lead to ignorance and arrogance in leadership that are all too common in this world.

Let us turn now to the central component of the Jewish Leadership Model—the leader's Actions. Simply put, Action is the employment of leaderly expert competencies, strong character, and authority, all integrated in accomplishing the mission. The military leader is given America's best, the soldier, and it is his or her Actions with respect to the soldiers—training, education, motivation, providing equipment, etc.—that result in accomplishment of the assigned mission.

Leader competencies can be viewed as the expert knowledge of the officer to be applied within the Situation at hand. There is, ultimately, no way to impart this skill set to a future leader except through practice and experience. Like all professions, it is this constant honing of the skill set through experience that makes the leader a true professional. It is the work of a lifetime requiring constant perseverance in seeking excellence.

Repetition, repetition, repetition of common knowledge and basic officer skills is an important technique that the military uses in building this human expertise. This repetition is also critical in terms of an officer's spiritual development. It needs daily workout, daily exercise, daily prayer, and daily moments of private reflection and meditation. This constant activity of experience, practice, and reflection, whether physical or spiritual, will lead the young officer to understand that such practice is a lifetime requirement that can never be slacked if one is to be a professional officer of high competence and, we should add, moral character, the second leaderly attribute required if Action is to be successful.

The leader's moral character as a prerequisite for successful Action has already been treated en passant in the course of this chapter, but we shall pause to emphasize a vital aspect of character not ordinarily recognized as such—a determination on the part of the leader to provide the necessary resources for those he sends into harm's way. It is axiomatic that soldiers must be provided with the materials of warfare required to accomplish the mission. No combat mission ever begins with all the ammunition, units, or supplies commanders would ideally want. But that said, if they are to lead effectively, there must be a minimum baseline of resources available to accomplish the mission. As adaptive and creative as leaders may be, only G-d can create *ex nihilo*. It is a challenge for young officers to decide the minimum resources that they as leaders require to accomplish the mission. But it is a greater challenge for them to summon the moral courage to tell their commander honestly and fearlessly when they are allocated insufficient resources to accomplish the job. It may in a given case be unfeasible for a commander to provide all the resources that his officer subordinate feels are necessary. But it is always the officer subordinate's duty to make his unit's needs unmistakably known to his boss.

It is these first two leader components—competency and character—that many people sometimes mistakenly construe as sufficient to define a leader in successful pursuit of Action, but they are not entirely what such leadership is about. As explained earlier, leader competencies and character must be suffused with the transformative revelation that comes only with the burning bush experience. Such an experience is relatively easy to perceive if you have the right commo gear in your tool bag. A leader can have had the experience of merely communicating, but, as with the early Moses, without the larger vision, without the understanding of the Situation and the needed Results, the leader's view of leadership will remain superficial. Still, competency and character as prerequisites for successful leaderly Action are not to be underplayed. To be a soldier of whatever rank, one needs to be tactically competent. In fact, such competence is regarded as a moral imperative within the Army today. But it takes much more than tactical or technical competence to perform Action that produces the total result we speak of here.

Equally important in producing successful Action by the leader is the third prerequisite component—authority to accomplish the mission. Such authority entails access to the unit, the soldiers, and the materials necessary to translate plans and orders into the directed Result. This authority for leadership, as General Shinseki points out, is "an appointment to position—a set of orders granting title." For military officers, this authority ultimately comes from an act of Congress that grants the individual a commission and a rank. For political leaders, it comes from the will of the people as expressed at the ballot. For other types of leadership, like parenting or leading one's personal life, it comes from an inalienable right granted by G-d. Some have confused this authority with leadership. We all have encountered politicians who, despite the authority granted them, were not leaders. The history of the Civil War is filled with examples of politically appointed general officers who failed terribly on the battlefield despite the high authority granted them. To understand why this is so, we need to understand that authority comes in two guises.

The first, mentioned above, is the authority given by Congress to be an officer. This can be viewed as the legal right to lead. But as one stands in front of soldiers, the realization comes quickly that there is a second type of authority needed for leadership to work, a higher authority. It depends on the willingness of those we would lead to be led by us. This willingness cannot be ordered by Congress or even by the leader—it must be earned. Such moral authority to lead is conferred only on the leader who comes to merit it, through hard work, setting the example, and convincing the led that he/she will be there with them and for them. Such authority is a product of demonstrated moral character, proven trustworthiness, and a strong dedication to and caring regard for those led. They must believe that we are really a part of their team. As General Shinseki indicated earlier in this - chapter, they must feel that the leader is totally committed to them and the mission in self-abnegating love. Such is the moral authority to lead.

Both legal and moral authority are needed for successful leadership. It is important to realize that though legal authority persists, moral authority is a perishable commodity. It can be lost with one act of self-aggrandizement, one act of disloyalty, one act of dishonor. Unlike its legal counterpart, it must be re-earned every day the mantle of leadership is worn.

Conclusion

We have looked at a model of leadership as posited by Judaism. We have seen that the leader must understand the Situation in detail, including those whom he or she will lead, and must have a vision of the "promised land" where the followers are to be lead. However, those requisites are not enough. The leader must take the right Action to bring about the desired Results. The Action must reflect three components—competency, moral character, and authority to do the necessaries to actually perform the mission. Particularly, for the leader's Action to be successful, the leader must invest in that Action the moral character necessary to maintain a bond of earned trust between the leader and the led, between the officer and the soldier.

I would like to end with a rabbinical story that demonstrates many of the things I have talked about. This story will serve to focus the many concepts I have discussed and show them in a practical setting. It will help the reader to think clearly in analyzing what a faith-based concept of leadership is all about.

One of the longest and most complicated services in Judaism is the prayer series for Yom Kippur, the Day of Atonement. It takes many years to master these prayers in Hebrew, to understand their significance and meaning. Rabbis and holy people have spent their lives trying to reach levels of ecstatic holiness through these prayers, many times without success.

The story we speak of is a Hassidic tale of a rabbi who, on one Yom Kippur, came to the synagogue very early in the day to start his prayers so that he could be uniquely devout in them. His prayers were perfect in their syntax and grammar. He pronounced every word with the most perfect Hebrew inflection. He had brought to his prayers on this particular Yom Kippur decades of learning and study to achieve what he thought was one of the highest possible levels of perfection in prayer. He felt that he was surely touching G-d's ears with his words.

In the back of the congregation a man came in very late. He was late because he was poor and unlearned, one who lived alone in the woods far away from the village. He was a wood-gatherer for the community, a man of no importance in the eyes of most people. He walked quietly into the synagogue, stood in the back for about 20 minutes, and then left. At that very moment, a voice came to the rabbi from above and said, "Rabbi, do you know who has given me the most perfect of all prayers on this Holy day?" "No," said the rabbi in the false humility we all have perfected so well. He was sure he knew the answer, but wanted this Holy voice, who must be the Creator, to say it was he, the rabbi. "Who is it, most Holy One, who has given you the most perfect gift of the heart?" the rabbi asked. "It is the wood-gatherer," said the voice. "Go learn from him what your G-d requires of you."

This shocked the rabbi. How could an unlearned wood-gatherer's prayer on this Yom Kippur be holier than his? After all, the wood-gatherer came in late, spent only 20 minutes, and left. The rabbi ran out of the synagogue to catch up to the wood-gatherer. He stopped him and asked him what possible prayer could he have offered that took only 20 minutes when most learned men's prayers on this day lasted for 10 hours or more. The wood-gatherer said, "Rabbi, I am an unlearned man who cannot read or write, but I do know the Hebrew alphabet." He paused, embarrassed, and continued, "I just stood in back of the synagogue and recited the alphabet three times and prayed to G-d that He take the letters and form the words He needed in order to accept my prayer." The Rabbi was dumbfounded at the wood-gatherer's humility. Then he asked why he was late and why he left so early. The wood-gatherer said that since the weather was so cold, he spent the entire day before gathering wood for the elderly of the village so that they could stay warm during the night. He needed to leave early because he had to make sure that the old and poor had enough wood to cook their meals when the fast ended that evening.

In the foregoing exemplum, I challenge the reader to identify who the real leader is, whom he is leading, the vision of leadership the leader is following, the moral and/or legal authority he has to lead, and the knowledge and expertise that enable him to lead effectively. This story shows that good leadership comes in many shapes and forms, often revealing itself in the most surprising ways. For one to acquire the requisite moral authority for leadership, he or she in whatever style and form must embody the moral character described in the Cadet Prayer. And, as General Shinseki implied, regardless of who does the leading, of the leadership style employed, and of who does the following, the common factor must begin and end with the mandate from G-d, "And you shall love."

Notes

1. In Hebrew rabbinical writings, Moses is usually called Moshe Rabbeinu, which means "Moses Our Teacher," followed by ע״ה which stands for *Ailav Hashalom,* meaning "peace be upon him." One should note that this is very similar to the Islamic tradition of following Muhammad with *pbuh,* which in Arabic also means "peace be upon him."

2. This is an old Chasidic story I heard from my Rebbe, Rabbi Chaim Freidman. It is a story used to show what purity in prayer is. The spellings G-d and L-rd in this chapter require explanation. Based upon the Third Commandment, "Thou shall not take the name of the L-rd thy G-d in vain," Jewish tradition is very strict in observing conventions for assuring that verbalizations of the Holy Name, whether spoken, written, or printed, never profane the name. For example, one must be in a religious rapture and have experienced a ritual immersion before writing the Holy Name in Hebrew, and whatever it is written on must subsequently be buried in a grave and never be dishonored. Since any paper bearing printing can become garbage or worse, care is taken to avoid spelling out the Holy Name in printed material, thus the hyphenated forms G-d and L-rd.

3. For Jewish prayer, see Yitzchok Kirzner and Lisa Aiken, *The Art of Jewish Prayer* (New York: Judaica Press, 2002). For Christian prayer, see Enrrico A. Rocco, *Setting a Trap for G-d: The Aramaic Prayer of Jesus* (Unity House, 1997). For Islamic prayer, see Muhammad *Ashraf, Salat or Islamic Prayer Book* (Lushena Books, 2002). These are only a sample of the hundreds of books available on these topics.

4. Rambam is an abbreviation for Rabbi Moshe Ben Maimon. It is an ancient Jewish tradition to call great Rabbis by such shortened forms of their titles and names.

5. Moshe Ben Maimon, *Mishne Torah* (Jerusalem: Moznaim Publishing Corporation, 1989). Translation by the author.

6. A description of His will can be seen in the words of the Prophet Isaiah in Isaiah 58:6-7, ". . . to loose the bonds of evil, to untie the bonds of yoke, and to let the oppressed go free. Is it not to break your bread with those who are hungry, and to bring those poor with no home into your house, when you see the naked to clothe them. . . ."

7. President Kennedy's Inaugural Address can be found at http://www.yale.edu/ lawweb/avalon/presiden/inaug/kennedy.htm.

8. Deuteronomy 6:4-5, the Hebrew text having been taken from Nosson Scherman, *The Complete Art Scroll Sidur* (New York: Mesorah publications, 1984). Translation from the Hebrew by author.

9. 1 Corinthians 13:13. The New American Standard Bible.

10. Lex Hilton and Fariha Al-Jerrahi, *101 Diamonds From the Oral Tradition of the Glorious Messenger Muhammad: Collected by Ibn Arabi* (New York: Pir Press, 2002).

11. A copy of General Shinseki's speech may be found online at http://www.army.mil/ features/ShinsekiFarewell/farewellremarks.htm. Emphasis supplied.

12. Thomas Merton, *Thoughts in Solitude* (New York: Farrar-Straus-Giroux, 1956).

13. Deuteronomy 6:5.

14. For a good overview of ancient Jewish sources on medical ethics, see Avraham Steinberg and Fred Rosner, eds., *Encyclopedia of Jewish Medical Ethics* (New York: Feldheim Press, 2003).

15. For modern examples, see Naomi Wiener Cohen and Jacob H. Shiff, *A Study in American Jewish Leadership* (Brandeis University Press, 1999), or Hal M. Lewis, *Models and Meanings in the History of Jewish Leadership* (New York: Edwin Mellen Press, 2004).

16. Exodus 2:11-14.

17. Exodus 3:5.

9 | Islam and The Cadet Prayer: An Islamic Reflection on Prayer and Moral Leadership

Sherifa Zuhur

Introduction

Islam is the youngest of the three monotheistic traditions. As in the Judaic and Christian traditions, religious belief is intended to be a way of life. In that endeavor, man is concerned with Allah and his relationship with Allah. Nonetheless, the most important aspect of his life, during which his *islam* (submission to God) is tested on a daily basis, is his relationship with his fellow human beings. Many attitudes and precepts, particularly in this area of ethics, are held in common by the three great religious traditions. For example, with regard to their respective mystical traditions, it is possible to compare their ideals of spiritual development in both historical and modern writings. The Muslim tradition produced ascetics, most famously early figures in Islamic history like Hasan al-Basri (d. 728), a pious ascetic to whom many miracles are attributed; or Rabi`a al-`Adawiyya, similarly, an ascetic and celibate (d. 752 or 801)[1]; or Ibrahim al-Adham (d. 782), whose journey from palace life as the King of Balkh to nine years of meditation in a cave, and thence to Mecca where he earned his bread as a carpenter, resembled the path of Siddhartha Gautama, the man who became the Buddha.[2]

While these individuals became famous for their solitary dedication to prayer and the Highest and for the miracles emanating from their special gifts, the ordinary Muslim is not required to live a life of extreme asceticism or celibacy. One *hadith* (a text relating the Prophet Muhammad's [s.a.w.s.[3]] deeds, words, or precepts) states: "In the matter of religion, Allah has not put on you any undue constraint."[4] Mainstream Islam counters its own ascetics with this hadith. The supreme challenge to the future Muslim leader is to develop spiritually in both dimensions, that is, in his relationship with Allah and with human society.

No doubt, a number of noticeable similarities in the three faiths stem from the shared history, topography, and cultural traditions of the Middle East, where these faith systems developed. Nonetheless, it is common to hear that Christianity, or Christianity and Judaism, are "Western," whereas Islam represents the Eastern world. This misperception has progressed even further in political analyses, which often propose cultural or "civilizational" distinctions as well.

Another very interesting point for comparison stems from Muslim scholars' orientation toward the question of the proper balance between faith on the one hand, and logic, reason, or scientific thought on the other. This was a grave concern in the medieval period, and St. Thomas Aquinas' position on this question owes something to the Muslim philosopher, Ibn Sina, known as Avicenna (d. 1037). Aquinas cites Avicenna more than 250 times in his *Summa Theologica,* as well as making frequent references to Averroes (Ibn Rushd), and we know that other Christian theologists and scholars of his time were also influenced by Muslim scholarship.

The influences of Islam on Christianity are, however, not well known to educators and students in the United States, including the schools devoted to officer training. But for Muslims, Christians, Jews, and others alike, the task of becoming morally and spiritually motivated leaders bears on issues of faith, loyalty, and character development. Of course, these vary somewhat from religion to religion, particularly regarding the contemporary environment, political factors, and the manner in which each faith has expressed its core concerns. Prayer, as Rabbi Huerta has pointed out (see Chapter 8 of this volume), differs stylistically and in its performance and emotional impact from faith to faith. It may even be distinct methodologically. For Muslims, prayer is a duty, a ritual, a means of acknowledging God, and the appropriate way to begin all tasks.

Prayer is one of the required duties of Muslims, described in English as the "Five Pillars" that encompass (1) *shahada,* the declaration or testimony of faith; (2) *salat,* prayer, to be performed five times daily; (3) *zakat,* an obligatory portion of one's income and wealth given as charity, or in support of Islam;[5] (4) *sawm,* fasting during the month of Ramadan from dawn until dusk; and (5) *hajj,* the pilgrimage to Mecca to be performed at least once, if possible. Beyond the Five Pillars, Muslims share certain rules, principles, and prohibitions, for instance dietary restrictions and the forbiddance of consuming alcoholic beverages, primarily because one must be clear-headed in order to pray. Muslims are concerned about what is allowed, forbidden, or neutral according to Islamic law. Certain things, ideas, or practices are forbidden, or strongly discouraged, because they lead to crimes as defined in the Qur'an, or in Islamic law.

The principles of the Five Pillars can also be found in Judaism and Christianity, for instance, the idea of declaring one's faith is expressed in Hebrew, *"Shma Isra'il, adonai elohainu, adonai echod"* (Hear O Israel, The Lord Your God, the Lord is One). Charity is essential in Christianity. Likewise, *tzadaka* is a virtue in Judaism; the same notion, payment of charities *(sadaqa),* exists in Islam. Jews fast from dawn to dusk on Yom Kippur, the Day of Atonement, and Christians of various denominations fast, or give up certain types of food, as a spiritual discipline. Religious pilgrimages, especially to the burial sites of holy figures throughout the Mediterranean, draw Jews and Christians, and many Christians visit Jerusalem to view the Holy Sepulcher and the Stations of the Cross; Jews visit the Wailing Wall along the side of the Haram al-Sharif; Muslims participate in pilgrimages to Mecca, Medina, and Jerusalem; and the Shi`a visit Mashhad, Qum, Najaf, and Karbala. Prayer is performed regularly in Judaism and Christianity, although the idea of Muslim individual prayer performed singly or collectively contrasts with the Christian practice of a prayer service or Mass. In fact, in the United States, Muslim "services" have evolved more along Christian lines, as have prayer traditions of other faiths like Buddhism.

There is, however, a difference in that Muslims are required to pray five times a day, in a particular format, facing Mecca, and at precisely specified times, often a very difficult task in American workplaces or schools. The frequency of ritual prayer in Islam is attributed to Moses, who is recognized as a prophet by Muslims. According to a hadith narrated by Anas bin Malik, the Prophet Muhammad (s.a.w.s.) visited heaven in a miraculous journey known as the *mi'raj*. During this journey, Allah directed Muhammad to require Muslims to pray 50 times a day. The Prophet then descended to a lower level of heaven and met Moses, who advised him that the Muslims would not be able to meet this requirement. The Prophet therefore returned to Allah, who reduced the number of required prayers until there were only five, each one being like a good deed with the value of ten prayers (thus totaling 50). Although Moses warned that the Prophet's people would not be able to meet even this requirement, Allah did not reduce the number beyond five, and the Prophet did not care to press Him further.

Prayer is relatively brief, and, with the provision of running water and a prayer space, Muslims can be accommodated. A more significant difference between the religious faiths may be their respective responses to secularism in contemporary Western society. Some cadets may be more comfortable with the idea of religion as a personal, compartmentalized activity, that being a popular approach within American society. Others may instead be more actively involved with their faith, attuned to its historical interpretation as a way of life and not just a religious identification. In any case, because the Cadet Prayer itself legitimizes those cadets who recognize the presence of faith in their lives to help meet moral demands, it could be attractive to many Muslims.

A Muslim View of the Moral Precepts in the Cadet Prayer

In considering the role of the Cadet Prayer, let us try to view it from the perspective of the soldier-faithful, and thereby work our way toward the Islamic attitude to spiritual development. A master truth of the Islamic faith is the principle of *tawhid*, the Oneness of God, or his "unicity."[6] *Tawhid* is spelled out in the Muslim declaration of faith, or *shahada,* the first of the Five Pillars. The *shahada's* first phrase is "There is no God but Allah." The next phrase is "And Muhammad is the Messenger of Allah." This simple declaration is part of the vocalized call to prayer that resounds five times every day in the Muslim world. Converts to Islam recite this phrase to express their commitment.

The phrase is whispered in a newborn's ear. It is recited when one is dying. It is also a part of the five daily prayers, recited after the cycles of bowing and prostrating oneself before God in a prayer segment called the tashahud.

Tawhid pervades all aspects of modern Islam. It can be understood in a metaphysical sense as the principle that simultaneously explains Allah's close relationship to all living beings and empathy with them *(tashbih)*, depictable as lines streaming outward from Allah's presence as the Center of All, and explains as well his ommipotence *(tanzih)*, depictable with Allah as a central point surrounded by concentric circles. Superimpose one image over the other, and one arrives at *tawhid*. It is a principle reflected in Muslim prayer, art, architecture,[7] and social praxis. Therefore it is perfectly fitting for a Muslim to acknowledge God, as the Cadet Prayer does from the outset, since He guides all human pursuits. Moreover, these first lines of the Cadet Prayer describe the historical experience of Muslims whose aim is to draw closer and closer to God, in fact, to experience unity, *wahdah,* with him.

The foundational sentiment of the Cadet Prayer, and the way it demonstrates the natural impulse to pray, is also captured in the very first *surah* (chapter) of the Qur'an. While the *shahada* encapsulates the truth of Islamic monotheism, this first surah, entitled the Fatiha (the Opening) is different in tone from the supplicatory tone of the Cadet Prayer. It is the key refrain of the five required daily prayers and indeed all prayer cycles. The Fatiha is recited with the undertaking of every new task. Thus, it is recited when planting a spring seedling or beginning a journey, written at the beginning of students' examinations, and uttered by a groom and a bride to formalize their marriage:

> *Bismillahi al-rahman, al-rahim. Al-hamdu li-lah, rabb al-`alamayn.*
> *Al-rahman, al-rahim. Maliki yawm al-din. Iyyaka na`budu wa-iyyaka nasta`in. Ihdina al-sirat al-mustaqim. Sirat alladhina ana`mata `alayhum ghayri al-maghdub `alayhum wa-la al-dhallin.*
> [In the name of Allah, the Most Gracious and Most Merciful. Praise be to Allah, the Cherisher and Sustainer of the Worlds. Most Gracious, Most Merciful. Master of the Day of Judgment. Thee we worship and thine aid we seek. Show us the straight path. The path of those upon whom Thou has given Thy Grace. (Of) those whose lot is not wrath, and who do not go astray.]

The Fatiha is recited at the opening of each unit of prayer, followed by the exclamation "Amen," (said by Sunni Muslims aloud if praying alone, but silently if an imam leads prayer); thereafter, the believer bows and prostrates himself. By means of the Fatiha and the *shahada,* even the non-Muslim can discern the Muslim's conception of the nature of Allah, and orientation to Him.

The powerful metaphor of the "straight path" conveys that one cannot simply *be* a Muslim, one must live as a Muslim. Only when traversing Allah's path can the qualities of leadership be created, nurtured, and demonstrated. And performance of prayer keeps one on the straight path.

The full meaning of the instrumentality of prayer cannot be fully conveyed here. The injunctions to pray even when one is sleepy, or ill and unable to assume the postures of prayer, are part of its discipline. That discipline and inherent repetition are also a force for unity. At prayer time all Muslims are facing Mecca and praying with precisely the same words to their Master, leaving behind their other daily tasks, worries, or preoccupations. Following the Fatiha, the bowing and prostrations in cycles, and the *tashahud*, the believer requests Allah's protection and may ask for blessings and favors for himself/herself, family members, or other Muslims.

While there are strong attractions for Muslim cadets in the sentiments of the Cadet Prayer, there are also negatives. For example, the very first words of the clearly supplicatory Cadet Prayer, "O God, Our Father," may even offend Muslims, for Allah cannot represent more than one entity, and has fathered none, nor is he a Father:

> Say: He is Allah. The One and Only.
> Allah, the Eternal, Absolute.
> He begetteth not, Nor is He begotten.
> And there is none Like unto Him. (*al-Ikhlas*, 112:1–4)[8]

Muslims also reject the concept of the Trinity, though Jesus is acknowledged as a Prophet. This significant difference between Christianity and Islam means that Muslims do not want to be treated as just another variety of Christian. Nor are all Muslims comfortable in Christian surroundings, or in being asked to perform grace at a meal when offered as a Christian prayer.

In any case, this preliminary identification in the Cadet Prayer is followed by the description of God as the Searcher of human hearts, one identical to an oft-repeated theme in the Qur'an:

> And know that Allah, Cometh in between a man
> And his heart. . . . (*al-Anfal*, 8:24)
> And verily thy Lord knoweth, All that their hearts do hide
> As well as all that, They reveal. (*al-Naml*, 27:74)

God's omnipotence and knowledge of the human heart inspire the reflexive feeling and knowledge of Him through human emotions:

> For Believers are those, Who, when Allah is mentioned,
> Feel a tremor in their hearts, And, when they hear
> His Signs rehearsed, Find their faith strengthened,
> And put [all] their trust, In their Lord. (*al-Anfal*, 8:2)

Indeed, Islam is sometimes called the "language of the heart" both in the mystical traditions of Islam known as Sufism, and in the modern-day populist evangelism of contemporary religious leaders like the Egyptian television preacher, `Amr Khaled. The most intense emphasis on emotional knowledge, or learning of the heart as opposed to intellectual reasoning, can be found in the tradition of Sufism and its poetry, or *inshad*,[9] which is performed in a prayer ritual called the *dhikr*, or remembrance of Allah.

As in the Cadet Prayer, "honest dealing" and "hatred of hypocrisy and pretense" are important precepts in Islam. Along with the acknowledgment of Allah comes the Muslim's duty to provide for those less fortunate, and to ensure that justice, `adala, prevails in the Muslim community. Usually defined as social justice, `adala can be required of the state, but it further implies honest dealing in business. Honest dealing was prized and ensured in the past through the office of the *muhtasib*, one who supervised the market weights, measurements, and exchanges, assuring they were fair. Truthfulness, sincerity, and generosity toward those less fortunate are all required on the straight path. For this reason, *zakat*, a portion of one's income and wealth to be given in charity and to support Islam, is another of the Five Pillars. *Zakat* is a necessary task for Muslims, not merely a suggested good practice or a virtuous deed. Though wealth comes from Allah, people must ensure the creation and preservation of justice and fair treatment.

Similarly, the sentiment of choosing "the harder right instead of the easier wrong" has echoes in the basic principles of Islamic law, *shari`a*. Qur'anic, Prophetic, and divine values inform the complex pattern of Islamic jurisprudence. Under this system, all actions, practices, things, etc. are classified as "permitted," "forbidden," or "neutral." Whether the Muslim has to choose a course in the context of Western values and laws that might not forbid the same activity or thing, or has to choose, as a leader, to pursue a more difficult, riskier course in a particular situation, the Muslim is guided by a principle called the *hisba*, related etymologically to the office of the *muhtasib* described above. The *hisba* states that the Muslim must command the good and forbid the evil:

> For He commands them [to do]
> what is just and forbids them what is evil;
> He allows them as lawful what is good
> and prohibits them what is bad.
> He releases them from their heavy burdens
> and from the yokes that are upon them. (*al-A'raf*, 7:157)

Political and social disagreements have arisen over how to gain compliance with the *hisba:* Should others enforce the *hisba* on their fellow Muslims, as in Saudi Arabia where voluntary morals police (the *mutawa`in*) claim a right to enforce the public practice of Islamic behavior? Or is individual responsibility the appropriate path, since Allah will on the Day of Judgment punish those who practice evil? Certain authorities like Yusuf al-Qaradawi, a moderate Islamist (or New Islamist[10]) and a widely popular preacher who is watched by millions of viewers on Al Jazeera television, interpret this verse in a less prescriptive way. Al-Qaradawi explains that because Islam is meant to be liberatory (releasing people from their burdens), one may choose the simpler or more flexible interpretation of Islamic rules when possible.[11] This interpretation can draw as well on a different Qur'anic idea, namely, that "there is no compulsion in religion" (al-Baqarah, 2:356), which is meant to remind Muslims that "they could not force another's heart to believe."

Leadership Values

The Cadet Prayer identifies values essential to military leaders. Nearly all of the qualities mentioned in the Cadet Prayer—courage, loyalty, nobility, eschewing moral compromise, fearlessness, reverence, friendship, fellowship, sympathy, and honor—are characteristics required of the Muslim leader. Many of these same qualities were prized prior to the rise of Islam, in the idealized behavior of tribal Arab warriors. In that age, the *jahiliyya* (the barbarous era before Islam), the warrior's loyalties were to blood relations—tribe and clan. With the arrival of Islam, loyalty was extended to the Muslim *ummah*, or community, instead of the individual's blood ties. However, these clan and tribal loyalties persisted and created different types of factional problems and cultural traditions for Muslims.

Today, the Muslim cadet's loyalties are to his country, the United States; the Constitution (the Army's central loyalty); the U.S. Army itself; and his fellow cadets. Beyond that, family and community are primary. It is a point of honor to Muslims in the military that their loyalty to the United States is as strong as that of any other religious or national group. Unfortunately, such loyalty has sometimes been challenged, as with the Japanese-American community during World War II. At the same time, their own co-religionists, families, or co-nationalists of origin may ask Muslims how they can support a war on Muslims, or how they can rationalize certain aspects of American foreign policy that are detrimental to their national community of origin.[12] At this particular time, Americans who emigrated from Afghanistan, Iran, Lebanon, and Iraq might all encounter such questions. Such inter-Muslim tensions make it increasingly clear that while the *ummah*, the international Muslim community, is a point of reference, the nation-state as locus of citizenship is far more compelling. This is, in fact, a primary complaint of Islamists, particularly militant ones. It means that military leaders, whether from Pakistan, Yemen, Egypt, or the United States, may share a religious framework of reference, but their political loyalties and concomitant military goals are defined by their active nationality.

There are subcurrents within the Cadet Prayer that will also resonate with Muslim listeners. For example, the appeal to "guard against flippancy and irreverence in the sacred things of life" is a sort of pledge to Muslims that during their development as leaders, such qualities as piety, morality, and dedication to a Higher Being are not to be mocked as they might be in other endeavors or environments.

The phrase "knows no fear when truth and right are in jeopardy" is a deeply attractive sentiment to Muslims. Fearlessness is further an essential quality in a military leader. Muslims are enjoined in the Qur'an to fear Allah, but not men and not Satan or his agents.[13] The fearlessness of a believer is different than that, say, of the pre-Islamic Arab with his conviction that fate ruled all, and would determine his life and death. Fear has specific purposes. Believers are tested by fear and hunger (al-Baqara, 2:155–7; al-Nahl 16:112). At the same time, fear of hellfire, of punishment after death, has a different purpose. This type of fear is to promote piety, prayer, and other religiously required activities. But fear should not produce frozen anxiety. According to the neo-Platonist ethicist Ahmad Ibn Muhammad (Ibn) Miskawayh, fear of death is an evil. Death is inevitable, and one can responsibly prepare for death by living ethically and observing Allah's commandments.[14]

The actions of others may also jeopardize pursuit of "truth and right." The early history of Islam concerns the persecution of a small group of individuals, the Prophet Muhammad (s.a.w.s.) and other early believers in Islam, who were not protected within the Meccan patronage system, and who threatened its polytheistic economic structure. The tribes congregated at Mecca and traded with each other during the months of peace, when no feuding could be conducted. The site of such trade and market activity was the pre-Islamic pantheon, under the guardianship of the Meccans. The early Muslims, who denied the status of gods and goddesses other than Allah in that pantheon, therefore fundamentally threatened Meccan prosperity and its power structure. In their aim for truth and a moral way of life, Muslims, despite their small numbers, defied the Meccans. Under persecution, it was impossible to lead that moral way of life unmolested, so they emigrated from Mecca with their Prophet to the city of Yathrib, thereafter known as Madinat al-Nabi (City of the Prophet), known today as Medina. This event, the founding of the Muslim community, was so important that all of Islamic history henceforth dated from the Emigration *(hijrah)*. The Meccans did not, however, leave them in peace. Consequently, the Prophet prepared his followers for battle against the Meccans and their allies, waging jihad in order to defend the practice of Islam through submission to the one Allah. Many Muslim war traditions, and the ethics of battle, or warfighting, are based on the history of these early struggles against the oppressors of the Muslims.[15]

Islamic views have, unfortunately, often been stereotyped and essentialized in Western news media and political discourse in the most negative possible terms. For instance, Muslims are described as fatalistic, mindless destructive forces. Some news media explanations of Islamist "extremism" have simplistically blamed it on socioeconomic deprivation. Some have claimed that mujahidin (those who engage in jihad) are fixated on the promise of virgins in Paradise.[16] Islam is described as being incapable of democracy and tolerance. Quite a few of the related debates revolve around the nature of political authority in the Muslim world, rather than religious or military leadership.

Throughout, Muslims are characterized in a binary manner as being either "militant" or "moderate."[17] Non-Muslims frequently define Muslim values as those of a civilizational Other. Muslims, however, commonly agree that their personal values are affected in a positive way by the Islamic faith and doctrine.

Leadership and Its Qualifications

Historical examples of Muslim leadership inevitably begin with the *sira*, or life story of the Prophet Muhammad (s.a.w.s). Discussions of the Prophet's personal qualities may be found in the *hadith* literature encompassing the Prophetic Tradition. It is the secondary source of jurisprudence following the Qur'an. The individual *hadiths* consist of short recountings of the Prophet's words, deeds, or habits, or those of his companions or, in some cases, his wives. One of the most frequently utilized collections for instructive purposes is the *Niche for Lamps* of al-Khatib al-Tabrizi (d. 1337),[18] which deals with political, economic, religious, and social issues. Much of the popular commentary and explanation of *hadith* is like a mirror reflecting the Prophet's life as the Beautiful Model for all other Muslims. This reverence for his leadership came from the multiplicity of Prophetic functions, including political leadership, legislation and mediation, spiritual leadership, and, in his military role, service as Commander of the Faithful, *amir al-mu'minin*. Following the Prophet Muhammad's death, the succeeding Caliphs relied on various generals to conduct their campaigns, and eventually on the office of the sultan and his generals. They all endeavored to emulate the *sunnah*, the "way" or example of the Prophet. The purpose of *hadith* literature was to demonstrate that *sunnah* in a detailed fashion.

When asked by `Ali ibn Abu Talib, the Prophet Muhammad's cousin and son-in-law, and one of the earliest Muslims, about the nature of his *sunnah*, the Prophet answered as follows:

> Knowledge is my capital/Intellect is the basis of my religion
> The love of Allah is my foundation/The yearning after Him is my vessel
> Remembering[19] Him is my companion/Confidence in Him is my treasure
> Science is my armament/Patience is my garb
> Satisfaction is my booty[20]/Certitude is my nourishment
> Truth is my intercessor[21]/Obedience is my love
> And striving along the straight path of Allah is my ethics,
> And the delight of my heart lies in prayer.

It is instructive that he speaks here of morality, knowledge, and love of God; consequently, these values form the very basis of what leadership—military, political, or religious—should be. Commentators emphasize the Prophet's compassion and kindness, and also that he was resolute once a decision was taken. Further, `Ali ibn Abu Talib himself explains that a leader cannot be greedy, ignorant, unjust, or harsh. He cannot "fear states," i.e., other nations, accept bribes, or ignore the Prophet's *sunnah* or the *shari`ah* (Islamic law).[22]

Warfare and Leadership

In Islam, the function and history of the military, indeed of warfare itself, is fighting "on the path of God," as jihad or rightful struggle.[23] This concept is often considered by Christians and Jews to be at odds with their own present-day orientation. If we consider the many wars of Christendom, including the Crusades, and the military and political struggles of the Jewish people in history, parallels with jihad can be discerned. It is useful to remember that the early battles of the Muslims were conceived not only as a struggle for religious freedom, but also as a battle to the death in what was a civil war. Though many followed the new path led by the Prophet, some family members remained loyal to the pre-Islamic Meccan aristocracy. Then, after the Muslim community was finally established at Medina, a second period of civil war followed in which Muslims were pitted against Muslims; this encompassed the first and second *fitnas,* or schisms, in which the two branches of the faithful fought for ascendancy.[24] This type of conflict was proscribed, though in actuality it occurred again and again in history. Later on, as the Muslim empire expanded, the political leadership was deeply concerned with the question of their military's loyalties. Different solutions were attempted, but the most successful were meritocratic military systems. For example, in the "volunteer" army of the Ummayad period Syrian troops held fierce loyalties to the Caliph. These troops clashed with others from different regions, but they were essential in suppressing the `Alids (the followers of `Ali who opposed the Ummayad Caliphs).

As the Islamic empire divided, it became preferable, on both economic and strategic grounds, to man military forces from prisoners or military slaves who might not have such strong regional or tribal affiliations. Consequently, the *ghulat* (slave) armies of the Safavids, whose most attractive characteristics were their alternate ethnicity; the mamluks of Cairo, Damascus, Baghdad, and other large cities; and the Janissaries of the Ottoman sultans, were composed of such elements. These were meritocratic forces. At the same time, the military was frequently linked with the mystical Sufi orders. Their dervishes, noted for such devotional exercises as bodily movements leading to a trance-like state, were called on in Salah al-Din's campaigns against the Crusaders, staved off Portuguese inroads in the Maghreb, and participated in the siege of Constantinople.[25]

Salah al-Din, the founder of the Ayyubid dynasty, provided another exemplary model of military leadership for Muslims. Of Kurdish rather than Arab origin, he served at first as the lieutenant in Egypt of Nur al-Din, the Zanjid.[26] His daring expansive and defensive policies were effective, leaving their imprint on the area in a chain of Ayyubid fortresses extending from Aleppo, Damascus, and Bosra in Syria all the way to Jerusalem, the Sinai, and Cairo.

Salah al-Din gained the admiration of his adversary, Richard Coeur de Lion, and a series of stories about their chivalrous behavior is contained within the larger framing of Salah al-Din's defense of the Islamic world from European conquest.[27]

Muslim political leadership (like its Christian counterpart) claimed religious legitimacy in the past, indeed infallibility, and that claim was put to the test on the battlefield, for instance, in the long war between the Ottoman and Safavid empires. Though only Allah is Infallible, the political leaders' claims to infallibility seem to have been a universal phenomenon. The link between religious and political authority is still a powerful force in the Muslim world today. Nevertheless, claims of infallibility faded as modern professional armies developed since the 19th century. In Muslim countries, the military has played and continues to play a very important role in politics in Egypt, Syria, Algeria, Jordan, Tunisia, the Sudan, Turkey, Pakistan, and other nations.

Wanton killing and violence are anathema in Islam, hence the embarrassment and deep concerns that Muslims feel at being identified with terrorism today, or with the militant and uncompromising brand of jihadi-salafism that has emerged in the Muslim world through groups such as the recently-killed Abu Mus`ab al-Zarqawi's al-Qa'ida fi Bilad al-Rafidhayn.[28] The guiding principles of warfare and truces with the enemy for Muslims do not allow for the kind of unspeakable barbarity and terrorist outrages practiced by extremist groups.[29] I've already alluded to the fact that Christianity has an equally bloody history—wars between sects, the conquest of the New World, the Inquisition, and the inhumane treatment of the Jews. It is fair to say that if one looks closely at the three monotheistic faiths, both militaristic and peace-loving traditions may be found.[30]

Muslims in America

Being a Muslim and practicing Islam in America does not present an exact parallel to the Christian or Jewish experiences in the practice of their faiths. In discussing West Point's ideals of faith, patriotism, and service through an Islamic lens, it seems insufficient to remark on the congruence of the Cadet Prayer with Islamic thought in the abstract. It is important to ask in what way these ideals affect contemporary Muslims in the U.S. military and what kind of challenges face today's Muslim cadets.

We do not know exactly how many Muslims live in America. Estimates range from 1.1 million to over 7 million.[31] The Muslim community in America is comprised of Muslims who attend mosques and others who are unaffiliated, or "unmosqued." It should be remembered that women are not required to attend mosques, and that, except within the more recent Islamist trend toward sahwa (awakening), mosques are not the center of social life in the Islamic world as is frequently the case in the West. Men should attend Friday prayer, but in the United States such impediments as national, linguistic, and sectarian divisions; travel time; and work schedules might discourage Muslims from participating in their local *masjid* or mosque. With the rise in salafism, a term encompassing both Islamic reform and the groups aiming at a stricter cleansing of Islamic tradition, Sunni prayer leaders have discouraged Shi`a Muslims from participating in some local mosques.[32] Different sects and national groups have tended to group separately in prayer facilities, except where specific mosques make an effort to be inclusive (for instance, in Quincy, Massachusetts, or at the Islamic Center of Los Angeles). Even with such efforts, however, mosque communities can split or express tensions, as in Cleveland, Ohio, basically along the lines of Indian and Pakistani versus Palestinian members.[33]

The uncertain size of the Muslim population is largely due to a sizable, but indeterminate convert population. Data for immigrants exists, but the numbers of converts are unrecorded within census data, as are the numbers of Muslim-American children of each group. Within the military today, estimates of Muslims range from 4,500 to 15,000. A probable reason for that wide range is that individuals are reluctant to reveal their religion if it might lead to discrimination. In 2005, at the U.S. Naval Academy, there were 10 Muslim midshipmen out of 4,200. There are nine Muslim International Fellows at the Army War College in a class (2007) consisting of 348 officers. In 2005–2006, there were 21 Muslim students at West Point, and that included international cadets. Clearly, Muslims are a minority in the nation and the military, and a tiny minority at the service academies.

Life and faith in the United States for Muslims are difficult on several levels. Outside of major cosmopolitan urban areas, Americans express high levels of xenophobia towards immigrants. These fearful attitudes wax and wane in response to local economic pressures as much as by international events. National catastrophes like the assault on the World Trade Center and the Pentagon on September 11, 2001, will of course leave a more lasting impression.

It may be difficult to acknowledge that America the melting pot has a very distinctly Christian culture in broad swaths of the country, and that non-Christians encounter discrimination, or at least difficulties, in connecting with those outside their faith. Non-Christians must adapt to a Christian-based working environment beginning with an employment calendar determined by the Christian Sabbath and holidays. Muslims usually have to protest to employers, or work for each other, in order to observe their own religious requirements such as the daily prayer schedule, dietary restrictions, and fasting during Ramadan. Similar problems face Muslims attending American schools. Today, more often than not, accommodations that involve compromises on both sides may be made in public or federal settings, but more rarely in the private sector. Intense pressures are felt by Muslim families who try to encourage Islamic practices and attitudes in their children, who are surrounded by peers often reflecting the antithesis of their families' own values. Some American Muslims try to uphold their religious customs as scrupulously as if they were in their homeland, but by and large that is nearly impossible.

Moreover, immigration, which has taken place in distinctly different historical waves, did not provide Muslims with guidelines about how to live "in" their faith outside of a Muslim environment.[34]

The military, as a federal entity, has obligations to racial and religious minorities, at least to the extent of ensuring nondiscrimination, equal opportunity in recruitment, retention, and promotion, and the opportunity for military personnel to practice their faith. For Muslims, this latter obligation entails accommodating designated prayer times, providing appropriate venues for prayer, allowing participation in ritual fasting, and cooperating with dietary restrictions. Businesses, public schools, universities, and the military have often not provided the necessary practical assistance and cooperation, yet claimed that students, workers, and soldiers were free to practice their religion without discrimination.

Within the military and other federal entities, there have been wide variations in the degree of accommodation to the special religious needs of Muslims. The typical focus has been on accommodating a student population or the enlisted soldiers rather than staff, faculty, or civilian employees. In contrast, one notices frequent prayer breakfast meetings, Bible study groups, and other types of activities for all groups of Christians at these facilities. As one might expect, greater and more frequent accommodation has been made for local Muslim citizens when American military facilities are located in Muslim countries, as in Iraq. Prayer rooms were provided for Kosovar refugees at Fort Dix, New Jersey, during Operation Provide Rescue. Perhaps closer proximity to Muslims in Afghanistan, Iraq, and elsewhere is helping to advance changes in the United States as well. Here, military educational facilities are transitioning from a situation in which there were no Muslims, to one where a few international cadets or officers were Muslims, to the present one where many Americans, including military members and civilian employees, might be Muslim. Most Army facilities currently appear to be between that second and third stage.

The Cadet Prayer acknowledges God even outside of worship situations. Finding or creating a place for Muslims to worship remains a hurdle in some military facilities. Nevertheless, Fort Leavenworth, Kansas, provides a Muslim prayer room. Fort Bragg, North Carolina, has made arrangements for Muslim prayers,[35] and Muslims at the Pentagon gather for a Friday prayer service. Moreover, the Pentagon group has now offered its second annual iftar reception, the traditional meal breaking the day's fast during Ramadan. While there are only two Muslim Army chaplains (and two Muslim Navy chaplains) to date,[36] there are a number of civilian imams who serve prayer facilities.

One problem is that Muslim mosques may not exist in towns close to military installations. Thus, without prayer space on campus or barracks, Muslims can't easily fulfill one of their basic duties. The requirements of prayer as well as Muslim traditions about their prayer spaces are not well understood. In years past, at the Army War College Muslims were invited to pray in the Christian chapel complex, which is located in an area some distance from the instructional facilities. Students do not have permission to leave their classes for prayer, meaning that only during a limited part of the year do noon prayers fall during the lunch break. There have been no Friday prayer services. Also, it perhaps was not realized that Muslims might be reluctant to worship in buildings expressly set aside for Christian study and worship. Later, a very small room in the War College library was set aside for prayer. Since the two genders cannot pray together in such a confined space, however, the practical consequence was to exclude either men or women. Those responsible for providing appropriate space might have assumed that Muslims use the space for individual meditation, perhaps not understanding the requirement of established prayer times. A larger temporary space is now in use, giving Muslims a sense that the institution cares about their needs.

At West Point in 2005, Muslims shared a building with Christian groups. The arrangement meant that the space had to be vacuumed for each use by Muslims since non-Muslims using the space at any prior time wore shoes. Muslims remove footwear in their prayer spaces since they pray on the floor surface itself, which must be clean. In October of 2006, the Academy opened a new prayer space that could accommodate an increase in Muslim cadets up to 32. The presence of an imam and a regular Friday service, like that at the Pentagon, now provides a sense of community.

When trying to negotiate such issues as group prayers, dietary alternatives, or differing schedules, Muslim cadets have to choose between silence, or a kind of advocacy and persistence that is quite difficult to sustain, even for established career professionals. The Global War on Terror has sparked a great interest in all that is connected with Islam, which by and large is very poorly understood and elucidated within the military. That makes Muslims' knowledge of Islam both suspect and valuable. To their credit, the military leadership has recognized the needs and value of Muslims in the military at some locations, but much more remains to be done.

Since the events of September 11, 2001, prejudice against Muslims has heightened in the United States in general, as has Muslim defensiveness concerning their faith, and the role of violence in what Americans call "fundamentalist" Islam. In the abstract, Americans perceive Islam more negatively than they do flesh-and-blood Muslim-Americans. Views about Islam and Muslim-Americans improved somewhat from 2001 to 2005. A 2005 survey by the Pew Research Center and the Pew Forum on Religion and Public Life showed that a majority of Americans, 55 percent, regard Muslim-Americans favorably, although 59 percent feel that Islam is very different from their own religion.[37] With the heightened red alert in August 2006, increasing restrictions on air travelers, and rising prices at the gas pump, however, it has become quite difficult to know whether American perceptions of Muslims will continue to improve.

Muslims have a right to be protected from discrimination, as we observed earlier, and their small but increasing numbers in the military present other challenges besides that of changing the institution so as to accommodate

Muslim worship. The most pressing of these challenges is the need to respond to ignorance, and in some cases bigotry, with regard to Islam and Muslims. For example, Muslim students report feeling ill at ease with peers' alcohol use and discussion of dating. They are not unique in such misgivings; some Christian students face similar issues. Fasting during Ramadan is quite difficult since the students' physical education or team sports commitments, as well as course papers and examinations, are scheduled according to the Western calendar year. At West Point, Muslim cadets faced with such challenges try to meet a higher level of moral discipline. This experience probably adds to their overall moral training in an important way—sacrifice for one's fundamental beliefs is not a bad thing.

Another challenge for Muslim as well as Arab cadets hinges more on national or ethnic identity than on religious identity. There are Muslim-Americans who are not, or at least were not, primarily concerned with their religious identity. At West Point, however, as part of a unique self-selected, highly motivated student pool, Muslim (and Arab) cadets believe that because of their origins, or their parents' origins, their classmates often hold them responsible for faraway events, for example, jihadist beheadings, Sunni-Shi`i conflict in Iraq, and violent responses to the Danish cartoons published in European newspapers in 2006. Trying their best, given their very different backgrounds and levels of knowledge, they tried to enlighten their peers. The camaraderie growing out of the Academy's developmental activities is at risk when, as during the Danish cartoon incident, Muslim cadets feel compelled to respond to unfounded accusations and slurs circulated by e-mail. With the overall context of U.S. foreign policy in the Middle East being so incredibly complex, serving as religious and political ambassadors is beyond the abilities of Muslim cadets. They are themselves acclimating to their military environment and learning about themselves as Americans, human beings, and Muslims. They are not experts on the Muslim world nor on their families' countries of origin, and they are horrified by acts of violence committed in the name of Islam. Often they try to clarify the misinterpretation of Islamic doctrines by resorting to arguments for inclusion and multiculturalism that have until recently represented America positively. But they, like foreign students elsewhere in our military establishments, schools, and training centers, are not subject-matter experts. On the other hand, their efforts, whatever they may be, probably enhance the very same self-learning process that was mentioned a few lines above.

Arabs in America, who are only a small fraction of the world's Muslim population, have encountered stereotyping for some time. This impacts Christian as well as Muslim Arabs. In response to 9/11, several hundred formed a group called the Association of Patriotic Arab Americans in the Military. They speak about their identity and try to educate military audiences.[38] Another group, Muslims in the Military, was established well before 9/11, and there is now an American-Muslim Armed Forces and Veterans Affairs Council. These organizations do not seek to separate their members from military culture; rather, they seek to enrich military culture. The only parallel to such organizations at West Point is the fraternization among Muslim and international cadets. They are, on the one hand, very much like other international students in the United States, sometimes bonding due to shared schedules, hardships, and experiences. The option of a more robust faith community might help cadets of minority faiths, including Muslim, to recognize that the Academy is vitally interested in their spiritual development and its contribution to their total development as future officers of character.

Conclusion

Ultimately, Muslim cadets are sociologically more similar to their cadet peers of other religions than to many other Muslims within the United States or overseas. Their youth and progress on the path of individual growth and development toward being an officer, their patriotism, and their idealism bind them in a special relationship with other cadets. The significance of the moral precepts of the Cadet Prayer, like the steps already taken to make it possible to practice Islam at West Point, is that they encourage moral development—the pursuit of the best, the truest, the most honest and spiritual. And all of this is congruent with the Islamic faith and its values.

Cadets may or may not know much about the Islamic tradition of just war, the major figures in Islamic history, or the philosophical or theological debates within Islam. But the Cadet Prayer suggests that there is a space for their education in these matters that, along with their general developmental pursuits, will help them to be better persons, soldiers, and Muslims. The awkwardness of being a Muslim in America and in the military at this time is actually a blessing in disguise for those who would become leaders of moral character, since it balances the critical scrutiny of their faith and background against their own quests for knowledge, faith, and understanding.

Notes

1. Fariduddin Attar, *Muslim Saints and Mystics: Episodes from the Tadhkirat al-awliya,* trans. and ed. A.J. Arberry (London: Arkana, 1966), 19-25 and 39-51.
2. Ibid., 62-79.
3. S.a.w.s. stands for *salat 'alayhu wa-salam,* blessings and peace be upon him.
4. *Al-Kafi,* vol. V. Scholars also explain "there shall be no monkery" [in Islam]. See Ayatullah Murtada Mutahhari, "Distinguishing Features of Islam," and Annemarie Schimmel, *And Muhammad Is His Messenger: The Veneration of the Prophet in Islamic Piety* (Chapel Hill, NC, and London: University of North Carolina Press, 1985), 50.
5. *Zakat* in support of Islam could mean payment to support a mosque, institute of Islamic learning, publications, or funds necessary to support *da`wa,* the mission or spreading of Islam. In addition to being an alms tax and charity, it is justness, integrity, and the principle of recycling wealth.

6. Fazlur Rahman, *Major Themes of the Qur'an* (Minneapolis, MN: Bibliotheca Islamica, 1980).

7. Seyyed Hossein Nasr, *Islamic Art and Spirituality* (Albany: State University of New York Press, 1987).

8. Unless otherwise indicated, the English "interpretation" (the Qur'an may not be translated) is from *The Meaning of the Holy Qur'an,* trans. and ed. Abdullah Yusuf Ali (Beltsville, MD: Amana Publications, 1422/2001).

9. Michael Friskkopf, "Tarab in the Mystic Sufi Chant of Egypt," in Sherifa Zuhur, ed., *Colors of Enchantment: Visual and Performing Arts of the Middle East* (New York and Cairo: American University in Cairo Press, 2001).

10. According to Raymond Baker, *Islam Without Fear: Egypt and the New Islamists* (Cambridge, MA: Harvard University Press, 2003).

11. Yusuf al-Qaradawi is one of the most influential Islamist moderate figures. He resides in Qatar and turned down an offer to become the Muslim Brotherhood's General Guide in 2004. He is the author of some 50 books.

12. Andrea Elliott, "Sorting Out Life for Muslim Marines," *New York Times,* August 7, 2006.

13. Therefore fear not men, But fear Me and sell not My Signs for a miserable price (*al-Ma'ida,* 5:44); "It is only the Evil One [Satan] that suggests to you the fear of his votaries: Be ye not afraid of them, but fear Me, If ye have Faith (*al-`Imran,* 3:175); "But it is for those, Who fear their Lord, That lofty mansions, One above another, Have been built" (*al-Zumar,* 39:20).

14. Akbar Muhammad, "Fear in the Islamic Tradition," *Yale Journal for Humanities in Medicine* (2004).

15. Youssef H. Aboul-Enein and Sherifa Zuhur, *Islamic Rulings on Warfare* (Carlisle Barracks, PA: U.S. Army War College: Strategic Studies Institute, 2004).

16. Actually, the pleasures of paradise pertain to Muslims in general, excluding sinners. While the Qur'an does not specify a number of "dark-eyed maidens" (assumed to be virgins), hadith sources promise there will be 72. Muslims feel that emphasis on this idea as a motivation for jihad trivializes their belief, both in paradise and in pursuing the straight path in their lifetime.

17. As in Akbar Ahmed, "Islam's Crossroads-Islamic Leadership," accessed at http://www.islamfortoday.com/akbar02.htm.

18. The topics of this collection are discussed in Carl Ernst, *Following Muhammad: Rethinking Islam in the Contemporary World* (Chapel Hill, NC, and London: University of North Carolina Press, 2003), 112-115. Among the other most frequently used *hadith* collections are those of al-Bukhari and Muslim.

19. A reference to the ritual of *dhikr,* which means remembrance.

20. Islamic armies shared in the booty. At times, controversy arose over shares, pitting earlier converts to Islam against later ones.

21. A Prophet, or `Ali ibn Abi Talib as an Imam, according to the Shi`a sect, can intervene (*shafa`a*/intercession) with Allah for the believer on the Day of Judgment. See Sherifa Zuhur, "Intercession (*Shafa`a*)," *Dictionary of the History of Ideas* (New York: Charles Scribner's Sons, 2004).

22. *Nahj al-Balagha* (Sermons of `Ali ibn Abi Talib), p. 50, as cited by Imam Khomeini, "Islamic Government," in *Islam and Revolution: Writings and Declarations of Imam Khomeini,* ed. Hamid Algar (Berkeley, CA: Mizan Press, 1981), 67.

23. As opposed to mere *qital,* killing.

24. *Fitna* means a schism or split within the ummah, or in society. These schisms led eventually to the doctrinal divide between Shi`i and Sunni Islam.
25. J. Spencer Trimingham, *The Sufi Orders in Islam* (Oxford: Oxford University Press, 1971, 1998), 240-241.
26. Many English language histories contain only brief information about Salah al-Din. See, for instance, Marshall Hodgson, *The Venture of Islam,* Vol. III *The Establishment of an International Civilization* (Chicago, IL: University of Chicago, 1974), 266-268.
27. Salah al-Din's restoration of Egypt to Sunni Islam (the preceding Fatimid dynasty was governed by Isma`ili Shi`a) is an idea emphasized in contemporary historiography.
28. Aboul-Enein and Zuhur, *Islamic Rulings on Warfare;* Fawaz Gerges, *Journey of the Jihadist: Inside Muslim Militancy* (Orlando, FL: Harcourt Inc. 2006).
29. Ibid.
30. Karen Armstrong in a discussion based on her book, *The Battle for God* (New York: Albert Knopf, 2000) at Dickinson College, Carlisle, PA, April 25, 2005.
31. Some of these estimates are: 7.0 million (2004), Council on American-Islamic Relations; 2.8 million (2001), American Jewish Committee; 4.1 million (2001, 2004), *Britannica Book of the Year.*
32. In larger American cities, Muslims will have a choice of mosques established for Nation of Islam members, usually for groups of mixed backgrounds, and sometimes for Shi`i or Ahmadi groups. There are even Sufi orders with their own teaching and worship centers. However, in smaller cities or towns, it has been more common for prayer facilities to be inclusive.
33. In this unfortunate incident, the imam of the largest mosque in Cleveland was indicted under charges of promoting terrorism a decade earlier. The mosque split appeared as one group supported their co-nationalist, the Palestinian imam, and others sided with Indian and Pakistani members of the mosque board until the indictment proceeded.
34. Yvonne Yazbeck Haddad, *Not Quite American? The Shaping of Arab and Muslim Identity in the United States* (Waco, TX: Baylor University Press, 2004).
35. Lloyd J. Matthews, "Introduction: Primer on Future Recruit Diversity," in *Population Diversity and the U.S. Army,* eds. Lloyd J. Matthews and Tinaz Pavri (Carlisle Barracks, PA: U.S. Army War College, Strategic Studies Institute, 1999), 3.
36. Linda D. Kozaryn, "Muslim Troops Highlight National Diversity," *Armed Forces Press Service,* October 19, 2006.
37. This was a telephone interview survey conducted with 2000 American adults. "Views of Muslim-Americans Hold Steady After London Bombings," Pew Research Center for the People and the Press, July 26, 2005.
38. "Arab-Americans in Military Battle Against Stereotyping," *Association of Patriotic Arab Americans in the Military.* Accessed at http://www.patriotic apaam.org, March 7, 2003.

10 | Four Sermons on the Cadet Prayer: The Protestant Perspective

*John J. Cook III and
James R. Carter*

Introduction

Taking their worldview from the Word of God, Protestant Christians understand leadership and leader development in the context of God's eternal plan and purpose for his creation. God has created humankind to reveal his glory here on earth. Giving us dominion over everything he has created, the Sovereign Ruler of the universe is the author and giver of all authority on earth, both individual and state. All leaders to whom he grants authority, therefore, are accountable and responsible to be good stewards of that authority. After his comprehensive search for the purpose and meaning of life, King Solomon came to the following conclusion: "Fear God and keep His commandments, for this is the whole duty of man. For God will bring every deed into judgment, including every hidden thing, whether it is good or evil" (Ecclesiastes 12:13–14). The Christian officer, then, is a man with authority who understands that he is also a man under the supreme authority of God, and that he must lead accordingly.

Having received their salvation solely through the atoning work of Jesus Christ, Protestant Christians rightly understand that their lives are not to be lived for themselves but for the One who both created and redeemed them for his service and for his glory. Christ is not only their Redeemer but the epitome of leadership. His life of love and his example of selfless service are the model for all human leaders in any capacity. It is Christ's likeness to which God desires to conform every Christian. For Protestant Christians, his example and his teachings are the basis for leader development.

Correctly understanding their role in God's plan and purpose, then, Protestant Christian officers do not separate their faith and their profession. They understand that all of life belongs to God and that each day is a gift from God to be lived for His glory. Contrary to the thinking of some that faith and the profession of arms are mutually exclusive, the Christian officer cannot be true to himself or to his God unless he integrates the two in the performance of his duty. Duty within the profession of arms is secondary to and subsumed within the Christian leader's duty to God. The shared professional identity and the principles of officership[1] are remarkably consistent with the values of the Christian faith, so much so, in fact, that the Christian leader living out his faith in obedience to Biblical teaching will naturally lead a life that exemplifies all of the Army's professional ethos.

This does not mean the Christian officer should wear his religion on his sleeve. That is neither necessary nor desirable. Recent examples of senior Army officers unintentionally creating the perception that their personal faith is preferred over others, or that officers and soldiers under their authority might be disadvantaged if they do not share that particular faith, have underscored once again the need for the military profession to ensure that all faiths are respected equally and that all uniformed personnel are free to practice whatever religious faith they desire or no religion at all. That is certainly the case here at West Point.

At the same time, the Christian officer need not hide the fact that he is a Christian or the fact that his personal life as well as his duty performance are guided by his Christian faith and informed by Biblical principles. Being true to his own worldview and beliefs, as well as to the Army's ethos, is what makes him a man of integrity and a leader of character.[2]

In remarkable congruity with West Point's approach to leader development in the Cadet Leader Development System (CLDS), John Maxwell in his book *Developing the Leader Within You* identifies integrity as the most important ingredient of leadership:

> A person with integrity does not have divided loyalties (that's duplicity), nor is he or she merely pretending (that's hypocrisy). People with integrity are "whole" people; they can be identified by their single-mindedness. People with integrity have nothing to hide and nothing to fear. Their lives are open books. V. Gilbert Beers says, "A person of integrity is one who has established a system of values against which all of life is judged."
>
> Integrity is not what we do so much as who we are. And who we are, in turn, determines what we do. Our system of values is so much a part of us we cannot separate it from ourselves. It becomes the navigating system that guides us. It establishes priorities in our lives and judges what we will accept or reject.
>
> We are all faced with conflicting desires. No one, no matter how "spiritual," can avoid this battle. Integrity is the factor that determines which one will prevail. We struggle daily with situations that demand decisions between what we want to do and what we ought to do. Integrity establishes the ground rules for resolving these tensions. It determines who we are and how we will respond before the conflict even appears. Integrity welds what we say, think, and do into a whole person so that permission is never granted for one of these to be out of sync.[3]

The author of the Cadet Prayer, Chaplain Clayton Wheat, the United States Military Academy Chaplain from 1918 to 1926, understood the importance of faith in developing the wholeness, or the integrity, of leaders of character and the importance for cadets preparing to be officers to integrate their faith with their future profession. His purpose in writing the prayer was to help facilitate that human development and integration:

> I have been asked to say a word about the motives which prompted me to compose the Cadet Prayer. When I came to the Academy in 1918 as Chaplain I was straightaway impressed with the high ideals and deep-rooted principles which have always governed and determined the action and life of the Corps. Corps honor, corps justice, corps integrity, corps loyalty, corps trustworthiness, are instinctive group virtues which have long dominated the action of the Corps, even though the individual member may at times have failed in his effort to live up to those ideals.
>
> I have found some of these virtues and ideals set forth in the Alma Mater and The Corps—songs that are cherished by the cadet—*but I found no expression of the Corps virtues in a form which the cadet might use in voicing his desire to attain those qualities and standards which the Corps expects and demands of its members.*
>
> In the Cadet Prayer, I attempted to compose a petition which would set forth in simple phrases the aspirations of young men who earnestly desired to realize in their own lives the ideals and principles which have long been fostered in the Corps.

As we seek to develop leaders of character at West Point within the Protestant view of the Christian faith, we pray in the Cadet Prayer each Sunday that God will "strengthen and increase our admiration for honest dealing and clean thinking," that we will "choose the harder right instead of the easier wrong," that we will "never be content with a half-truth when the whole can be won," and that we will "maintain the honor of the Corps untarnished and unsullied, *showing forth in our lives the ideals of West Point in doing our duty to God and to our Country*" (italics added by author). These moral precepts as contained in the Cadet Prayer are at the very core of what it means to be a leader of character. Character is about more than what we do. It is about who we are on the inside. As noted earlier, it is about integrity, that is, consistency between what is seen on the outside and what is unseen on the inside. Our character stems from what lies within us: the attitudes of our heart, the thoughts of our mind, and the values we hold dear. For the Christian officer, all of these are shaped by his Christian faith.

The chaplains at West Point understand that all cadets will naturally continue their search for moral meaning during their four years at the Academy. The chaplains are thus committed not only to facilitating that search for all cadets, but to helping Christian cadets mature in their chosen faith and understand the importance of integrating their faith and their profession as future officers. It is absolutely essential to their professional and spiritual development, because it will make them both a better Christian and a better officer. In addition to including the Cadet Prayer every Sunday as an integral part of the worship service at the Cadet Chapel, the chaplains periodically preach a series of expository sermons based on the Cadet Prayer that teach the Biblical principles and moral precepts upon which the prayer is built. Though not written exclusively for those of the Christian faith, the prayer is clearly grounded in and consistent with the teachings of the Protestant view of the Word of God.

What follows in this chapter are four sermons out of a series of 15 that were preached at the Cadet Chapel in the fall semester of 2001. They highlight four of the moral precepts contained within the Cadet Prayer as understood and interpreted from a Protestant perspective.

Living Above the Common Level of Life—John J. Cook III[4]

As a prisoner for the Lord, then, I urge you to live a life worthy of the calling you have received. Be completely humble and gentle; be patient, bearing with one another in love. Make every effort to keep the unity of the Spirit through the bond of peace. There is one body and one Spirit—just as you were called to one hope when you were called—one Lord, one faith, one baptism; one God and Father of all, who is over all and through all and in all. But to each one of us grace has been given as Christ apportioned it.... It was he who gave some to be apostles, some to be prophets, some to be evangelists, and some to be pastors and teachers, to prepare God's people for works of service, so that the body of Christ may be built up until we all reach unity in the faith and in the knowledge of the Son of God and become mature, attaining to the whole measure of the fullness of Christ. Then we will no longer be infants, tossed back and forth by the waves, and blown here and there by every wind of teaching and by the cunning and craftiness of men in their deceitful scheming. Instead, speaking the truth in love, we will in all things grow up into him who is the Head, that is, Christ. From him the whole body, joined and held together by every supporting ligament, grows and builds itself up in love, as each part does its work.

—Ephesians 4:1–7, 11–16

In the inspiring book *Rising Above the Crowd,* Zig Ziglar tells the story of Ben Hooper:

When Ben Hooper was born many years ago in the foothills of east Tennessee, little boys and girls like Ben who were born to unwed mothers were ostracized and treated terribly. By the time he was three years old, the other children would scarcely play with him. Parents were saying idiotic things like, "What's a boy like that doing playing with our children?" as if the child had anything at all to do with his own birth.

Saturday was the toughest day of all. Ben's mom would take him down to the little general store to buy their supplies for the week. Invariably, the other parents in the store would make caustic remarks just loudly enough for both mother and child to hear, comments like, "Did you ever figure out who his daddy is?" What a tough, tough childhood.

In those days there was no kindergarten. So, at age six, little Ben entered the first grade. He was given his own desk, as were all the children. At recess, he stayed at that little desk and studied because none of the other children would play with him. At noon, little Ben could be found eating his sack lunch all alone. The happy chatter of the children who shunned him was barely audible from where he sat. It was a big event when anything changed in the foothills of east Tennessee, and when little Ben was twelve years old a new preacher came to pastor at the little church in Ben's town. Almost immediately, little Ben started hearing exciting things about him—about how loving and nonjudgmental he was. How he accepted people just as they were, and when he was with them, he made them feel like the most important people in the world. Reportedly, the preacher had charisma. When he walked into a group of any size, anywhere, the entire complexion of that group changed. Their smiles broadened, their laughter increased, and their spirits rose.

One Sunday, though he had never been to church a day in his life, little Ben Hooper decided he was going to go and hear the preacher. He got there late and he left early because he did not want to attract any attention, but he liked what he heard. For the first time in that young boy's life, he caught just a glimmer of hope.

Ben was back in church the next Sunday and the next and the next. He always got there late and always left early, but his hope was building each Sunday. On about the sixth or seventh Sunday the message was so moving and exciting that Ben became absolutely enthralled with it. It was almost as if there were a sign behind the preacher's head that read, "For you, little Ben Hooper of unknown parentage, there is hope!" Ben got so wrapped up in the message, he forgot about the time and didn't notice that a number of people had come in after he had taken his seat.

Suddenly, the service was over. Ben very quickly stood up to leave as he had in all the Sundays past, but the aisles were clogged with people and he could not run out. As he was working his way through the crowd, he felt a hand on his shoulder. He turned around and looked up right into the eyes of the young preacher who asked him a question that had been on the mind of every person there for the last twelve years: "Whose boy are you?"

Instantly, the church grew deathly quiet. Slowly, a smile started to spread across the face of the young preacher until it broke into a huge grin, and he exclaimed, "Oh! I know whose boy you are! Why, the family resemblance is unmistakable. You are a child of God!" And with that the young preacher swatted him across the rear and said, "That's quite a heritage you've got there, boy! Now, go and see to it that you live up to it."[5]

I can remember my dad talking to me when I was a young boy about how my behavior reflected not just on me, but on our family. When I became a Christian at the age of nine, he emphasized that my actions now reflected as well on my Lord and Savior, Jesus Christ. Those conversations with my dad had a profound impact on me, helping to shape my conduct as I was growing up. Like Ben Hooper, I had a heritage to live up to.

When I later received my call to the ministry, I realized how important my conduct was, not just for my reputation, but for the reputation of the church and my Savior whom I proclaim as my Lord. I knew that my life had to be lived to a higher standard. What I want to share with all of you in this sermon is that the calling to live above the common level of life, to live to a higher standard than the rest of the world, is not unique to ministers. All of us have been called to a life of holiness.

God told the entire assembly of Israel in Leviticus 19:2, "Be holy because I, the Lord your God, am holy." Holy simply means set apart, different, above the common level of life. What we find in both the Old and the New Testaments is that the people of God are called upon to display God's holy character in their lives. God's Word instructs us repeatedly, particularly in the New Testament, to live a life worthy of God and of our relationship with him.

I want to quote four of these scriptures, one of which comes from our text. From prison, Paul wrote these words to the Philippians: "Whatever happens, conduct yourselves in a manner worthy of the gospel of Christ" (1:27). He went on to say that whether he was able to get out of prison and see them again, or whether he was only able to hear about them, he wanted to know that they were living lives in a manner worthy of the gospel of Christ. The same applies to us—whether anyone we know is watching us or not. Whether it is Sunday morning or Saturday night, we need to conduct our lives in a manner worthy of the gospel of Jesus Christ.

We read the same admonition in Colossians 1:10: "And we pray this in order that you may live a life worthy of the Lord and may please him in every way." First Thessalonians 2:12 adds, "Encouraging, comforting, and urging you to live lives worthy of God, who calls you into his kingdom and glory." From our text in Ephesians 4:1, Paul says, "As a prisoner for the Lord, then, I urge you to live a life worthy of the calling you have received." The Word of God thus commands us to live lives that are different from, and above, the common level of life. What does this life look like? And how can we accomplish this?

First of all, it is a life that is lived in response to God's love for us—a love which he demonstrated very clearly in Christ. Too often when we read God's Word, we glance right over words like "then" and "therefore." Paul says, "As a prisoner of the Lord, then, I urge you." The "then" refers to the first part of Paul's letter to the Ephesians in which he talks about what God has done for us in Christ. By the grace of God we have been saved through faith in Him. And this is not a reward for works done, so no one can boast. It is a gift of God (Ephesians 2:8–9). In Chapter 3, beginning with verse 16, Paul expresses his prayer for the Ephesians: "I pray that out of his glorious riches he may strengthen you with power through his Spirit in your inner being, so that Christ may dwell in your hearts through faith. And I pray that you, being rooted and established in love, may have power, together with all the saints, to grasp how wide and long and high and deep is the love of Christ, and to know this love that surpasses knowledge, that you may be filled to the measure of all the fullness of God."

Based on what God has done for us in Christ, Paul then says, "I urge you to live a life worthy of the calling you have received." God's call comes to each of us at the cross of Jesus. God has called us out of darkness into his wonderful light. He has called us out of spiritual death into spiritual life. He has called us out of separation from him into relationship with him. The purpose of God's call is to redeem us for that for which we were originally created. It goes all the way back to Genesis when God created us in his image so that we could live in fellowship with him. Our sin broke that fellowship. God has redeemed us through his Son, Jesus Christ, so that we can have what he originally created us to have, an intimate relationship with him.

The word "redeem" means to buy back, to free from captivity by payment of ransom. Someone has to pay the price, normally a costly one, to redeem another. The cost to God of our redemption was the life of his Son, Jesus Christ. That is why God's Word says that we are not our own. Paul writes in First Corinthians 6:19–20, "You are not your own; you were bought at a price. Therefore honor God with your body."

God's grace is often misunderstood. Grace is free, but it is not cheap. I heard about a preacher who was trying to illustrate for his congregation the freeness of God's grace. He called a young boy from the congregation forward during his sermon and told the boy he was going to show him what it means to receive God's grace. He offered the boy a coin he had in his hand and said, "This coin is my gift to you. All you have to do is reach out and take it. It's free." The little boy took the coin and the minister told him to go back to his seat.

That illustration demonstrates a powerful truth about God's grace, but it leaves out an equally powerful truth. God's grace is free in the sense that there is nothing we can do to earn it or buy it. But what we need to understand is that while God's grace is freely given to us, it was not free to God. It cost him dearly! Because God has paid the necessary ransom to free us from captivity to sin and death, we completely belong to him. Our lives are to be lived out every day in service to him.

In many of his New Testament letters, the apostle Paul refers to himself as a bond servant of Christ. Paul understood that he owed everything to Christ and he willingly became his servant on this earth. Paul found purpose in life by responding positively to God's call to live in relationship with him through Christ. We, too, will find purpose and meaning in life when we respond to God's love for us in Christ.

King Solomon wrote about his search for the meaning and purpose of life in many different things. He had wisdom. He had pleasure. He had wealth. He had every material thing a man on this earth could possibly want. He found it all meaningless because he discovered that purpose and meaning in life come only by living in a right relationship with the God who created us and redeemed us. As we live each day conscious of what God has done for us through Christ, we will live lives worthy of the calling we have received—and we will live above the common level of life.

Second, we live above the common level of life by living in unity within the fellowship of the body of Christ. Close study of the context of these scriptures that talk about living a life worthy of the gospel and the calling we have received reveals that they all deal with our relationship with other believers. In fact, Paul wrote these words to different churches in his day to address the problem of disunity in the body. The biblical command to live a life worthy of the calling we have received is a command to live that calling in unity within the body of Christ.

An integral part of our calling is membership in the body of Christ. The Bible says that none of us lives to himself or herself. Living for oneself is living at the common level of life. We have been called to live above the common level of life. Life is not about us, our family, our friends, or our career. Life is about something greater than you and I as individuals can ever be. In Christ, we are all part of something greater than ourselves. The church, as Christ's body, is the context in which we as believers live out our calling in a manner worthy of the gospel. God has given the Church, not the individual, the mission to fulfill his purpose here on earth. He expects every Christian to participate in the body in unity with others so that, working together, we can accomplish God's purpose.

I have thought about this from both a military perspective and a Christian perspective. It is one thing to be squared away by yourself, either as a soldier or as a Christian. It is an entirely different thing to live and work in harmony and unity with others on a daily basis. It is a higher, more difficult standard, but it is the standard to which God has called us.

There are two parallel thoughts with respect to unity within the body that are worthy of further comment. The first one is this: Unity is created within the one body by the one Spirit. That is the theme of the fourth chapter of Ephesians. The Spirit of God has already bonded us together. We as Christians are commanded to maintain and cherish that unity by living in harmony with everyone else within the body. And we are to do so at all costs. Paul writes in Ephesians 4:3, "Make every effort to keep the unity of the Spirit through the bond of peace." He writes in First Corinthians 1:10, "I appeal to you, brothers, in the name of our Lord Jesus Christ, that all of you agree with one another so that there may be no divisions among you and that you may be perfectly united in mind and thought."

In Philippians 1:27, living lives worthy of the gospel is defined in terms of unity in spirit and mind as we work together for the faith of the gospel. That is not easy. It is not easy for God's people to live in unity and harmony all the time with every other member of any local body of Christ, but it is what we are called to do. The qualities we need to do so are mentioned right here in Ephesians 4:2: "Be completely humble and gentle; be patient, bearing with one another in love."

Humility, gentleness, patience, and love are four of the qualities we need to live in unity within the body of Christ. Humility literally means lowliness of mind, versus high-handed or haughty. It means never considering yourself as better than others. Christ demonstrates throughout the New Testament a genuine attitude of humility. Even though in heaven he was with God and was God, he gave up his position of glory in heaven to take on the form of a servant on earth. He humbled himself and became obedient to death, even death on a cross. We are called to have the same attitude. Our humility should flow from a realization of our own dependence on God's grace and the genuine worth of fellow believers within the body of Christ.

The Bible says we are to treat everybody else with complete humility and gentleness. How do you define gentleness? We see gentleness in a mother's care for her newborn baby. She gently handles her child as she takes care of its every need. Jesus described himself as gentle and humble in heart. Gentleness is a fruit of the Spirit which will be more and more evident in our lives, particularly in our relationships with others within the body, as God's Spirit conforms us to the image of Christ.

Patience is another fruit of the Spirit and has to do with understanding and forgiving the shortcomings of others. Love is the fourth necessary quality. Agape, or unconditional love, is absolutely essential if we are going to be able to live in harmony and unity within the body of Christ.

All of this applies to smaller groups within the body. God wants us to live in unity and peace within our marriages and within our families. Such relationships should be exceptional, above the common level of life in our society and world. Those outside the church should see something special in our marriages and our families. They will be something special if we follow the specific instructions in God's Word, particularly the instructions to live in unity and harmony with one another.

The second parallel thought with respect to unity is that we are to live in service to each other, particularly to those within the body of Christ. The Bible says that *all* Christians have been given a spiritual gift (Ephesians 4:7). We have not been given that gift for our own benefit, but for the common good (Ephesians 4:7), to serve and build up the body of Christ. We are not a random collection of individuals. No local body of believers, including the West Point Chapel congregation, is a random collection of individuals. Revisit what Paul wrote in First Corinthians 12:18: "But in fact God has arranged the parts in the body, every one of them, just as he wanted them to be." When God calls us into relationship with him, he simultaneously calls us into relationship with the body of Christ. He endows each one of us individually with spiritual gifts for the common good, and he places us exactly as he wants us in the body of Christ where he commands us to live in unity and harmony with one another. That will happen only if each one of us does his or her part. The Bible says, "As each part does its work, the whole body, joined and held together by every supporting ligament, grows and builds itself up in love" (Ephesians 4:16).

Thus, according to what God is saying in his Word, to live above the common level of life means we have to live in unity within the fellowship of the body of Christ. We are his church and his body to which he has given the mission to share the gospel of Jesus Christ with the world. We ought to look different. We ought to be different. People should look at us and see something special as we work together in harmony and unity, by his grace, within his body.

Third and finally, we live above the common level of life by living in obedience to the Word of God. I was surprised at seminary to learn that some Christian writers and thinkers, both past and present, have expressed the belief that the Sermon on the Mount (Matthew 5–7) does not describe life here on earth. They see it as a picture of what life will be like after this earthly life, when we are all in heaven. In their view, human beings in this life cannot live up to the ethical ideals Jesus insisted upon in the Sermon on the Mount.

I have heard similar comments about the Honor Code at West Point. Is it reasonable? Is it realistic to expect young people from today's society to live up to a code and a standard that is so lofty? I would argue that it is not only realistic, but absolutely essential, because we are here to produce leaders of character, leaders who will stand a stout cut above the common level of leadership. We need leaders with the highest values of honor and integrity, leaders who will not lie, cheat, or steal, or tolerate those in our profession who do. Yes, it is a tough standard. So is the Word of God.

The rest of Paul's letter to the Ephesians describes the life as commanded by God to be clearly above the common level: "In your anger do not sin. Do not let the sun go down while you are still angry" (Ephesians 4:26). Anger is a human emotion. Sometimes we get very angry. We are to resolve our anger within the day. Ephesians 4:29 says, "Do not let any unwholesome talk come out of your mouths," not even in the locker room or on the playing field. Ephesians 5:3–4 tells us, "Among you there must not be even a hint of sexual immorality, or any kind of impurity, or of greed, because these are improper for God's holy people. Nor should there be obscenity, foolish talk, or coarse joking, which are out of place." Ephesians continues in a similar vein: "Do not get drunk . . . ."(5:18); "Wives, submit unto your husbands as to the Lord . . . in everything" (5:22); "Husbands, love your wives just as Christ loved the church and gave himself up for her to make her holy and . . . blameless" (5:25).

Are these higher and tougher standards? Absolutely! But they are the standards to which we have been called. God has called us to live above the common level of life. The Bible says, "We are God's workmanship, created in Christ Jesus to do good works, which God prepared in advance for us to do." In God's love and by God's strength and with God's grace, we can strive to meet his standards.

Too often, we as Christians excuse ourselves or take consolation in the belief that "everyone is doing it." It is common, even for Christians, to judge ourselves and our actions by the example of others. Yet, the only relevant basis for judgment remains: "Is it worthy of Christ?"

If you had stood at the foot of the cross watching your Savior die for you, would it make a difference in how you live today? If you had stood at the empty tomb and saw the resurrected Lord who conquered even death that you and I might have eternal life, would it make any difference in the way you live each day? As you picture yourself standing before our Judge, the Lord Jesus Christ, as all of us will one day, does it make a difference in the way you live now?

After experiencing the emptiness and meaninglessness of wisdom, pleasure, work, and wealth, Solomon speaks these words of manifest truth to all of us: "Fear God and keep his commandments, for this is the whole duty of man" (Ecclesiastes 12:13). If we will simply live in obedience to the Word of God, we will live above the common level of life.

We have been called from above to a higher standard in our daily lives. To live above the common level of life means walking every day—individually and collectively—in response to God's love, which he demonstrated in Christ, in unity within the fellowship of the body of Christ, and in obedience to the Word of God.

Recall Ben Hooper from the hills of east Tennessee and the young preacher who taught Ben his true parentage. Whose son or daughter are you anyway? Now, go and make sure you live up to it.

Choosing the Harder Right—James R. Carter[6]

> At this time, the administrators and the satraps tried to find grounds for charges against Daniel in his conduct of government affairs, but they were unable to do so. They could find no corruption in him, because he was trustworthy and neither corrupt nor negligent. Finally these men said, "We will never find any basis for charges against this man Daniel unless it has something to do with the law of his God.
>
> —Daniel 6:4–5

Daniel was a leader of great influence, and when facing a very difficult decision he chose the harder right instead of the easier wrong. He made a tremendous stand for the glory of God and was a significant leader of character for the nation of Israel.

As a young Hebrew boy, he was taken captive by the Babylonians during their seizure of Jerusalem. It was normal for the conquering king to take the best and brightest young male captives and train them in the ways of his nation and religion. The conqueror wanted to conform them to the standards of his nation and win them over to his customs and traditions. He wanted to break them down and rebuild them so they would follow his false gods. They were aware of the young men's ability to impact other Israelites and bring them into the worship of false gods and idols. And indeed, Daniel rose up through the ranks as a prominent leader in this new government.

Later in Chapter 6 of the Book of Daniel, we learn the Babylonian empire fell to the Persians. Their leader, King Darius, was so impressed with Daniel and his leadership ability that he appointed him one of his top three officers. We read in Daniel 6:1–2: "It pleased Darius to appoint 120 satraps to rule throughout the kingdom, with three administrators over them, one of whom was Daniel. The satraps were made accountable to them so that the king might not suffer loss."

Daniel was a leader working in a foreign land among a people who worshiped a false god. He was different from many around him, but he was determined to serve with dedication those placed in authority over him and strive for excellence in all his daily activities. Many became jealous of his devotion to duty and his desire to please and honor others and his God. We read in Daniel 6:3–5: "Now Daniel so distinguished himself among the administrators and the satraps by his qualities that the King planned to set him over the whole kingdom." So the administrators and satraps devised a devious plan. They went to King Darius as a group and encouraged him to decree that anyone who prayed to any god other than the King during the following 30 days would be executed. They persuaded him to put his decree in writing and seal it with his official seal. The King agreed to do this and the trap was set for Daniel. What a difficult bind Daniel found himself in. Would he continue to worship the true God of Israel or would he agree to kneel and worship the false god and King of Persia?

We read in Daniel 6:10–11 what Daniel decided to do. When he learned that the decree was signed, he went home and in his upper room with his windows open towards Jerusalem, he knelt down on his knees three times a day and prayed and gave thanks before his God as was custom. The assembled men found Daniel praying and making supplication before his God, so they went before the King and spoke concerning the King's decree, "Have you not signed a decree that every man who petitions any god or man within 30 days except you, oh King, shall be cast into the den of lions?" The King answered, "This [decree] is true according to the law of the Medes and Persians which does not alter."

They responded that Daniel, who was one of the captives from Judah, "does not show due regard for you, oh King, for the decree that you signed, but makes his petitions three times a day." And the King, when he heard this, was saddened and set his heart on saving Daniel, laboring till sunset to think of a way. Later, the men approached the King again and said, "Now, oh King, that it is the law of the Medes and Persians that no decree or statute which a king establishes may be changed." Daniel is an example of a man who chose the harder right instead of the easier wrong. The King reluctantly ordered Daniel thrown to the lions, and Daniel stood fully prepared to accept the consequences of refusing to obey the King's edict, whatever they were. We shall return to the subject of Daniel's fate at the end of the sermon.

At first glance it seems that obeying the lines of the Cadet Prayer should be fairly simple. As Christians we're called to do what's right before a righteous God. However, on reflection we know that is not always easy. Military leaders, which cadets aspire to become, will be called upon to make the right choice, and oftentimes the right choice as a leader in the military will be a very hard and difficult choice. Throughout life, regardless of our vocation, we are called upon to make difficult choices. Many will be called upon to make a crucial decision. It will be a defining moment. What will you choose?

We are always impressed with people who choose the harder right instead of the easier wrong. I once heard a story about a racquetball player who had trained for years to play on the pro tour and finally made it to a tournament final. The crowd was filled with excitement. This underdog player was playing the champion of the past few years, and it appeared he was going to pull a major upset. It was a critical time in the match. The challenger hit a great kill shot in the corner that he was sure would be good, but suddenly heard a slight squeak. He was the only one to hear the sound because his shot was in the corner. The linesmen looked puzzled and unsure of the call but finally called it a good shot. The challenger, however, turned around and waved it off. He told them his shot had hit the floor before hitting the wall, thus negating the point. His opponent went on to win. The challenger made a very hard decision, but the right decision. This great player realized that he could always win another match, but he could never regain his lost integrity. Oftentimes we can have things officially in our favor, but we must make the right call and not the convenient call.

Robert E. Lee, the great Confederate general, stood before President Jefferson Davis as an adviser early in the Civil War. Davis was asking the general's advice about an appointment he was going to make of another general. He asked Lee his opinion of this man, and Lee said, "Mr. President, he is a great man of great commitment and dedication. He is extremely competent and he will serve you well." The President thanked him, shook his hand, and Lee left the room. Another general, who had been in the room at the same time, looked at Lee and said, "How could you say these complimentary things about this man? Don't you know what he thinks about you? Don't you know what he says about you? Don't you know what his opinion is of you?" Lee looked at his friend and said, "The President did not ask me his opinion of me, but my opinion of him."

In other words, Lee, being the leader he was, would not violate his integrity by exacting petty revenge. He knew the officer in question was competent and committed. He didn't get into personality conflicts. What about you today? There are many other examples of leaders who made honorable decisions. I think of Eric Little, the great Scot sprinter in the 1924 Olympics, who chose not to compete on the Sabbath day because he felt compelled to obey Scripture.

Daniel also had to make a difficult decision, but what was different about Daniel's decision was that his life was at stake. Daniel was a model of strong character. He was on display as a man of integrity in a world that hated his God. If you are striving to be a better leader, you can draw three important lessons from Daniel's example. First, Daniel was a *leader of conviction*. He was uncompromising in hewing to his beliefs. He was uncompromising because he built his goals on the foundation established by God's priorities.

His world was defined by the view that the God of heaven reigns on the throne. To Daniel, God was not just his Savior who would bail him out in times of crisis, but rather God was his Lord who sees all that Daniel did. He lived under His presence and in His presence. God sat on the throne of Daniel's life. He was taken as a young boy from home, where he enjoyed stability and peace, and was thrust into a different culture, the Babylonian culture. This culture hated his beliefs and his God and despised the teachings of the Old Testament. The culture was aggressive and lacking in values, one determined to break down the convictions and values of young Daniel. Daniel lived in Babylon, but Babylon did not live in Daniel.

As Christians you and I are called to be in the world but not of the world. How was Daniel able to stand firm? How was he able to live in Babylon but not let Babylon live in him? The answer: he was a leader of conviction. He was a leader of conviction about the truth of God's word. He took God's word to be his road map, to direct him and lead him on a daily basis.

What are your convictions? What do you hold dearly to? Daniel was completely different from another leader we read about in Scripture. His name was Pilate. The Jews arraigned Jesus before Pilate, hoping he would have Jesus killed. Pilate interviewed him and consulted others, and in Luke, 24:3 Pilate says, "I find no fault in the man." Despite Pilate's finding that Jesus is innocent, the Jews persist. Pilate continues to interview Jesus and still finds nothing wrong in him. However, Pilate was not a leader of conviction, but a leader who was willing to compromise. He couldn't choose the harder right. He decided to choose the easier wrong. How? He looked at Jesus and then he looked at this influential group known as the Sanhedrin, realizing their power. He must have thought to himself, "These people are very influential. If I don't try to appease them, I may be on the next boat to Rome to stand before Caesar and I might lose my job." So Pilate stood before the world, he stood before Jesus Christ the King of Kings, and chose the easier wrong. He compromised his integrity, and that is the everlasting legacy he left.

Compromise is of great value in marriage, in business, and political negotiations. However, compromise in the area of values, in the area of morality and spirituality, is always a bad thing. Pilate was no Daniel. Daniel was a man of conviction, a man of principle. His principles were not for sale. He couldn't be bought either emotionally or financially. No price could make him swerve from what was morally right, from honor and reverence due the King of Kings. Can you be bought? What is your price to shade the truth? You may think that you can't be bought, but you have heard it said: "Everyone has a price." What is your price? I am thankful that Daniel was a servant leader of principle and could not be bought, that he would not compromise and trusted the Lord with his future. He did not know what the future held, but he knew who held his future.

Secondly, Daniel was a *leader of consistency*: "And in his upper room with his windows open toward Jerusalem, he knelt down on his knees three times that day and prayed and gave thanks before his God as was his custom since earlier days" (Daniel 6:11). Daniel didn't just wake up one morning and say, "I think I'm going to do the right thing today." That is not at all what happened. He made the right choice because he had consistently lived a life of righteousness by praying and depending on the Lord. He had cultivated the habit of spending time in the word and prayer. It is a challenge for some of us to pray once a day, but this man formed the habit of praying three times a day. This consistency comes from a conscience that was bound to Scripture. Martin Luther was another example of a man who chose the harder right. As he stood at his trial facing excommunication, he said: "My conscience is bound. It's bound to Scripture. Here I stand. I can do no other." He continued, "I believe that salvation in God rests in faith alone, that we cannot merit our salvation but that it is a free gift, lest no one should boast." These words were in total opposition to the doctrine of the day, but Luther, like Daniel before him, stood firm.

Daniel could have rationalized that the King's decree was in effect for only 30 days. He could have simply gone in his house, closed the windows, knelt down, prayed silently, and kept it a secret. But he chose to continue praying the way he had done for years. He wanted to give glory and honor to God, even though he knew how high the cost might be. Daniel lived a consistent life.

Thirdly, he was a *leader of commitment.* Daniel was committed to God with a sense of peace and comfort in the knowledge that God was in control. Daniel understood that he served a sovereign God who was in control of the entire creation. As Daniel knelt in prayer that morning to Almighty God, he did not have a stressed, anxious mind. Rather, he had a deep sense of peace that passes all understanding, He felt no fear, only faith that God was in charge of Daniel's life circumstances. Whether Daniel lived or died, he knew that God would reign. It's this peace that the world needs to see. It's what our soldiers need to see, as they look at their military leaders: stability and strength in the midst of crisis, a deep abiding peace knowing that God is sovereign and in control.

Just as Daniel and Martin Luther were called, we are called to live our lives with a reliance on God's sovereignty. In spite of pain or suffering and even in the face of death, we achieve victory as believers in Jesus Christ. When we commit to a life like this, we are going to be criticized, possibly even ostracized, for choosing the harder right. You might not be very popular because of your decision. The Apostle Paul writes in 2 Timothy 4:16, "No one came to my support, but everyone deserted me." We need to understand that when we make hard decisions we might feel alone for a while. There are many examples of leaders who were left alone after their difficult decisions. Noah was alone when he built the ark. Elijah was alone when he sacrificed to our Lord. Jeremiah was alone when he prophesied and wept, and Jesus was, in a sense, alone when he died. Can you handle being left alone for choosing the harder right? Are you willing to be a modern-day Daniel? Are you willing to make the stand that may cost everything? Are you willing to be a leader of conviction, consistency, and commitment? The real comfort is that God promises never to leave us or forsake us. Daniel understood this principle and lived fearlessly for the Lord.

I want you to learn what happens at the very end of Daniel's story. We noted that King Darius ordered Daniel to be thrown into the lion's den, certainly to all appearances a death sentence. Darius is filled with pain because he loved and appreciated Daniel and all he stood for. Secretly, Darius is beginning to be influenced by the moral tenor of Daniel's life, and he hopes Daniel will survive. God in his mercy closes the mouths of the lions and Daniel lives. Darius learns that Daniel is alive and rushes to see him. Daniel says, "Oh, King, live forever." Daniel continues to honor and respect the King who just threw him in the lion's den! Then Daniel exclaims, "My God sent an angel and shut the lion's mouth so that they have not hurt me, because I was found innocent before him and also, oh King, I have done nothing wrong to you." The King was exceedingly glad for him and commanded that he be taken up out of the lion's den. Then the King commanded that the men who had connived against Daniel be thrown in the lion's den themselves.

Later, King Darius decreed "that in every dominion of my kingdom men must tremble and fear before the God of Daniel" (Daniel 6:26). Thanks be to God! Look at the influence of a Godly leader over an ungodly country. Can one person make a difference? Yes! Can you be a catalyst for revival? Yes! Can you bring renewal? Yes! Can you bring transformation in your workplace? You'd better believe it! One day at a time, one decision at a time. May God empower us as his church to choose the harder right instead of the easier wrong.

Winning the Whole Truth—John J. Cook III[7]

All the believers were one in heart and mind. No one claimed that any of his possessions was his own, but they shared everything that they had. With great power the apostles continued to testify to the resurrection of the Lord Jesus, and much grace was upon them all. There were no needy persons among them. For from time to time those who owned land or houses sold them, brought the money from the sales and put it at the apostles' feet, and it was distributed to anyone as he had need.

Joseph, a Levite from Cyprus, whom the apostles called Barnabus (which means Son of Encouragement) sold a field he owned and brought the money and put it at the apostles' feet. Now a man named Ananias, together with his wife Sapphira, also sold a piece of property. With his wife's full knowledge he kept back part of the money for himself, but brought the rest and put it at the apostles' feet. Then Peter said, Ananias, how is it that Satan has so filled your heart that you have lied to the Holy Spirit and have kept for yourself some of the money you received for the land? Didn't it belong to you before it was sold? And after it was sold, wasn't the money at your disposal? What made you think of doing such a thing? You have not lied to men but to God. When Ananias heard this, he fell down and died. And great fear seized all who heard what had happened. Then the young man came forward, wrapped up his body, and carried him out and buried him. About three hours later his wife came in, not knowing what had happened. Peter asked her, "Tell me, is this the price you and Ananias got for the land?" "Yes," she said, "that is the price." Peter said to her, "How could you agree to test the Spirit of the Lord? Look! The feet of the men who buried your husband are at the door, and they will carry you out also." At that moment she fell down at his feet and died. Then the young men came in and, finding her dead, carried her out and buried

her beside her husband. Great fear seized the whole church and all who heard
about these events.

—Acts 4:32-5:11

The older I get, the more intrigued I am by what experiences from my past
stand out in my memory while I have long forgotten so many other things.
When my dad was stationed at West Point as a tactical officer from 1965 to
1968, I was about eight or nine years old. We lived close enough to the school
for me to walk to and from it every day. On my way home from school with
a friend one day, we saw some squirrels and threw a few acorns at them. It was
one of those relatively harmless things that little boys sometimes do. I don't
remember hitting any squirrels that day, but while we were engaging in this
mischief, some big boys—at least relative to us—came out of one of the
houses on the street. They ran over to us and pushed us around a little bit.
They didn't hurt us, but I can remember experiencing a little fear at the time.

Later that evening I told my dad that some big boys had roughed us up
on the way home from school. Being the protector he was, my dad was concerned. He asked me some questions. I told him what had happened, but con-
veniently left out the fact that I had been throwing acorns at the squirrels,
which was probably why the boys had come out of the house in the first
place. They did not want us to hurt the squirrels. Lacking that relevant bit of
information, dad put me in the car that evening and drove over to the house
where the boys lived. He left me in the back seat of the car and walked up to
the door to talk with their parents. When he came back to the car he said,
"You didn't tell me that you had been throwing acorns at squirrels." I don't
remember him giving me a big lecture that night, but I do remember the tone
of disappointment in his voice because I had not told him the whole truth.
He had made a decision to do something to protect his son based on incom-
plete information.

I have replayed that childhood memory in my mind many times over the
course of my life because it taught me a valuable lesson. I learned early on in
life that it is harder sometimes to tell the whole truth, and that half-truths usually result from having something to hide. I learned that sometimes by telling
a half-truth you can significantly alter the story in a way that can influence and
manipulate the decisions and actions of others. I learned as a little boy that
half-truths really are an attempt to deceive. I had deceived my own father by
not telling him the whole truth. I have grown since that time to understand
that the whole truth is better than a partial truth.

We continue the sermon series on the Cadet Prayer with the phrase,
"never to be content with a half truth when the whole can be won." As this
sermon began to take shape, I focused on the word "won." To win implies a
contest or a battle. We witness contests frequently on the fields of friendly
strife, as at Army football games. Winning implies that there are both winners

and losers. In the contest for winning the whole truth, this is precisely true. It is a critical battle with profound implications.

Truth is important as it relates to the gospel of Jesus Christ. Truth is important as it relates to one's character. Truth is important as it relates to our profession as soldiers. Before we address this phrase within the context of the Cadet Prayer, I want us to see the bigger picture first. We need to understand the larger context of the battle for truth that affects every one of us every day.

Several major themes in the Bible are identified in terms of battles of eternal consequence. One is the theme of light versus darkness. The Bible describes Jesus as the Light God sent into the world. There is an ongoing battle between that Light and the spiritual darkness of this world. We read in John 3, beginning with verse 19, "This is the verdict: Light has come into the world, but men loved darkness instead of light because their deeds were evil. Everyone who does evil hates the light, and will not come into the light for fear that his deeds will be exposed. But whoever lives by the truth comes into the light, so that it may be seen plainly that what he has done has been done through God."

This battle is exemplified in the sermon text. Why did Ananias tell a half-truth? Because he had something to hide! His deed was evil and he was attempting to hide in the darkness. This battle between light and darkness will rage until Christ returns, at which time we will enter either heaven or hell. The Bible describes heaven as a place of eternal light. There is no darkness in heaven. Hell, by contrast, is described as a place where there is no light. In our world, light and darkness will contend with each other until that day when light emerges eternally victorious.

Another battle described in God's Word is that between the Spirit and the flesh. In Romans 6, Paul describes this battle, in which even as a leader in the early church he struggled with his old sinful nature. He did not always do the things that he knew he should do. At other times he did things he knew he should not do. He asks rhetorically, who would deliver him from this constant struggle. He refers to the same struggle in Galatians 5:16–17: "So I say, live by the Spirit, and you will not gratify the desires of the sinful nature. For the sinful nature desires what is contrary to the Spirit, and the Spirit what is contrary to the sinful nature. They are in conflict with each other, so that you do not do what you want."

In Ephesians 4:22–25, writing to new Christians, Paul says: "You were taught, with regard to your former way of life, to put off your old self, which is being corrupted by its deceitful desires; to be made new in the attitude of your minds; and to put on the new self, created to be like God in true righteousness and holiness. Therefore each of you must put off falsehood and speak truthfully to his neighbor." In describing how their new life in Christ should differ from their old, the very first instruction he gives them is to put off all falsehood and speak truthfully.

We need to understand this admonition in the bigger picture. There is a monumental battle raging in our world today between truth and falsehood.

On one side of the battle line is Jesus Christ, who is the Truth along with the written Word of God, the Holy Bible, which contains absolute truth. On the other side is Satan, who is described in scripture as a liar and the father of all lies. John 8:44 says, "He was a murderer from the beginning, not holding to the truth, for there is no truth in him. When he lies he speaks his native language, for he is a liar and the father of lies."

Truth and falsehood are mutually exclusive. Jesus Christ is the Truth. There is no deceit or falsehood in him. Satan is a liar and the father of all lies. There is no truth in him. This battle raging in the heavenly realms has a directly significant impact on us today. The battle is currently complicated in our society by what we call "postmodernism." Postmodernists would have us believe that all truth is relative, that there is no absolute truth . . . even in religion. In postmodernist thought, all religions are equal in terms of goodness and truth.

Within this larger context, there are two critical battles being fought. One of these is the battle for the truth of the gospel of Jesus Christ. Jesus unequivocally proclaimed that salvation is through him, that he alone is the Way, the Truth, and the Life. He declared that no one can come to the Father except through him. Satan is decisively engaged in combat to do everything he can to undermine that central truth. You see his activity in the parable of the sower and the seed. As soon as the seed (the Word of God) is scattered, the evil one (Satan) immediately tries to snatch it up because he does not want people to understand their need for salvation through Jesus Christ. He knows how important it is for him to strike early and hard in this battle. And strike he will! Second Corinthians 4:3–4 says, "And even if our gospel is veiled, it is veiled to those who are perishing. The God of this age has blinded the minds of unbelievers, so that they cannot see the light of the gospel of the glory of Christ, who is the image of God."

One of Satan's most effective weapons in this battle is the half-truth. He uses them as nothing more than an attempt to deceive. At the very beginning of the Bible in Genesis 3, when the serpent approached Eve in the Garden of Eden, what did he tell her? He deceived Eve with a partial truth. He told Eve that her eyes would be opened and that she would be like God if she ate the fruit that God told her not to eat. Her eyes indeed were opened, but she certainly was not like God. Instead, she and Adam saw that they were naked and they tried to hide from God. Satan deceived Eve with a partial truth to get her to disobey God. Because she did, sin entered the world through her and through her husband Adam.

Satan's temptation of Jesus in the desert is another great example of his attempt to deceive with half-truths. Jesus was very hungry. He had been fasting for 40 days. Satan approached him and used actual scripture to tempt Jesus. He did not change the words of the scriptures, but he took them out of context and presented the resulting half-truths to Jesus. He knew that if he could get Jesus to sin, we would have no salvation from our sins because we would have no Savior. Jesus recognized the half-truths for what they were, and responded with other scripture—in context—to refute Satan.

Similarly, there are distortions and perversions of the gospel of Jesus Christ in our world today. There are whole religions based on partial biblical truths that have been embellished by other doctrine that is not biblical. Each of these religions has many adherents who are sincere in their faith, but their religion is not based on the whole truth. This has been true from the very beginning of the early church. Paul says in Galatians 1:6, "I am astonished that you are so quickly deserting the one who called you by the grace of Christ and are turning to a different gospel, which is really no gospel at all. Evidently some people are throwing you into confusion and are trying to pervert the gospel of Christ." Paul had preached that salvation was by grace through faith in Jesus Christ. The Judaizers followed him in Galatia and told these new Christians that Paul had not spoken the whole truth, that they also had to obey the laws that had been given in the Old Testament, specifically the requirement to be circumcised. In essence, they were saying that salvation is not complete by grace alone, but that God's grace must be accompanied by our works. That is a perversion of the truth of the gospel of Jesus Christ. Unfortunately, many believed the Judaizers and began to be swayed from their new faith. Christians in every era need to be very careful not to be deceived by half-truths when it comes to the central gospel of Jesus Christ. In this battle for the truth of the gospel, half-truths can be dangerous if not deadly. A half-truth is not the truth! Do not settle for half-truths when it comes to rightly dividing God's Word of truth.

I want to zero in on a second strategic battle within the context of truth versus falsehood, and that is the battle for truth in our individual lives. It is not just a battle for our souls as we have already discussed. It is a battle for our integrity, our character, and our witness. Satan's objective is to undermine our character as Christians and subsequently our witness for Jesus Christ. His tactics have not changed much since he approached Eve in the Garden and Jesus in the wilderness. He wants to get us to compromise our integrity by settling for half-truths in our lives. Half-truths, at best, are utterances less than completely honest. They are a compromise with Satan himself, who is the father of lies. In reality, half-truths amount to deception and deceit, which are sins according to God's Word. Do not allow Satan to entice you to settle for or accept or be content with a half-truth in your life and in your dealings with others.

Satan played an active role with Ananias in our sermon text. Acts 5:3 says, "How is it that Satan has so filled your heart that you have lied to the Holy Spirit . . . ?" What Ananias did was not bad in and of itself. He sold some property. He did not have to sell the property. It was strictly voluntary. He could have sold the property and simply said, look, I need a quarter of this money. I need half of this money. I need three-quarters of this for myself. I will give you the rest. That would not have been a problem.

What Ananias did when he presented the offering was to imply that the amount was the total payment he had received for the property. He did this for personal gain because he wanted a reputation for generosity like Barnabas. He sacrificed his integrity by telling a half-truth. His half-truth cost him his life.

The establishment of the church on earth was a significant part of God's plan. That made it a key battleground for Satan. Satan's goal was to infect the brand-new Christian community, to gain a foothold in the early church through which he might bring it down and thwart the plan of God. Satan's foothold was Ananias' heart. His tactic was to tempt Ananias to tell a half-truth.

Satan tried the same thing with the Israelites in the Old Testament. Achan's sin in Joshua 7 was catastrophic to the people and purpose of God. God had commanded them to conquer the promised land. God had told them to destroy everything they captured from these evil people. They were not to keep any of it. A man named Achan saw some things he wanted. He did not think that it would be a big deal to bring them back as booty from the war, so he hid them under the floor in his tent.

When the Israelites then went up against the city of Ai, they expected another successful battle. Instead, they suffered a humiliating defeat at the hands of their enemies. They retreated, wondering what was going on. God told Joshua he had a serious problem in his own camp, that someone had disobeyed God's instructions. They had compromised their character, their values, and their integrity. The consequence would be continued defeat until Israel cleaned out its own camp. So they drew lots and found out about Achan's disobedience and deceitfulness. They put him and his family to death. The penalty was so severe in both of these cases because the stakes were so high. Satan was trying to infect the community of faith by getting Achan and Ananias to compromise their integrity. The result for both Ananias and Achan was death.

Satan would love to undermine your character and your integrity and your witness for Jesus Christ in the same way. Our faith and our profession demand that we be men and women of absolute integrity and honesty. The Cadet Honor Code is critical to who we are as members of the profession of arms and as Christians. It is the spirit of the code, and not legalistic compliance, that is key. The goal is not to have a cadet finish four years at West Point without an honor violation. The goal is to produce leaders of character committed to a lifetime of unwavering honesty and integrity.

General Dwight Eisenhower said, "In order to be a leader a man must have followers. And to have followers, a man must have their confidence. Hence, unquestionably, the supreme quality for a leader is integrity. Without it, no real success is possible, no matter whether in leading a work gang, a football team, an office staff, or an army. If a man's associates find him guilty of being phony, if they find that he lacks forthright integrity, he will fail."[8] In a similar vein, General Alexander Haig stated unequivocally, "In an era marked by at least the appearance of questionable integrity and moral courage by many contemporary leaders, the demonstration of absolute integrity by a leader is the most important principle that any leader must follow."[9]

Integrity is of course more than just being honest; but one cannot have integrity without complete honesty. There is no profession in which this is more important than our own. In times of combat, lives are at stake. Leaders need to have the whole truth before they can make decisions that will affect the lives of those they lead. That is one reason why the phrase about half-truths is included in the Cadet Prayer.

In his book, *The Stuff of Heroes,* William Cohen writes about Second Lieutenant George Brown, who joined the 377th Regiment of the 95th Infantry Division as a platoon leader during the advance into Germany in late November 1944:

> *George Brown had never been in combat before. He was replacing a popular officer who had been not only well liked by his men, but well thought of by his superiors. This officer had a reputation for both courage and quick thinking in battle. George knew that he had big shoes to fill and had to win the respect of both his subordinates and his superiors.*
>
> *Unfortunately, nothing seemed to go right. On his first day in command, a hidden German sniper caught the platoon strung out on the open road and suddenly opened fire. Until then, no one knew of his existence. Eventually, his platoon got the sniper with mortar fire, but they were tremendously fortunate to suffer no casualties. The unwelcome surprise of the sudden fusillade may not have been George's fault, but he was responsible. A few days later, several Gestapo officers his company sought to capture got away. Then his company commander sent him to lead a night patrol to capture prisoners. As luck would have it, the patrol stumbled into an unsuspected minefield, suffering two wounded and capturing no prisoners. Again, George had done nothing wrong directly, but he was in charge when things went wrong. He knew that he suffered from comparison with his predecessor. He suspected that his boss thought him incompetent. At best, his soldiers probably thought him unlucky. In combat, some feel that being unlucky is just as bad as being incompetent, maybe worse.*
>
> *The following day the platoon ran into a hidden machine gun. Lieutenant Brown and a private, himself a new replacement, were separated from the rest of the platoon. The machine gun held George's platoon immobilized. They could not even raise their heads without coming under a hail of fire. But George and the private were out of the enemy's line of sight. Moreover, the private carried a bazooka. This weapon fired a rocket with a highly explosive warhead.*
>
> *George motioned the private to follow him, and they began to maneuver so they could attack the machine gun with the bazooka. As they got closer to their objective, a German rifleman guarding the machine gun spotted them and opened fire with his assault rifle.*
>
> *George loaded the bazooka from the rear and told the private to fire. Then he rapidly fired a burst from his carbine at the German and started to move forward. He missed. At almost the same time, he was temporarily blinded from the blast of the rocket as the private, who was now somewhat in front and to his right, fired the bazooka. Apparently, the private had been hit by the German rifleman. He fell to the ground immediately after firing, mortally wounded. As George continued forward, the bazooka rocket that the private had fired struck near the machine gun and exploded. Without thinking, George scooped up the bazooka from the fallen private. The*

surviving Germans were confused and demoralized. They immediately stood up and raised their arms in surrender.

George's men saw the rocket explode. Then they saw their lieutenant charge the position and capture the Germans. He had the bazooka slung over one shoulder and his smoking carbine held at the ready with his other arm. His men left their positions of concealment and joined him. Before George could say a word, they enthusiastically congratulated him. "Way to go, Lieutenant! Wow, better than Sergeant York! He's a one-man army!"

Almost immediately, the company commander arrived. George's men gave the commander a dramatic account of the incident, giving George credit for destroying the enemy position by himself after the private who had been with him was killed. George's company commander congratulated him on his feat. He told George he would be recommended for a high decoration, the Distinguished Service Cross. George knew that if he said nothing, not only would he be a hero, but he would have completely erased any bad impressions made during his first few days with the unit. No one knew the truth. Even the surviving Germans thought that George had fired the bazooka, which destroyed their position.

After all of George's earlier problems, it was very difficult for him to choose to do what he knew to be the right thing. That's the real test of integrity—to do the right thing when no one is looking. He did.

"That's not what happened," he told his platoon and his company commander. He then went on to give an accurate account of the incident. George stated he was recommending the private for the posthumous award of the medal that the company commander wanted to give him.

George Brown went on to become a very effective combat leader. Everyone respected him. It did not matter that he didn't fire the rocket that destroyed the gun emplacement. What did matter was that George was a leader whom both subordinates and superiors could trust absolutely. They knew he could be counted on to do the right thing even when no one was watching.[10]

Allow me to share some suggestions with you as we fight this battle for truth. First, understand God's desire for absolute truth in your life. King David, speaking to God, said, "You desire truth in my inner parts" (Psalm 51:6). Peter wrote that we are to be established in the truth (2 Peter 1:12) and that we are purified by obeying the truth (1 Peter 1:22). John said we are sanctified by the truth (John 17:17). God has called us to know the truth, walk in the truth, and speak the truth. The biblical standard is absolute truth and complete honesty.

Second, beware of Satan's goal and schemes. In military parlance, know your enemy! When you find yourself tempted toward secrecy, shamefulness, deception, and distorting the truth, you are treading on thin ice. Satan would love to get a foothold in your life to destroy your character, your integrity, and your witness for Jesus Christ by getting you to accept a half-truth when the whole could be won.

Third, in putting on and using the full armor of God, "Stand firm, then, with the belt of truth buckled around your waist" (Ephesians 6:14). Truth is our main defense against the father of lies. Arm yourself with truth. Grow in the knowledge of the truth of God's Word. Let the Spirit of truth be Lord of your life.

Finally, in the campaign for truth, commit yourself to a standard of absolute truth in all that you say and do. Part of that is accepting the cost of the truth. Proverbs 23:23 says, "Buy the truth and never sell it." The whole truth can sometimes be very costly, but never as costly as falsehood and deception. The truth cost Lieutenant George Brown the Distinguished Service Cross, but he kept his integrity, which is of far greater value. A violation of the Cadet Honor Code here may cost you the opportunity to graduate from West Point and be commissioned as an officer. If it comes down to a choice between telling a half-truth but escaping punishment, and walking 200 hours on the punishment area but telling the whole truth, walk the hours! Accept the cost of maintaining absolute integrity in your life.

John Naber was an Olympic swimming champion. In 1976 at the Olympic Games in Montreal, he won four golds, all of which were records, and one silver. He was the first Olympic swimmer in history to win two individual medals in the same day. In 1977 he won the Sullivan Award, which recognizes the nation's outstanding amateur athlete. Len Marrella, in his book *In Search of Ethics*, tells a powerfully revealing story about John Nabor:

> It has been said that athletic competition doesn't build character, it reveals character. That notion prompts me to describe a defining moment in John Naber's life—a defining moment that revealed his character. The moment occurred in 1973 when John Naber, as a recent high school graduate, competed in the U.S. National Championships. His goal was to win a position on the World Championship Team, which for an 18-year-old high schooler would be quite an achievement.
>
> Despite his young age, John was favored to win the 100-meter backstroke event, but his hand did not touch the wall as required. When the starter fired the gun, John got off to a quick start and at the end of the first lap he reached for the wall behind his head and initiated his flip turn. His feet swung around and he pushed off to proceed on his final leg of the event. As he surfaced he saw the official standing over his lane raising a hand to signal a rule violation. He swam a fast final lap and reached the finish line ahead of the rest of the swimmers. The applause from the spectators was deafening and the congratulations from other swimmers was exciting, but John was more concerned by the conference taking place at the other end of the pool. Finally, the head referee walked up to John and said, "I'm afraid you've been disqualified. The turn judge says she didn't see you touch the wall." John's shoulders dropped and his chin hit his chest. The crowd seemed to be pulling for him and John's teammates and his supporters hoped that the official had made a mistake. John's coach approached him and asked, "Do you want to fight this thing? Do you want to protest the call?" John's coach thought he could win if he protested strongly. There was a potential world title at stake and John's head was swirling. I suspect that John Naber didn't realize that this would be a turning point in his life, but he did know that how he handled this situation

would follow him the rest of his life. "My decision whether to fight the judge's call or to accept her decision was made in the blink of an eye. I knew what I had to do. My parents didn't raise a cheater. With moist eyes, I looked at my coach, the man who was offering a way out of my disappointment, and I admitted, , I didn't touch the wall." John Naber would rather be disqualified than dishonor himself. And it was after this huge disappointment and after his courageous display of character that he went on to become one of the outstanding athletes of his time.[11]

Integrity is not a given in anyone's life. It is a result of self-discipline, inner trust, and a decision to be relentlessly honest in all situations in life. Truth is absolute. God requires absolute honesty in our relationship with him and in our relationships with others. May we never be content with a half-truth when the whole can be won.

Maintain the Honor—James R. Carter[12]

It is not to angels that he has subjected the world to come, about which we are speaking. But there is a place where someone has testified: "What is man that you are mindful of him, the son of man that you care for him? You made him a little lower than the angels; you crowned him with glory and honor and put everything under his feet." In putting everything under him, God left nothing that is not subject to him. Yet at present we do not see everything subject to him. But we see Jesus, who was made a little lower than the angels, now crowned with glory and honor because he suffered death, so that by the grace of God he might taste death for everyone.

—Hebrews 2:5–9

One of the supplications to God in the Cadet Prayer is to "help us to maintain the honor of the Corps untarnished and unsullied and to show forth in our lives the ideals of West Point in doing our duty to thee and to our country." What does it mean to maintain the honor of something? The word "honor" is oftentimes translated to mean "dignity." As Christians, we have to answer the question, "How do we respect the dignity of others and honor our gracious Lord?"

Alexander the Great was a powerful warrior, leader, strategist, and general who conquered the known world. Alexander was also known as a strict disciplinarian, a leader whom his soldiers respected. Alexander hated cowardice and did not tolerate soldiers who deserted. A story in the book *The Christian Message for Contemporary Life: The Gospel's Power to Change Lives* by Stephen Olford describes Alexander's attitude as follows: "History records that on one occasion while he was sitting in judgment on a number of state matters, a young soldier was brought before him, charged with being a deserter. Alexander was a general who demanded total and complete allegiance; yet here was a deserter. What was he to do? He questioned him and the young soldier pleaded guilty and asked for clemency. Surrounded by his aides, the face of the great general slowly relaxed and they heaved a great sigh of relief. Would the culprit be released? There was a pause. Then Alexander bent forward and addressed the young man, "What is your name?" Back came a feeble reply, "Alexander." "What is your name?" demanded the Macedonian monarch. The young man said politely, "Alexander, sir." Rising to his feet, the king grabbed the soldier and knocked him to the ground, pinning him to the floor and thundered, "Either change your name or change your behavior."[13]

My friends, you have been given a special name. Your name is Christian. Those of us who have confessed our sins and placed our faith and trust in Jesus Christ alone for salvation are called "Christians." How we live is important and how we display our Christian mode of living is important to the watching world. The name Christian was first used in the New Testament town of Antioch. There was something different about this group. Set apart, they were called to preserve the honor of a trinitarian God.

I ask you as Christians, how do you seek to honor God and those in the Corps? As leaders of character, servants of the nation, members of a noble profession, and spiritual war-fighters, what motivates you to bestow honor and dignity on those around you? As servant leaders we are called to a higher standard. Earlier in the Cadet Prayer we read that we are called to live above the common level of life. And so it is for Christians. One of the first questions asked within the Westminster Confession of Faith is, "What is the chief end of man?" In other words, why have you been created and what is your purpose here on earth? The answer is: "To glorify God and to honor Him forever."[14] To glorify God and to honor his holy name is the chief end of man. That is why we have been created: to bring glory and honor to His name. How do we honor those around us and maintain the honor of the Corps? The answer is that we do so by bringing honor to our Lord and our Savior Jesus Christ.

There are four main ways that we can honor God. The first way that we honor God is through our Word. We honor Christ with our words. It's important that our word become our bond. Psalm 15:1 asks, "Lord who may dwell in your sanctuary? Who may live on your holy hill?" That person, we then learn, is he whose life is "blameless and who does what is right and righteous. Who speaks the truth, who speaks the truth from his heart and has no slander on his lips." Yes, we honor God through our word and with our speech. It is so important that we learn to build and edify one another with our words. Enormous destruction can result from our speech. Throughout my ministry I have counseled people whose marriages have deteriorated as a result of harsh words and cruel statements. We are called upon to honor others through our words. James 3:4–9 notes that a huge forest can be set ablaze by only a small spark. Just so with wickedness ignited upon the world, man's tongue being the fire. Man can tame the earth's mighty creatures, yet can't manage to tame that tiny member, the tongue. Huge ships, despite gales and storms, can sail anywhere in the world, guided only by a small rudder. In man, the tongue can act as an equally powerful rudder, guiding us to use words to inflict great harm—or to bring great good—depending on the will of its owner.

Too often we praise God yet curse men. But our language should never be tarnished or sullied. It must be used to honor one another because we have been created in the image of God with dignity and worth. We honor God by taking a stand for the Gospel and not being ashamed of the truth.

We also honor God through our Walk. Psalm 1:1 says, "Blessed is the man who does not walk in the counsel of the wicked or frequent the path of sinners or sit in the seat of mockers." What we say and what we do begin to synchronize. Congruency forms in our life. Hypocrisy and pretense disappear, and our hearts develop a strong sense of integrity. That integrity becomes the navigating principle in our life. With a willingness to live right before God, as we are led by the Holy Spirit, we begin to trust God and others. We decide to take off the mask of performance, that is, calculated moral or religious acts, and simply trust God's love to flow through our soul. We do not allow our lips to violate what is in our hearts. Our conscience is guided by the word of God and our strength comes from his leading. It is not based on our performance or acts but rather on the person and work of Christ working in us. As we surrender to the Holy Spirit, we become more like Christ because we are moving, however slowly and haltingly, toward the ideals modeled by Christ in the New Testament. As we spend time in prayer and join together in corporate worship, we become as one, and our lives begin to body forth a biblical perspective. Biblical standards and principles become a beacon, constantly warning us away from the rocky shore of moral destruction.

We live in a postmodern culture believing that truth is at best relative and at worst unknowable or inexpressible in language. But we of the West Point community live, work, and breathe in an institution which espouses noble ideals and believes in absolute standards. We will not lie, cheat, steal, or tolerate those who do. We believe in a code, a code of conduct. A code of honor. Why? Because such a code lays a moral foundation that every leader, officer, and member of the profession of arms must have to undergird the superstructure of character. Our profession is built on that moral bedrock.

I read a highly relevant piece posted on the internet titled, *Catch of a Lifetime*. In depicting how we should "walk," the author tells a funny and moving fishing tale from his experience as an 11-year-old boy. I can relate to this tale because as a little boy I used to go fishing with my dad. The author begins with the day he and his dad went to their cabin on a beautiful lake in New Hampshire:

> *On the day before bass season opened, he and his father were fishing early in the evening, catching sunfish and perch with worms. Then he tried on a small silver lure and practiced casting. The lure struck the water and caused colored ripples in the sunset, then silver ripples as the moon rose over the lake.*
>
> *When his pole doubled over, he knew something huge was on the other end. His father watched with admiration as the boy skillfully worked the fish*

alongside the dock. Finally he very gingerly lifted the exhausted fish from the water. It was the largest one he had ever seen, but it was a bass.

The boy and his father looked at the handsome fish, gills playing back and forth in the moonlight. The father lit a match and looked at his watch. It was 10 p.m.—two hours before bass season opened. He looked at the fish, then at the boy. "You'll have to put it back, son," he said.

"Dad!" cried the boy. "There will be other fish," said his father. "Not as big as this one," cried the boy. He looked around the lake. No other fishermen or boats were anywhere around in the moonlight. He looked again at his father.

Even though no one had seen them, nor could anyone ever know what time he caught the fish, the boy could tell by the clarity of his father's voice that the decision was not negotiable. He slowly worked the hook out of the lip of the huge bass, and lowered it into the black water.

The creature swished its powerful body and disappeared. The boy suspected that he would never again see such a great fish. That was 34 years ago. Today the boy is a successful architect in New York City. His father's cabin is still there on the lake. He takes his own son and daughters fishing from the same dock.

He was right. He has never caught such a magnificent fish as the one he landed that night long ago. But he does see the same fish . . . again and again . . . every time he comes up against a question of ethics.[15]

The young boy caught more than a fish that day. He caught a life lesson in integrity. He caught a lesson in character and what it meant to have a biblical ethic that lives itself out honoring God's law. How important it is that we walk the walk. The world is watching. It decides who we are by our walk and by our love. Our world does not want clever leaders, it wants *credible* leaders. We want leaders who will emphasize integrity instead of image, leaders who have nothing to fear and nothing to hide. Their public and private lives are joined together as one under the gaze of God almighty. They are willing to surrender to the sanctifying magic of the Holy Spirit.

The third way we honor God is through our *Work*. As students, you are to honor God through your work, which is your studies and military requirements. As faculty and staff, your job is to honor Him through your teaching and support role. As mothers and fathers, your job is to honor God through the raising of your children. Colossians 3:23 says, "Whatever you do, work at it. Work at it with all your heart as working for the Lord. Since you know that you will receive an inheritance from the Lord as a reward." It was later in my own life before I really understood that labor is a good thing. It is a gift. Work was ordained by God before the fall. If you study Genesis 1 and 2, you will come to realize that work was ordained and instituted as a gift from God. God himself says, "I worked six days and on the seventh, I rested from all my labor." In time, I began to see my profession and my work as a gift from the Almighty. This realization began literally to transform my vision of life and how I entered into the day. My alarm clock quit being an alarm clock and became an opportunity clock. I believe strongly that as Christians we are called upon to prepare for and through our work, because the day is coming for some of you to do great things for the Lord. Right now you are at a fork in the road in which you have to make a choice for God. For some of you it may be in your cadet life as a student; for others, it may be later in life, but I believe that the moment will come when you have to make a stand for the glory of God. You will be able to make that stand if your heart is ready and you have prepared. Usually, this moment of courageous decision will take place in your workplace. May we honor Christ in our work.

Finally, we honor God through our *Worship*. What exactly is worship? Worship is an expression of love for and to God. There is much up for discussion throughout our society and our land today about worship. Should we have contemporary worship, or should be have traditional worship? Should we have blended worship? We go to different churches, and every church has a different style of worship. But when people ask me what I think, I say that I am less concerned about the style of the worship than the heart in the worship. Is your heart preparing for worship? The goal of worship is not simply for us to be blessed; the goal of worship is to bring honor and glory to God.

A transformation took place in my life when I began to realize that the end state of worship is not just for the body and life of Jesus Christ to be reconsecrated and recelebrated, but for God to be glorified. He can be glorified in many different ways as long as our hearts seek to honor Him as the corporate body of Christ. What is worship? It is an expression of love to the Almighty. Worship is being a participator in the Kingdom of God rather than a spectator. It is when we leave the stands and come down to the playing field and say, "Lord, I want to be on your team and I want to worship you in spirit and in truth." Worship does not start with us. It starts with God. Our life should be an act of worship. God is the object of our worship. We maintain honor through our worship of God.

Among my professional readings, I encountered a great book titled *The Raising of the Modern Day Knight* by Robert Lewis. Lewis writes about the qualities of a medieval knight, focusing on the qualities that were prerequisites for membership in the exalted circle of knighthood. One requirement was to live life as a champion. Another was to honor women, to show them dignity and respect. Still another was to practice generosity in all of one's dealings with people. Finally, he writes, "A knight was called upon to train and to teach those around him. Every knight was given a page and a few understudies who were known as apprentices. He was to train and teach them certain qualities and attributes of what it meant to be a knight. The knight would sit around the campfire at the end of the day and fix in their minds an image of what it meant to be a knight. The knight told stories of glory and honor with the hope that as the young boys fell asleep they would dream about glory and honor."[16]

On a personal note, last night as I began to prepare for sleep, I prayed that our cadets would fall asleep dreaming dreams of glory and honor in behalf of

God. May we pray today that our gracious Lord will help us to maintain the principles that give rise to such dreams. These are timeless biblical principles, written in Holy Scripture, that have been instilled in the Cadet Prayer. Let us use them to maintain our honor as Christians. God has called us to a great task, but I believe that we as the body of Christ are prepared. May God be with you as you honor him through your word, work, walk, and worship.

Notes

1. See chap. 1 of this volume.
2. This fact is discussed in much more detail in chap. 4 of the present volume.
3. John C. Maxwell, *Developing the Leader Within You* (Nashville, TN: Thomas Nelson, Inc., 1982), 36.
4. This sermon was delivered originally by Chaplain (Lieutenant Colonel) John J. Cook III at the Cadet Chapel, United States Military Academy, West Point, New York, on September 30, 2001. All Biblical quotations here and in the following three sermons are from the New International Version.
5. Zig Ziglar, "Do You Know Who His Daddy Is?" *Stories for the Heart*, ed. Brian Harbour (Sisters, OR: Multnomah Books, 1996), 223.
6. This sermon was delivered originally by Chaplain (Major) James R. Carter at the Cadet Chapel, United States Military Academy, West Point, New York, on October 7, 2001.
7. This sermon was delivered originally by Chaplain (Lieutenant Colonel) John J. Cook III at the Cadet Chapel, United States Military Academy, West Point, New York, on October 28, 2001.
8. Dwight D. Eisenhower, cited in *Great Quotes from Great Leaders,* ed. Peggy Anderson (Lombard, IL: Great Quotations, 1989).
9. Alexander Haig, source unknown.
10. William A. Cohen, *The Stuff of Heroes* (Marietta, GA: Longstreet Press, 2001), 33.
11. Len Marrella, *In Search of Ethics* (Washington, DC: DC Press, 2001), 140.
12. This sermon was delivered originally by Chaplain (Major) James R. Carter at the Cadet Chapel, United States Military Academy, West Point, New York, on December 2, 2001.
13. Stephen F. Olford, *The Christian Message for Contemporary Life: the Gospel's Power to Change Lives* (Grand Rapids, MI: Kregel Publications, 1999), 107.
14. *The Shorter Catechism with Scripture Proofs* (Carlisle, PA: The Banner of Truth Trust), 1.
15. "Catch of a Lifetime," author unknown (www.joyfulministry/com/catchf.htm).
16. Robert Lewis, *Raising a Modern Day Knight* (Colorado Springs, CO: Focus on the Family Publishing), 66.

About The Contributors

Captain Erica Borggren graduated from the U.S. Military Academy in 2002 as the class valedictorian. A Rhodes Scholar, she spent her lieutenant years at Oxford University, England, where she earned an M.S. degree in Comparative Social Policy in 2003 and a Postgraduate Diploma in Theology in 2004. Since then, she has been stationed in Yongsan, Korea, where she served as the Executive Officer for Headquarters and Headquarters Company, 18th Medical Command, and then as the Management Officer in the Resource Management Division of the 18th MEDCOM. She now commands Alpha Company, 121st Combat Support Hospital, in Yongsan, Korea.

Colonel Donna Brazil is an Academy Professor in the Department of Behavioral Sciences and Leadership at the U.S. Military Academy. She holds a B.S from the Academy and an M.A. and Ph.D. in Social Psychology from the University of North Carolina at Chapel Hill. She has eight years experience on the faculty at the Military Academy, teaching Military Leadership, Group Dynamics, Leadership Theory, and Marriage and the Family.

Chaplain (LTC) James R. Carter attended the Reformed Theological Seminary in Jackson, MS, and, after receiving ordination as a Presbyterian Minister, he entered the Army Chaplain Corps in 1988. He holds a B.A. from Belhaven College in Jackson, MS, and a Master of Divinity and M.A. in Marriage and Family Therapy from the Reformed Theological Seminary. He is a graduate of the Combined Arms Service Staff School (CAS3) and the Command and General Staff College at Ft. Leavenworth, KS, and is currently a Doctorate of Ministry candidate at Erskine Theological Seminary. He has held chaplaincy assignments in Germany and Korea as well as during Operations Desert Shield and Storm in the Middle East. Chaplain Carter was also Senior Pastor of the West Point Cadet Chapel, and is presently the 4th Infantry Division Chaplain at Ft. Hood, TX.

Chaplain (Colonel) John J. Cook III is a 1979 graduate of the U.S. Military Academy where he served as First Captain of the Corps of Cadets during his senior year. Upon graduation, he served five years as an artillery officer before leaving active duty to attend the Southern Baptist Theological Seminary in Louisville, Kentucky, during which time he also served as Pastor of New Bethel Baptist

Church for three and a half years. He reentered active duty in January 1989 as a chaplain and has served in various positions at home and abroad ranging from battalion chaplain to Deputy Third Army Chaplain. He was the Deputy Chaplain of the Coalition Land Forces Component Command, Arifjan, Kuwait, in 2004–2005. Currently assigned as the Military Academy Command Chaplain since July 2005, Chaplain Cook had two previous assignments at West Point as the Protestant Cadet Chaplain and later the Pastor of the Cadet Chapel. Two of his children, twins Jonathan and Joshua, are in their third year as cadets at the Military Academy.

Lieutenant General F. L. Hagenbeck is the 57th Superintendent of the United States Military Academy at West Point, New York. He was commissioned in the Infantry from the Military Academy in 1971. Later, at Florida State University, he earned a Master of Science Degree in Exercise Physiology and served as an assistant football coach. While assigned to the U.S. Military Academy's Department of Physical Education, he earned a Master of Business Administration from Long Island University. He is also a graduate of the Army War College and the Army Command and General Staff College. General Hagenbeck has commanded at every level from company through division, culminating as Commanding General of the 10th Mountain Division. He has also served in the 25th Infantry Division, 101st Airborne Division, 82nd Airborne Division, including the Grenada operation in 1983, and TRADOC. Before becoming Superintendent, General Hagenbeck served as the Army's Deputy Chief of Staff, G-1, and in numerous staff positions, including Chief of Staff, 10th Mountain Division; Director, Officer Personnel Management Directorate, U.S. Total Army Personnel Command; and Assistant Division Commander (Operations), 101st Airborne Division. General Hagenbeck has served in numerous Joint assignments, including Exchange Officer and Tactics Instructor at the Royal Australian Infantry Center; Deputy Director for Politico-Military Affairs, Strategic Plans and Policy Directorate (J5); and Deputy Director for Current Operations, J33, Joint Staff. General Hagenbeck served as Commander, Coalition Joint Task Force Mountain, Operations Enduring Freedom/Anaconda, and Deputy Commanding General, Combined Joint Task Force 180 in Afghanistan.

Lieutenant Colonel Sean T. Hannah is the Director of Leadership and Management Studies, Department of Behavioral Sciences and Leadership, U.S. Military Academy. He has 20 years experience leading in infantry units in both peace and combat and at strategic levels working for the Chief of Staff of the Army, and later for the Assistant Secretary of the Army (Financial Management and Comptroller) at the Pentagon. He holds both an MBA and MPA from Syracuse University, an M.A. in Military Science from the Marine Corps University, and a Ph.D. in Leadership from the University of Nebraska. His scholarly research focuses on authentic and moral leadership, and his most recent publications on those topics include "Authentic Leadership: The Heart of High

Impact Leadership," in *Leadership Lessons from West Point*, ed. Doug Crandall (John Wiley and Sons, forthcoming); and co-author, "Veritable Authentic Leadership: Emergence, Functioning, and Impacts," and "Moral Leadership: Explicating the Moral Component of Authentic Leadership," both in *Authentic Leadership Theory and Practice: Origins, Effects, and Development* (2005), eds. W. B. Gardner and B. J. Avolio.

Brigadier General Anthony E. Hartle, U.S. Army Ret., received a B.S. from the Military Academy, M.A. in American and English Literature from Duke University, and Ph.D. in Philosophy from the University of Texas at Austin. Commissioned in the Infantry, he served two tours in Vietnam, commanded a battalion in the 101st Airborne Division (Air Assault), taught literature and philosophy and served as Vice Dean at USMA, and retired as the head of the English Department in 2004, 40 years after commissioning. While stationed at the Academy, he also served as a staff member for the Presidential Commission Investigating the Space Shuttle *Challenger* Accident. General Hartle authored *Moral Issues in Military Decision Making* and coauthored *Dimensions of Ethical Thought*. He has also published a variety of book chapters and journal articles. At West Point, he chaired the Superintendent's Honor Review Committee for many years and worked closely with the Center for Professional Military Ethics in the supervision of the Values Education Program for cadets. He was also the chairman of the Executive Board of the Joint Services Conference on Professional Ethics from 1993 to 2002.

Chaplain (Major) Carlos Huerta graduated from OCS and was commissioned as a Field Artillery officer. He served in various positions, to include Turkish translator for NATO forces in Turkey, Special Weapons Officer in Turkey and Korea, and Battery Commander in the 2nd Infantry Division, Korea. He received his Ph.D. in Mathematics in 1986, specializing in Topological Measure Theory and Quantum Logic, and his Rabbinical Ordination in 1991. In 1994, he was commissioned as a Chaplain in the U.S. Army. Assignments have included chaplaincies with the 3rd Special Forces Group (Green Beret) and the Jewish Community Chaplain's Office/1st Battalion, 1st Infantry, at the Military Academy in 2000. He has served two tours in the Iraq war, both times with the 101st Airborne Division. He has published widely in such diverse fields as mathematics, the Holocaust, Sephardic and Spanish culture, and many more. He was recently reassigned to chaplaincy duty at West Point.

Colonel Lloyd J. Matthews, U.S. Army Ret., received a B.S. degree from the U.S. Military Academy, M.A. from Harvard University, and Ph.D. from the University of Virginia, and is a graduate of the Army War College and Armed Forces Staff College. His military assignments included command at platoon, company, and battalion levels; advisory duty in the Vietnam War; editorship of *Parameters*, the Army War College quarterly; and an English professorship and the associate deanship at the Military Academy. Following retirement from the Army, he served as a project manager in Saudi Arabia and later Turkey. Colonel Matthews has published well over 100 articles, features, reviews, monographs, and editions on professional topics, including the edition, with Dale E. Brown, *The Parameters of Military Ethics* (Pergamon-Brassey's, 1989); the article "The Need for An Officers' Code of Professional Ethics," *Army* Magazine, March 1994; the entry on American Military Ideals, *Oxford Companion to American Military History,* ed. John Whiteclay Chambers (Oxford University Press, 1999); and the edition, with Don M. Snider, *The Future of the Army Profession* (McGraw-Hill, 2nd ed., 2005). Colonel Matthews also served on the editorial staff for the August 2004 *Final Report of the Independent Panel to Review DoD Detention Operations* [at Abu Ghraib] ("Schlesinger Panel Report").

General Eric K. Shinseki, U.S. Army Ret., holds the Class of 1951 Chair for Leadership Study in the Department of Behavioral Sciences and Leadership at West Point. He graduated from the Military Academy in 1965 with a B.S. degree and was commissioned in the Armor branch. He later obtained an M.A. in literature from the University of North Carolina, following which he taught philosophy and world literature at West Point. During his 39-year Army career, he commanded at troop, squadron, brigade, division, and army levels, and among other positions served as the Army's Deputy Chief of Staff for Operations and later as the Vice Chief of Staff. He served two combat tours in the Vietnam War and was twice wounded; served as the Commander of the NATO Stabilization Force during the campaign to pacify Bosnia-Herzegovina; and was the Army Chief of Staff during the period encompassing the terrorist attacks in New York and Washington on September 11, 2001, the Coalition campaign that ousted the Taliban government in Afghanistan in the late fall of 2001, and the campaign resulting in the capture of Baghdad and deposition of Saddam Hussein by Coalition forces in the spring of 2003. General Shinseki retired from the Army at the completion of his tour as the 34th Army Chief of Staff in June 2003. Asked how he wanted to be remembered by history, he replied, "Simply as a soldier."

Professor Don M. Snider, Colonel, U.S. Army Ret., received a B.S. degree from the U.S. Militry Academy, M.A. in Economics and M.A. in Public Affairs from the University of Wisconsin, and Ph.D. in Public Policy from the University of Maryland. He was appointed to the civilian faculty of the U.S. Military Academy in 1998. This followed a 28-year military career in the Army, five years in Washington, DC, as analyst and director of political-military research at the Center for Strategic and International Studies, and three years as the Olin Professor of National Security Studies at West Point. Among his most important early publications was a two-part series appearing in the September and December 1987 issues of *Parameters,* constituting at that time the definitive public explication of the 1986 Goldwater-Nichols legislation. Other publications include "The Civil-Military Gap and Professional Military Education at the

Pre-commissioning Level" in *Armed Forces and Society,* Winter 2001 (coauthor); and "The Future of Army Professionalism: The Need for Renewal and Redefinition" in *Parameters,* August 2000 (coauthor). Most recently he was coauthor of the article "Christian Citizenship and American Empire" in the fall 2003 issue of *Faith and International Affairs,* author of "Leadership by Example," *Army* Magazine, November 2005, and project director, *The Future of the Army Profession,* 2nd ed. (McGraw-Hill, 2005). He is a member of the Council on Foreign Relations, and serves on the Executive Committee of the Inter-University Seminar on Armed Forces and Society.

Colonel Patrick J. Sweeney is an Associate Professor and the Deputy Head of the Department of Behavioral Sciences and Leadership at the U.S. Military Academy. He is also Director of the Eisenhower Tactical Officer Leader Development Program for the Academy. Colonel Sweeney commanded the 3rd Battalion, 320th Field Artillery, in the 101st Airborne Division (Air Assault) at Ft. Campbell, KY, and served with the 101st during Operation Iraqi Freedom I. He received the M.A. and Ph.D. from the University of North Carolina at Chapel Hill. Colonel Sweeney was an Assistant Professor in the department from 1992 to 1995 where he served as an instructor of the General Psychology for Leaders course and Executive Officer/Researcher in the Center for Leadership and Organization Research. His research interests include trust and influence in combat, leader development, and cohesion. He currently teaches the Leadership in Combat course at the Academy.

Father Edson J. Wood, Order of St. Augustine, is the Brigade Chaplain at the Military Academy. Father Wood pursued his undergraduate degree (B.A in Philosophy) at Villanova University, Villanova, PA, and his graduate work (Licentiate in Sacred Theology) at the Catholic University of America, Washington, DC. He was ordained a priest in the Order of St. Augustine in 1972 and assigned to Archbishop Carroll High School as Dean of Students and Instructor of Theology. In 1979, he became Assistant to the President at Catholic University. In 1983, he was assigned to Malvern Preparatory School, Malvern, PA, as Chair of Theology and Director of Student Activities. In the summer of 1993, he was asked to spend a month at West Point to assist with Cadet Basic Training and remained at USMA until the present, first serving as Catholic Cadet Chaplain and then as Assistant Chaplain, USMA. In September of 2002, Father Wood was appointed "Chaplain to the Corps of Cadets" (or "Brigade Chaplain") by the Secretary of the Army.

Dr. Sherifa Zuhur is Research Professor of Islamic and Regional Studies at the Strategic Studies Institute, U.S. Army War College. She taught for 17 years prior to joining government service at institutions that include the Massachusetts Institute of Technology, University of California at Berkeley, and the American University in Cairo. During this period, she was a Fulbright senior scholar and

Rockefeller award recipient. She has published 12 books and monographs and more than 56 articles and chapters. Her most recent books are *The Middle East: Politics, History, and Neonationalism* and *Asrar Asmahan* (in Arabic). Recent military studies include *Iran, Iraq, and the United States: The New Triangle's Impact on Sectarianism* and *The Nuclear Threat and A Hundred Osamas: Islamist Threats and the Future of Counterinsurgency.* Outside of her official work, she engages in other Middle East scholarship, serving as Director of the Institute of Middle Eastern, Islamic, and Diasporic Studies, an independent resource center, and Assistant Editor of ABC-Clio's forthcoming *Encyclopedia of Arab-Israeli Wars.* She received a B.A. in Political Science and Arabic and Arabic Literature, a Master's in Islamic Studies, and a Ph.D. in Middle Eastern History, all from the University of California, Los Angeles.